Fulfilled in Our Hearing

Fulfilled in Our Hearing

History and Method of Christian Preaching

Guerric DeBona, OSB

Paulist Press
New York/Mahwah, N.J.

Cover design by A. Michael Velthaus
Book design by Lynn Else

Library of Congress Cataloging-in-Publication Data

DeBona, Guerric, 1955–
    Fulfilled in our hearing : history and method of Christian preaching / Guerric DeBona.
        p.   cm.
    Includes bibliographical references and index.
    ISBN 0-8091-4359-3 (alk. paper)
    1. Catholic preaching. 2. Preaching. I. Title.
BV4211.3.D42 2005
251—dc22

2005005980

Published by Paulist Press
997 Macarthur Boulevard
Mahwah, New Jersey 07430

www.paulistpress.com

Printed and bound in the
United States of America

CONTENTS

Passionate, Purposeful, liturgical, Scriptural
Kerygmatic, formational, logical

In thanksgiving to Almighty God
for my parents,
Glenn and Joan DeBona,
who brought me to the waters of baptism

ACKNOWLEDGMENTS

I owe my first debt of gratitude to Archabbot Lambert Reilly, OSB, and my dear confreres of Saint Meinrad Archabbey, both living and deceased. As we celebrate the sesquicentennial of our foundation from the venerable Abbey of Maria Einsiedeln in Switzerland, I am reminded that our work and prayer together as sons of Saint Benedict continue to shape us as silent hearers of the Word, discovering the mystery of God in Christ, hidden and dwelling within us. I am especially thankful to the late Brother Lawrence Schidler, OSB, who preached without words.

My appreciation also extends to Fathers Mark O'Keefe, OSB, and Justin DuVall, OSB, rector and vice-rector of Saint Meinrad Seminary and School of Theology, whose encouragement in my teaching and research has enabled me to complete this book; their own excellent preaching and writing inspires all of us to witness to the gospel of Jesus Christ. Additionally, some past and present members of the faculty of the school have been especially formative in my own education history; I count among these Archbishop Daniel M. Buechein, OSB; Drs. Bernard Brandon Scott, James Walter, and David Buttrick; Fathers Cyprian Davis, OSB, Timothy Sweeney, OSB, Eugene Hensell, OSB, and Harry Hagan, OSB; and the late Father Nathaniel Reeves, OSB, Msgr. Jerry Neufelder, and Msgr. Stephen P. Happel. I am also profoundly indebted to Professors James Naremore, Barbara Klinger, Patrick Brantlinger, Terry Martin, Donald Gray, Susan Gubar, and Stephen Watt of Indiana University for their influential contributions to my understanding of culture, narrative, and visual communication.

This project would never have been written without the advice and readership of my fellow faculty members and cherished colleagues near and far. As academic dean, Dr. Tom Walters's tireless optimism and integrity for the profession has been an inspiration. Dr. Richard Stern, a friend, mentor, and thoughtful partner in the homiletics department at Saint Meinrad, encouraged me to pursue a project on a short history and method of preaching. Father James Wallace, CSsR, of Washington Theological Union offered his wise and experienced perspective on the text. The late Robert Waznak, SS, was a formative influence on these pages long before the manuscript came to light. Father Raymond Studzinski, OSB, and the priests at Archbishop Curley Hall at Catholic University were unfailing in their hospitality and stimulating discussion during my sabbatical. As always, the staff of the archabbey library was gracious and eager to assist me in whatever I needed.

I wish to thank Father Gerard Sloyan in a special way for his valuable comments on the manuscript and the generous foreword to this text; few scholars radiate such personal warmth and zeal for the gospel. My appreciation as well to Father Larry Boadt, CSP, and Mr. Paul McMahon for their editorial skills, and to Dr. Nancy de Flon for her careful, cultivated, and expert guidance through the various stages of publication of this book. Finally, Mrs. Carol Heeke, ever the administrative problem solver at Saint Meinrad, removed any computer glitches along the way.

Last, and most important, I am overwhelmingly grateful to my students—seminarians, permanent deacon candidates, and lay students—of Saint Meinrad College and School of Theology, who over the years have given me more than they will ever know and certainly much more than I can possibly express in return. I continue to pray for them and for the up-building of the Church through the proclamation of the risen Lord, so that "in all things God may be glorified!"

FOREWORD

When reviewers and writers of an introductory word say in an outworn cliché (to use a tautological pleonasm), "This is a much needed work," the reader's immediate mental challenge is to ask, "Who needs it?" There is a small literary genre in our day—it was much larger in the nineteenth-century Protestant United States—of works on preaching. That genre can always use a good, new title. This book is such a one.

Congregations have been complaining about preaching since the apostolic age. Like Miniver Cheevey, they've had reasons. Effective preaching is a high art. It is no wonder that over the centuries many charged with it have not mastered the art. The reasons are chiefly two. The first is that the written Word of God chosen for proclamation on a Sunday or feast day is normally so sublime that human words in exposition of it can seem lame or banal. The second is that preachers need to have engaged in the hard work of plumbing the biblical text or texts and, equally important, to have reflected deeply on what may be going on at this time in the lives of their hearers. The inevitable result of not doing either is an often lengthy exhortation to exercise a virtue that most of those present are already practicing, or to avoid a vice to which the absent may be committed. The spoken word may go no deeper than the speaker's ordinary thought process, and that is not good enough.

This is a description of bad preaching. Good preaching, by contrast, is the fruit of hard labor that has not hesitated to seek out the thought of others on the biblical Word, to think long and hard about why this congregation might need this Word of God in its current situation, and to speak that Word clearly in words thought out carefully beforehand.

The reader of this book who may be in the majority will be a "dipper-in" who finds in it an ingenious mixture of the theoretical and the practical, lengthy passages useful to some but useless to others (no fault of the author), and overall a remarkable tour of the homiletic horizon. This is a book for those who have derived both pleasure and pain over the years as consumers of pulpit preaching and equally for those who find preparing the product a drudgery or a delight. Catholics will learn about Protestant styles of preaching they had not known of, and Protestants will be told of Catholic sermon types no longer in vogue and the ideal of preaching on a three-year lectionary since Advent of 1969. Is there anything that can be called distinctive of preaching by women? of preaching to Hispanic and Portuguese congregations besides preaching in those languages? of black preaching, as it is called, as if there were but a single mode? All these questions and their nuances these pages wisely deal with by listening to a variety of expert voices that speak from within those cultures. No foolish thing is said about the questions the author takes on.

There are a few important matters not dealt with in this near encyclopedic treatment of a theme. That is because they are the subject of a different handling at book length. What of the congregations who hear the voice of a single preacher for years on end, and what are the hardships of being that preacher? Has the Catholic Church in the United States faced the reality of the limited theological education—evenings and Saturdays—available to candidates for the order of permanent deacon, often with its stress on doctrine and morality when education in the Bible and the liturgy is what is needed? What can be done for bishops and priests to supplement what may have been the deficiency of their seminary education in the Old Testament and the Pauline writings? The high hopes for the richer fare provided by the *Lectionary for Mass* and the *Revised Common Lectionary* can go unrealized if there is clerical timidity about an exposition of anything but the gospels. Worse still, if there is fear of discussing the great questions of national and international life as these scriptures shed light on them.

But all of that is the subject of another book. The one in hand deals very well with each aspect of the skill of preaching it tackles. It could be called professional literature. *How to Be an Effective General Practitioner* or *The Skill of Honest Lawyering* is not a title that crowds the shelves of chain booksellers and airport book stores. Yet the entire population is affected by the small populations in those professions. Call preaching a vocation if you will, not a profession. It does not matter. Preaching matters profoundly to all who regularly worship God publicly through Jesus Christ in the community of the Holy Spirit.

Guerric DeBona has done something remarkable about this calling. He has written about it interestingly, even at times pleasurably. Can his work be given as a gift to one's favorite homilist or one's "unfavorite" homilist without offense? Surely it can, as a show of appreciation of the exercise of an extremely difficult art.

—*Gerard S. Sloyan*
Priest of the Diocese of Trenton

INTRODUCTION

It would be hard to exaggerate the explosion of interest that has occurred in preaching over the last thirty years. In the 1970s Christian preachers in the United States were introduced to what came to be called the New Homiletic, a radical departure from the models of preaching in the past. Yet, some of the methodologies of the New Homiletic were not exactly new. Most of these revisionist homiletic strategies tried to capture biblical preaching in a contemporary idiom that had been lost by centuries of complicated rhetoric and argumentation, stretching back as far as the fourth century to Saint Augustine in the West and the Cappadocian Fathers in the East. Searching for a new point of view for preaching in the midst of the twentieth century, the New Homiletic looked both to the past and to the future. How did Jesus preach? What grounds Christian preaching? How is the Word made real and vivid to the listeners, the people of God? These became the questions for those who introduced another voice into preaching, and they are some of the ones we will be asking here in this book.

Tracing a detailed "history" of preaching is a daunting task, and not within the scope of the present volume. Preaching itself has been so diffused over the centuries that constructing a comprehensive story of the evangelization of the Word is practically unmanageable in a single volume. It is possible, though, to isolate tendencies, trends, and even specific preachers who have contributed to Christian preaching over the ages. These events and people who inhabit historical moments open a window into the preaching of the past and help to guide our present homiletic circumstances. In addition to certain notable occurrences glimpsed as refractions of light in preaching history, we might take a long, hard look at the very substance of a homily itself in relation to its cultural context. Indeed, there are particular characteristics of the

1

speech-act that were more important than others in the history of preaching, and some of these traits have held fast well into the twentieth century. At some times, the rhetorical content of text was very crucial to the preaching, while the charismatic personality of the preacher became a central focus for the congregation at others. Then again, not all developments in the homily have concerned traditional preaching models. The 1970s saw the tremendous rise in television evangelism. And indeed, we know that the rise of media culture has changed the way we think about language and communication; such a shift is bound to renegotiate preaching. The old rules of Aristotelian rhetoric that have typically defined the homily were examined more closely by the contemporary homiletic methodologies in light of a quickly changing society.

This book takes a brief look at the history of preaching and its methods and tries to make sense of the evolution of the homily (or sermon) in a cultural context. Although I spend most of this work looking over the last twenty-five years of preaching, I frame our contemporary period with a developmental history in order to understand better our present condition. Beyond this, there remains the question of homiletic technique, newly and radically modernized for the modern age. A number of inductive "methods" were introduced in the 1970s and 1980s to account for the increasing role of the listener in preaching. There had already been numerous volumes written for preachers about rhetorical technique, but what about the Christian assembly, those were to "hear the word of God and keep it"? How would preaching increase their faith? Although the New Homiletic was a Protestant movement, the Catholic Church produced its own version in the remarkable NCCB document *Fulfilled in Your Hearing*, written in 1982. The bishops' statement articulated an innovation in the liturgical homily even as it powerfully acknowledged the insights of the Second Vatican Council's well-known statements on the role of the laity's full participation in the eucharistic liturgy. Ultimately, to trace the development of a homiletic method is to see the importance of the hearer in the speech-act for both Protestants and Catholics.

But more than thirty years after the New Homiletic and *Fulfilled in Your Hearing*, there has been expansion in preaching on almost every possible level, especially in relation to the *hearer* of the homily. Multiculturalism has blessed the church in North America with vast diversity in the last few decades alone. If we are going to welcome the stranger as a guest, then we can no longer preach out of the same models; we must begin to discover the newer and most effective ways to communicate to a congregation characterized and animated by linguistic and cultural difference. Moreover, insights from feminist writings on scripture, as well as newer thoughts on our postmodern condition, have further challenged our normative ways of preaching by suggesting a more collaborative environment for preaching the Word. Clearly, the hierarchical strategies of preaching are even now being replaced by homily preparation notable for its dialogue with the culture and the congregation. Such practices are reinforced by an educated laity searching for meaning in a society often marked by relativism and trivial entertainment. Technology has already changed the face of more than a few generations. What does it mean to preach liturgically in a techno-saturated, menu-driven environment? What kind of "new hearing" is open to those who have been bombarded with sound bytes, lightning-fast hip-hop lyrics, and dazzling cinematic digital photography? Finally, is a culture of endless choice and pluralism really open to being converted by the Word made visible?

This book is not an answer to the issues I have just mentioned but hopes to open a discussion about where Christian preaching has been and where it might be headed. What Pope John Paul II has called the New Evangelization is already upon us. That ambitious project for the third millennium continues to be one of the highest priorities for the church as it continues to ponder the mystery of God-in-the-world, indeed, the Word made flesh. Although this text has been written from a Catholic perspective, I see my efforts here to give an overview of Christian preaching as an ecumenical project as well. With preaching as our common ground, the Christian Church can learn a great deal from both its history and its homiletic methodology. At the moment we may have to stand before a divided table, but that does not mean that the churches cannot gather around a unified pulpit. As a people already transformed by the Incarnation, we await the graced moment when the Word will be fulfilled in our hearing.

—September 14, 2004
Feast of the Exultation of the Holy Cross
Saint Meinrad, Indiana

1

THE CHANGING VOICE OF PREACHING

Now go, and I will be with your mouth and teach you what you are to speak.

—Exodus 4:12

Preaching is the gifted expression of God's saving power inside human language. From what we know of salvation history, the impulse to preach has come from God's own initiative. Moses was commissioned by God to liberate a nation from the yoke of slavery, though he was slow of speech. Isaiah's lips were touched with a burning coal as he began to witness to God's majesty and glory in Zion. And Ezekiel was given a scroll to eat before he would speak to the house of Israel. The prophet Jeremiah describes his own call to preaching when he says that

> The LORD put out his hand and touched my mouth;
> and the LORD said to me,
>   "Now I have put my words in your mouth.
>   See, today I appoint you over nations and over
>   kingdoms,
>   to pluck up and to pull down,
>   to destroy and to overthrow,
>   to build and to plant." (Jer 1:9–10)

The disposition of the people of Israel toward the word of God might be summed up in the language of the psalmist: "Zion praise your God, who has sent his word to the earth."

Christian preaching celebrates the Word that has become flesh. The Word of the Lord came again one day to the quiet little

5

town of Nazareth in a synagogue full of those waiting to hear God's word unfold before them:

> When he came to Nazareth, where he had been brought up, he went to the synagogue on the sabbath day, as was his custom. He stood up to read, and the scroll of the prophet Isaiah was given to him. He unrolled the scroll and found the place where it was written:
> "The Spirit of the Lord is upon me,
> because he has anointed me
> to bring good news to the poor.
> He has sent me to proclaim release to the captives
> and recovery of sight to the blind,
> to let the oppressed go free,
> to proclaim the year of the Lord's favor."
> And he rolled up the scroll, gave it back to the attendant, and sat down. The eyes of all in the synagogue were fixed on him. Then he began to say to them, "Today this scripture has been fulfilled in your hearing." (Luke 4:16–21)

This is the foundational moment of Christian preaching; it occurs at the graced juncture of preacher, text, and hearer. The Word of the Lord has come definitively, dressed in radiant fullness and truth.

There are a number of useful observations about Luke 4:16–21 that might be made in a discussion of preaching. First of all, Jesus positions himself as a prophetic speaker who proclaims God's scriptural Word. He delivers that Word squarely in the midst of the Jewish prophetic and liturgical context. Further, Jesus' preaching on that passage not only comments on or explicates the reading but announces that he is literally the fulfillment—the culmination of that prophetic tradition. The weight of the preaching event then calls our attention directly to the *preacher* himself, the "anointed," the one who enfleshes the Word at the moment of proclamation. Jesus stands before us mediating God's Word, much like Ezra in the book of Nehemiah, who opened the Torah in the sight of all the people. "So they read from the book, from the law of God, with interpretation. They gave the sense, so that the people understood the reading" (Neh 8:8).

At the same time, though, we must also claim another aspect to this originating preaching event in Luke, since a great deal of the meaning behind the passage depends on the way that Jesus has disclosed meaning in a *text* within the context of the gathered faithful. Jesus preaches Isaiah's text (Isa 61) in his own culture, a world waiting for liberation from the political and social constrains of empire and oppression. By an act of interpretation the text is made present in a new way. God has sent forth his Word to the earth yet again. The process of mediation transforms the scroll of the prophet Isaiah into God's Word, living and active among the congregation of worshippers. Speaker and text merge as the Word becomes visible to the assembly. Hence, at the moment Jesus unveils God's Word, he is also disclosing himself as the Word made flesh. Preacher and text will never find more definitive or more substantial authenticity than at this moment; all other Christian preaching events are refractions of the seminal moment in Nazareth.

Finally, the preaching of this good news in Nazareth has occurred within a congregational setting, a liturgical space, for a group of *hearers*. The gathered assembly becomes the lightning rod for the transmission of a synergy, a vibrant interaction. So Jesus tells the congregation in the synagogue that the passage "today has been fulfilled in your hearing"; in other words, that the Word has come alive in the act of speech precisely because the Word has been heard. "All spoke well of him and were amazed at the gracious words that came from his mouth" (Luke 4:22). Clearly, the listeners are crucial to the preaching moment in Luke 4:16–21. Jesus says that at the very moment of proclamation, this ordinary group of people has cooperated with the dissemination of God's Word. Listening has accomplished and fulfilled the destiny of the Word. In fulfilling the Word, the hearers of the assembly have affirmed that God has come to change the lives of God's people.

As *Fulfilled in Your Hearing* makes clear in its initial commentary on Luke 4:16–21, "the three major elements of liturgical preaching are all here: the preacher, the word drawn from the Scriptures, and the gathered community."[1] Although the authors of *Fulfilled in Your Hearing* focused on liturgical preaching, the dynamics that occur among preacher, text, and listener are applicable to all kinds of Christian preaching, whether that form of evangelization is rooted in catechetical or sacramental teaching, kerygmatic witness or liturgical proclamation.

To trace the history of preaching is to follow a veritable road map of variables that has placed a distinctive weight on the importance of either the text, or the preacher, or the hearer (or, in classical terms, the *logos*, *ethos*, or *pathos*), depending on historical and cultural circumstances. Jesus' activity in the synagogue and throughout his ministry sets the stage for a dynamic that will play itself out in various ways in the history of Christian preaching. For the purposes of this chapter, then, I will suggest briefly how Christian preaching has negotiated the delicate balance among text, preacher, and hearer at particular moments in Western history. I use these three foundational aspects of preaching as a window into a discussion for considering homiletics in our own times, with special attention to the role of the hearer. With Jesus of Nazareth's originating moment in the synagogue as a kind of template for our exploration, I have structured the text, the speaker, and the listener as particular moments in the story of preaching not in order to shape a linear history, but to evoke an impression characterized by the various turns Christian preaching has taken over the course of two thousand years.

Early Preaching and the Prophetic Mode

Scholars have recently been very attentive to the biblical roots of Christian homiletics and have noted other sources beyond Luke 4:16–21.[2] Many have observed that Paul's address in Acts 13:17–41 in the diaspora synagogue in Pisidian Antioch parallels Peter's Pentecost exhortation (Acts 2:22–40; and Stephen's speech [Acts 7:1–53]); these speeches have similar rhetorical approaches, together with a recapitulation of salvation history.[3] Using a contemporary rhetorical style while proclaiming God's wonderful works seems evident from the very beginning of Christian preaching. Stephen's great preaching in Acts 7:2–60 is a recollection of God's saving power from the very start: "Brothers and fathers, listen to me. The God of glory appeared to our ancestor Abraham when he was in Mesopotamia, before he lived in Haran, and said to him, 'Leave your country and your relatives and go to the land that I will show you'" (Acts 7:2–3). Indeed, it is Stephen's revisionist interpretation of salvation history from Abraham, the patriarchs, and Moses that has provoked his murder. In the end his preaching literally falls on deaf ears: "But they covered their ears, and with a loud shout all rushed together against him" (v. 57).

Yngve Brilioth reminds us of the important link that the early Church had to the synagogue and marks the emergence of Christian preaching with three primary elements: liturgical, exegetical, and prophetic, all of which are constitutive of Jesus' activity in Luke 4:16–21.[4] Some other preaching events in the New Testament have become paradigmatic as well. C. H Dodd's *Apostolic Preaching and Its Developments* (1936) argued that the preaching in Acts—such as Paul's exhortation in Acts 13:15–41, or Peter's exhortation in Acts 3:12–26—are more or less case studies of the preaching of the early Christian community. And Hughes Oliphant Old surveys at least five major preaching genres that have emerged in the history of preaching: expository, evangelistic, catechetical, festal, and prophetic preaching. He traces their origin to the psalm genres developed by Old Testament scholars.[5] Biblical literary forms powerfully influenced the way in which God's Word would be proclaimed in the early church.

Jesus' preaching in Luke 4:16–21 and other biblical witnesses became templates for the early church, models for preaching. These seminal events would be duplicated in the liturgical life of the Christian community. Thomas K. Carroll explains that "within the experience of the divine liturgy, they, too, preached on the sacred scriptures in a prophetic and homiletic manner, and thus brought into being within the first two centuries of the Church a unique type of rhetoric, which came to full flower in the time of Origen (185–253) and was named by him a homily in Greek and afterwards a sermon in Latin."[6]

Origen distinguished *homilia (tractatus)* from *sermo (logos)*. The homily was direct and free, "a popular exposition and application of scripture." On the other hand, the sermon, Robert Waznak points out, "followed the shape of classical rhetoric."[7] Waznak says that the homily has five characteristics: biblical, liturgical, kerygmatic, conversational, and prophetic.[8] A useful way of thinking about the homily is by contrasting it with catechesis. While catechetical instruction sought to impart information on Christian living, the *homilia*—which can mean "conversation" or "casual discourse"—was originally meant to be an informal, oral exposition of the text of scripture, an act of interpretation whose primary function was to illuminate the passage. On the other hand, catechesis, especially as it would evolve in the early church and beyond, was designed for persuasive argumentation. "Catechetical instruction as we find it in the earliest documents did not open up the mysteries of eternal reality, nor try to speak of the nature of God or of the salvation of the world."[9] Catechesis also derived a form of preaching in its own right, separate from the liturgical homily. With more apologetic concerns than is usually typical of the liturgical *homilia*, catechetical preaching really evolves into its own distinctive subgenre; it is exemplified by the brilliant preaching done by the Cappadocian Fathers or Theodore of Antioch in the fourth century.[10] In contrast to catechetical preaching, liturgical preaching emerges from the scriptures in the context of a liturgical event. Free from high rhetorical design, the homily allows the speaker to be relatively transparent. The liturgical homily's own formal style would evolve over time, nevertheless. Doubtless, the patristic master preachers like Saint John Chrysostom practiced different kinds of homiletic styles in the course of their preaching. Moreover, these homiletic forms have varied greatly according to region and place of origin, as Thomas K. Carroll has shown, and there is a great deal of variety between Latin patristic authors and, say, the Greek fathers preaching in Alexandria.[11]

Text and Logos:
Patristic Preaching and Classical Rhetoric

The church's contact with the Greek world would shape the form and function of both the liturgy and the homily of which it was a part. Thomas K. Carroll explains that at least four things occurred in Church order and worship, all of which would affect early Christian preaching:

a) a transition in the notion of preacher from charismatic prophet to hierarchic priest.

b) An equally significant change in the notion of worship from Jewish *synaxis* to Christian Eucharist.

c) A totally new form of exegesis from Jewish allegory to Christian typology.

d) A new style of presentation as classical rhetoric replaces biblical diatribe.[12]

The inevitable influence of Greco-Roman rhetoric would ultimately move Christian preaching away from biblical, prophetic kerygma into a Hellenistic, stylized *homilia*. "In this context prophecy was no longer the dominant dimension of preaching and was replaced by *didache* or teaching, with its emphasis on the unity and authority of tradition as handed down from bishop to bishop."[13] For some scholars, an enormous loss occurred in the history of preaching at precisely this juncture of Hellenized rhetoric and Christian kerygma. Brilioth says that in the Greek homily of the apostolic fathers, the prophetic character of preaching has been silenced altogether and replaced by teaching and a sober *paranesis* or ethical admonition.[14] Such a transformation was by no means sudden. According to George A. Kennedy, the contours of the Christian homily began to change over the years, "as the Church gradually began to employ more artificial rhetoric addressed to cultured audiences."[15] Some in these educated assemblies eventually became erudite preachers. And, indeed, most of the great patristic preachers were trained as rhetoricians. The Cappadocian Fathers—Basil the Great, his brother Gregory of Nyssa, and Gregory of Nazianzus—deployed the stylistic Greek

11

rhetoric of late antiquity, "metaphor, comparison, ecphrasis, Gorgaianic figures and parallelism."[16]

The highly rhetorical Latin *sermo* exerted an even more powerful influence on Christian preaching. Augustine's *De Doctrina Christiana* (396) synthesized Latin Christian preaching into a distinct, rhetorical discipline and would echo classical rhetoric's emphasis on a balance of *logos*, *ethos* and *pathos*. In the *Rhetoric*, Aristotle had regarded the *logos* as one of the three principal parts of the act of oration or speech-act. Aristotle has an elaborate division of labor for the *logos* of speech, the most obvious characteristic of which is "argumentation."[17] Now such rhetorical argumentation would not necessarily need to appeal to proclamation and faith experience at all. It would be possible to "preach" a sermon without a congregation, since the perfection of the sermonic form was independent of the listener. That development may appear to underscore the literary sophistication of the sermon, but for George Kennedy, Augustine's weakness is his identification of rhetoric with style because he "gave still greater authority to the categorization of styles and figures which was already an obsession of classical rhetoric. Just as technical and sophistic rhetoric had absorbed and diluted philosophical rhetoric in the centuries after Aristotle, Augustine made it possible for classical rhetoric to absorb Latin Christian writing and preaching into its discipline and prescriptions."[18] Augustine himself said that it would be well for those who cannot write their own sermons "to learn by heart and preach those of acknowledged masters."[19] By the time of Gregory the Great at the end of the sixth century, for example, it had become the practice to read the text alone from what Brilioth calls "an acknowledged teacher of the church." Thus, "the practice indicated that the liturgy had smothered the sermon, making it a mere section of the liturgy, which could only happen in an era when exposition of Scripture had dried up and when the spirit of prophecy had departed from the church."[20]

Preaching in the Middle Ages and the
Ars Praedicandi

Tracing the movement of classical rhetoric into the Middle Ages may be clearly seen in a vivid analogy provided by Professor Paul Scott Wilson. Wilson describes the early church's structuring "the bones beneath the material" through classical rhetoric, which typically deployed the five traditional categories or laws: invention (argument); arrangement (structuring an argument); style (selecting the right word or image); memory; and delivery. As the rhetorical style became almost an end in itself, "the bones of the sermonic structure began to protrude."[21] It was as if the sermon text became an object, no longer conscious of either the character of the preacher or attentive to the reaction of the listener. The sacred text itself appeared to be swallowed by structural and stylistic architectonics, and this is especially evident in the Middle Ages.[22] Many of the medieval *Ars Praedicandi* manuals were quite derivative. They modeled a sermon that started with a scripture quotation that was then followed by a statement of the theme and a prayer. That theme was restated, and followed by (usually three) divisions relating to the theme. Robert of Basevorn's *Forma Praedicandi* was one of the many manuals that flourished during this period. A variant on this same model, based on an introduction, three points, and a poem has remained in use up to our own day.[23]

The Middle Ages consistently followed one kind of method of argumentation in designing the sermon. Aristotle claimed that there were two types of argument, *induction* and *deduction*, but these medieval manuals encouraged only one type of argumentation—*deduction*. The most obvious examples of this type of preaching by theological argument were the rationalistic "university sermons"; they usually found a quotation of scripture and followed it with points. These points were, in turn, supported with verses from other texts.[24] In general, we might say that during much of the Middle Ages a great deal of catechesis was incorporated into liturgical preaching. Consequently, the sermon became less liturgical and more doctrinal; such instruction was reinforced by deductive argument, often of the most refined and elaborate nature. That kind of deduction was not at all peculiar to Scholastic preaching but was also elemental to contemporary medieval homiletics. Certainly, the years that followed the Reformation and Counter-Reformation only saw an increase in doctrinal, theological arguments, catechetical sermons, and practical rhetorical guides that would benefit greatly from argumentation by deduction.[25] And indeed, neoclassicists such as George Campbell, Hugh Blair, and Richard Whateley produced works on rhetoric that helped to influence deductive preaching in the eighteenth and nineteenth centuries. Whateley argued in "Elements of Rhetoric" (1828) that Aristotelian rhetoric was an "offshoot of Logic."[26]

Although occasionally dismissed because of rhetorical "ornamentation," variations on preaching by theological argumentation were common enough, even in small parishes. The deductive model was popular until well into the twentieth century and adapted into successful textbooks for seminary education. In 1870, John A. Broadus, a Baptist preacher, published *A Treatise on the Preparation and Delivery of Sermons*, which became the most widely used textbook in homiletics in America. Broadus skillfully blended Aristotelian rhetoric with the application of deductive argumentation and stressed the importance of "arrangement" in the manner of the Philosopher. In his chapter "Classification by Pattern," for example, Broadus recommends several deductive outlines for preaching, such as "the ladder outline": (1) all people have sinned; (2) Christ suffered and paid the price for the sins of humanity; (3) through Christ, humans may be forgiven their sins. This strategy is followed by others, such as "the diagnosis-remedy outline" and "the analogy outline," to name just a few.[27]

The Preacher and Ethos:
Post-Enlightenment Europe

A new accent on preaching arose with the return to a more basic experience of God that emphasized personal religious experience; it surfaced in eighteenth-century Europe "among Europeans of widely different confessional traditions. These groups were disgusted with what corporate Christian states had done to each other since the Reformation, and disillusioned with 'objective' appeals to scripture and tradition; they turned inwardly to a more individualistic and (in a certain sense) 'subjective' appropriation of the Christian faith."[28] Often associated with the great preaching of John Wesley (1703–91) and George Whitefield (1714–70) in the eighteenth century, "this preaching grew out of an essentially Calvinistic and Puritan understanding that the election of those predestined to salvation generally occurs when the Word of God is opened to a congregation through preaching."[29]

If this style of preaching had a unique feature it was its emphasis on *ethos*, the second principal quality that Aristotle named as part of the speech-act.[30] For Aristotle, the orator should be "a good and trusted man." *Ethos* is an element of character and "cannot be a matter of authority or the previous reputation of the orator. The reason for this is that only ethos projected in this way is artistic."[31] The popular story is told of John Wesley, who was once asked by someone how he preached. The great reformer is supposed to have replied, "I just ascend the pulpit, catch on fire, and the people watch me burn." Wesley and Whitefield were supposed to have devised a way of speaking that was close to singing. The task was to preach passionately in order to elicit religious fervor.[32] We know now that, far from preaching spontaneously, Wesley developed a highly sophisticated rhetorical style, especially in his early mature years, but this language evidently only increased his ethos as a witness to the gospel.[33] Wesley's effect on the congregation was conversion, prioritizing the role of the preacher into what Robert Waznak has called "the witness" as one of the several models for preaching that have evolved over the centuries.[34]

Schleiermacher, the Modern Witness

Friedrich Schleiermacher (1768–1834), a famous preacher and theologian in Berlin in the early nineteenth century, was an enormously complex thinker. He is often referred to as the father of modern theology.[35] Schleiermacher helps to crystallize

15

the *ethos* of the preacher as one who exemplifies a "witness" and mediator of meaning for a congregation. Schleiermacher sought to make hermeneutics the basis of theology, thereby shifting the weight of objective dogma to more personal, subjective interpretation. His interest was exegetical and departed from the neoclassical rhetoric and moral prescriptions so prevalent in Western Europe at his time. For him, poetic speech, and all its range of meaning and experience, was capable of transforming the human subject. Half Romantic poet, half theologian, the preacher was the potential conveyor of this conversion in a community of believers. In his "Introduction" to *Hermeneutics and Criticism* (1809–10), Schleiermacher articulates the role of the interpreter as a kind of broker of divine grace. Augustine had hinted at this quality of *ethos* when he says of a biblical passage that "the good listener will not so much be instructed by its being diligently analyzed as fired by its being passionately recited."[36] But Schleiermacher takes the role of the speaker somewhat further, saying that "the art of explication is therefore the art of putting oneself in possession of all conditions of understanding."[37] As Richard Lischer says, Schleiermacher "is remembered for shifting the weight of the hermeneutical and homiletical task from the objectivity of dogma to the subjectivities of the God-consciousness of the preacher and the life-situation of the hearer....He single-handedly reinvented the sermon as a medium through which the speaker imaginatively imparts his or her own experience of God to those who are receptive to it."[38]

Schleiermacher would face significant challenges several years later from neo-orthodox theologian, Karl Barth, who would ask: "Where is the Word of God in this immanent sea of feeling?...Where is the ongoing seeking if all that is done is simply the expression of an inner possessing?"[39] Through *ethos*, though, the preacher is not a narcissistic spectacle but becomes the link in making meaning for the congregation. Unlike the tradition he inherited, Schleiermacher imagined that the topics for sermons would be realized from a pastoral, practical encounter, not from a logical sequence of deduction. The minister would be "continually formulating his thoughts more or less directly from life and reflecting on them before the congregation....Everything depends on how much one can trust himself to hold fast to what has arisen within."[40] Schleiermacher was acutely aware of the balance between the preacher and the listener: "The minister has two perspectives. On the one hand, he goes back to the context in the biblical passage. But with his congregation in mind, he also has to see what they are accustomed to. Because his own exploration in the text is quite extensive, he must remember the capacities of his congregation."[41] Schleiermacher's writings on hermeneutics have been tellingly prophetic; they suggested what would soon become a preaching legacy in the twentieth century, a focus toward the *20ᵗʰ cent.* hearer as the one for whom meaning is mediated.

The Listener and Pathos

The third and last component of the oration for Aristotle is *pathos*, which he discusses in the *Rhetoric*, Book II, Chapters 1–11. The careful use of pathos is an appeal to the feelings and emotions of the audience. Pathos is really the study of human emotions; to be aware of them places the speaker at an advantage, since the ability to evoke strong feelings in the audience situates them in the "correct frame of mind" (1358a). "Pathos occurs as a mode of artistic proof when the souls of the audience are moved to emotion: they will come to a different conclusion for example, when they are angry than when they are pleased."[42] Augustine also echoed the importance of attending to listeners and their disposition when he asked in *De Doctrina Christiana*, Book IV: "What profits correctness in a speech which is not followed by the listeners when there is no reason for speaking if what is said is not understood by those on whose account we speak? He who teaches should thus avoid all words which do not teach."[43]

No one would argue that the listener has been totally absent from homiletic strategies over the years. After all, *pathos* is one of the Aristotelian elements for the speech-act. But, as we have seen, sermonic arguments, for a variety of reasons, have traditionally occurred in the form of deduction rather than Aristotle's second element for argumentation, namely, *induction*.[44] Where deductive rhetoric starts from a general principle and then moves to specific examples, inductive preaching does the reverse: it is the concrete

17

example and life experience that open the speech from which general conclusions might be drawn. I am not suggesting that argument by deduction, per se, is either weak or faulty. But rationalistic argument by deduction in a homily tends to eclipse the listener, since the deductive sermon can resist the historical mediating circumstance of a human subject. In other words, deduction stands on its own; it is quite possible to construct an argument without account for the people listening to it. Inductive argumentation, however, presumes an audience by definition; the strategy is to begin with concrete examples drawn from human experience and draw conclusions or an induction. With Schleiermacher's hermeneutical tactics, the history of preaching shifts in a direction that gives priority to the preacher's effect on a listening congregation; that movement implicates an inductive argument that would be more fully focused a hundred years later. What becomes clear in the twentieth century and beyond is that the listener's engagement is crucial to the very performance of the homily itself.

Contemporary Communication: The Turn Toward the Listener

Along with Schleiermacher's influence on Christian hermeneutics, a variety of factors contributed to a movement toward the listener in preaching into the twentieth century. I will only suggest two trends. The first of these comes from the academic community itself, where we notice a rapid growth and interest in biblical studies in the nineteenth century and into the twentieth, especially with the strong attention to the historical-critical method and to the critical study of forms of the Bible by notable Protestant theologians. This biblical scholarship strongly influenced the condition of contemporary preaching, since much of the recovery of the ancient text disclosed a more urgent, kerygmatic form of preaching. C. H. Dodd said that "much of our preaching in church at the present day would not have been recognized by the early Christians as kerygma."[45] Dodd, who studied extensively the early preaching of Paul and Peter in Acts as well as the parables of Jesus asks the question: what was the Gospel, historically speaking, at the beginning, and during the New testament period? Kerygma. The task of preaching is to come to terms with this gospel discourse and preach it in the twentieth century.[46] Dodd is echoing the lament of many who have noted the loss of biblical forms as a constitutive element in preaching. As Sidney Greidanus has pointed out recently, those who practice expository preaching (as opposed to topical) will be informed by the kerygmatic form of the Bible, which can be classified into distinct genres.[47] Modern biblical scholarship wants to reclaim a more ancient form of preaching, informed by the kerygmatic activity of the New Testament.

From a biblical scholar's point of view, deductive preaching makes a grasp of kerygma practically impossible. How does the contemporary mind begin to absorb the essential impulse of the ancient text? The Roman Catholic Church's *Divino Afflante Spiritu* (1943) encouraged the work of textual criticism as a scientific discipline in order to understand better the biblical literary tradition rooted in ancient Semitic culture. Later, the Second Vatican Council's *Dogmatic Constitution on Divine Revelation (Dei Verbum)* echoed the long tradition of *lectio divina* in the church that encouraged the preacher to listen carefully to the Word and cultivate his reading of scripture in order to be effective.[48] Form criticism applied to scripture could help scholars discover genres that revealed how God's Word was disseminated in biblical times.

Not everyone agreed that historical-critical methods would be the best way to grasp the early text and preach it effectively. Indeed, some of these historical-critical methods were deemed by some as suspect and ineffectual, especially for effective preaching. For these scholars, historical methods never really apprehend the meaning "inside" the text; such strategies have led to what Hans W. Frei has called "the eclipse of Biblical narrative."[49] Frei and other narrative theologians suggest that the realistic quality of the Bible precisely as a story meant for hearers has been overshadowed by attention to history. Indeed, the literary, narrative impulse is at the core of the biblical text, allowing listeners to reorder their lives through an encounter with the narrative impulse and strategy of the text. The parables of Jesus are the most obvious examples of this: preaching captured in a narrative frame, sowed in a field to be cultivated or rejected. Jesus was, after all, the master storyteller, what Bernard Brandon Scott has called the "symbol-maker" for the kingdom, who effected his conversions by retelling conventional narratives in an unconventional way.[50]

But the second trend that turned preaching toward a hearer has been much more monumental even than the considerable work in biblical and literary studies in the last hundred years. That influence has come from the listeners themselves. Modern American culture has formed them into consumers, sports fans, movie-goers, television viewers—in other words, wholesale, corporate *receivers*. As an instance here we could certainly cite the astonishing rise of mass culture in the twentieth century, specifically the American film industry, which, since its emergence in the urban nickelodeons in the late nineteenth century, consciously produced narratives that were transforming and transformed by the audiences for whom they were written.[51] Film and radio culture has created an audience raised on media—radio, film, and television—that is utterly inductive.

Thus, there has been a profound epistemological shift, a change in our way of knowing, at least within the last hundred years or more; it has transformed almost everything, especially the way we hear and understand language. Our culture now educates entirely by induction, and indeed, the teaching profession in the 1960s was also very influential in applying a revolutionary system of inductive learning to millions of students. Consumer culture, by definition, is filled with those who actively receive everything, from the products themselves to the information about them (advertising). According to J. Randall Nichols, the definitive statement about how communication works appeared in the mid-twentieth century in a work by Claude Elwood Shannon and Warren Weaver entitled *The Mathematical Theory of Communication* (1963). The first of the author's six principles for communication is that "communication is a receiver phenomenon."[52] As Nichols explains it:

> Although much of traditional homiletics focuses
> on the preacher's work in constructing a sermon, a

communication approach recognizes that communication is an inherently constructive process in which the receiver of messages actively builds meaning on the basis of information at hand, both from the signals provided by the sender and from existing or ambient information in the receiver's field.[53]

Communication theory recognizes that the preacher must abandon a style that fails to attend to a listener. J. Dewey and A. F. Bentley were able to apply their own research in education to levels of receiver interaction in *Knowing and the Known* (1949).[54] These authors first introduced the popular terms *actional*, *interactional*, and *transactional* into social science.[55] *Actional* describes the least effective way to communicate, since its aim is "the transmission of information and therefore strongly emphasizes message formation."[56] As Leonora Tubbs Tisdale has remarked:

> In speaker-oriented communication, primary emphasis is placed upon the speaker's ability to communicate the message accurately and correctly. The goal is that the information reach the hearer without any adulteration or change. The speaker encodes the message in language and symbols familiar to the speaker, and may choose to do so in a very esoteric way. What is most important is that none of the essential content be lost in transmission of the message.[57]

Interactional communication, on the other hand, transfers "ideas from one person to another. Here the listener is admitted as part of the communicative situation. The focus, however, in research and training is upon the message formulator [speaker]."[58] *Transactional* communication describes what occurs *between* people because it "recognizes that the sender changes the message as s/he receives feedback from the listener."[59] If we take these communication perspectives very broadly, it is easy to see how they might apply to the ways of preaching we have been discussing in this chapter, namely, the principal components of the speech-act: *logos*, *ethos*, and *pathos*. When preaching is deductive, it is *logos*-centered, and it has a risk of becoming actional, or dominated by the transmission of a message alone. In this scenario the homilist has a potentially minimal effect on a listener, and the congregation remains incidental to the preaching moment. Having said this, though, we might remember that the text remains a constitutive component of the speech-act. Jesus' preaching in the synagogue in Nazareth was informed by a text of which he is the fulfillment. Moreover, the difficulty with moving too far afield from some kind of message is the evacuation of a theological and historical moment. Messages center both the speaker and the congregation in a particular framework or content. Preaching without *logos* devolves into talk shows and entertainment spectacles that are driven by the personality of the showman and his audience.

A certain kind of criticism also exists if the object of a homily is simply to transfer information from a talented formulator, *interactionally*; then preaching is dominated by *ethos*, or the charism of the preacher himself. Here, the homilist becomes a self-conscious actor, or worse, a kind of empty, theatrical spectacle. There is little scriptural "message," and the congregation is reduced to marginalized spectators who are there to be entertained rather than enlightened. Some would claim that preaching in many congregations is currently stalled at this stage. Having moved from a message-centered sermon, the Christian assembly now faces preachers and presiders who attempt to amuse their congregations by the sheer power of their own personality. And yet, *ethos* has functioned not only as a vehicle for the preacher but as a mechanism for witness, and ultimately conversion. A homily robbed of *ethos* lacks conviction, drama, and humanity. If Aristotle meant *ethos* to be indicative of character, then the *ethos* portion of the speech-act represents a moral center for the homily.

Finally, contemporary communication leans toward audience participation. If *pathos* centered, then the homily moves toward transactional communication and fully engages the congregation in a dialectical relationship, or in what John McClure has called, "a round table pulpit."[60] Simply put, under the conditions suggested by McClure and others, the assembly constructs the sermon in the course of the week, serving as contributors to an expansive series of personal narratives that are ultimately gathered into one, "unified"

sermonic text. There is a potential problem here as well, in my estimation. A completely audience-centered homily is something like
"art by committee." It robs the homilist and the text of authority;
no one seemingly claims responsibility for the interpretation.
Ultimately, under such conditions, even the text itself becomes
unstable, even unknowable. Moreover, the teaching accomplished
under these conditions is often problematic, for reasons that are
probably obvious enough. Ultimately, the roundtable homily may
engage the experiences of too many participants and be too diffused
to be absorbed in a single sitting. Listening to *his* words, not the
words of those who heard him, fulfilled the text that Jesus proclaimed in Nazareth.

It is important to recognize, though, that the attention
toward the listener is a mature and vital development in the history of preaching and a necessary one to contemplate in our own
culture. To be sure, this final stage in this level of communication
recognizes the full authority of the hearer, which will not be lost
on those who would give preaching a "new hearing." In a certain
sense, the history of preaching is a story about the rise of the listener in the homiletic act. First acknowledged as a partner in the
fulfillment of Jesus' work on earth, then eclipsed by high rhetorical style, the hearer is destined to return once again to the synagogue to hear the Son of God, the Word made flesh. By the
mid- to late twentieth century, a number of methodological tools
began to evolve and to be promulgated in Protestant schools of
theology in North America. I will turn in the next chapter to the
most significant and influential of these homiletic methods.

Notes

1. NCCB, *Fulfilled in Your Hearing: The Homily in the Sunday Assembly* (Washington, D.C.: USCC, 1982), 3.

2. See, for example, Alistair Stewart-Sykes, *From Prophecy to Preaching: A Search for the Origins of The Christian Homily* (Boston: Brill, 2001).

3. Ibid., 6–14.

4. Yngve Brilioth, *A Brief History of Preaching*, trans. K. E. Mattson (Philadelphia: Fortress Press, 1965), 8–10.

5. See Hughes Oliphant Old, *The Reading and Preaching of the Scriptures in the Worship of the Christian Church*, vol. 1, *The Biblical Period* (Grand Rapids, MI: Eerdmans, 1998), 8ff.

6. Thomas K. Carroll, *Preaching the Word* (Wilmington, DE: Michael Glazier, 1984), 18.

7. Robert Waznak, SS, "Homily," in *The New Dictionary of Sacramental Worship*, ed. Peter E. Fink, SJ (Collegeville, MN: Liturgical Press, 1990), 552. See also Domenico Sartore, "The Homily," in *Handbook for Liturgical Studies*, vol. 3, *The Eucharist*, ed. Ansgar Chupungco, 189–208 (Collegeville, MN: Liturgical Press, 2000); and L. Della Torre, "Homilía," in *Nuevo Diccionario de Liturgia*, 3rd ed., ed. D. Sartore, A. M. Triacca, and J. M. Canals (Madrid: San Pablo, 1987), 1015–37.

8. Robert Waznak, *Introduction to the Homily* (Collegeville, MN: Liturgical Press, 1998), 16–26.

9. Old, *Reading and Preaching*, 259.

10. See Hughes Oliphant Old, *Reading and Preaching*, vol. 2, *The Ancient Church* (Grand Rapids, MI: Eerdmans, 1998), 5–15, 224–34.

11. See Carroll, *Preaching the Word*, esp. 63–166. Carroll treats the variety of Greek and Latin Patristic authors in some detail, nicely distinguishing the Greek homily in the Alexandrian Church from the developments in the fourth century.

12. Carroll, *Preaching the Word*, 21.

13. Ibid., 21.

14. Brilioth, *A Brief History of Preaching*, 20.

15. George A. Kennedy, *Classical Rhetoric and Its Christian and Secular Tradition from Ancient to Modern Times* (Chapel Hill: Univ. of North Carolina Press, 1980), 136.

16. Byron D. Stuhlman, "Cappadocian Fathers," in *Concise Encyclopedia of Preaching*, ed. William H. Willimon and Richard Lischer (Louisville, KY: Westminster John Knox, 1995), 65.

17. For a useful summary of the artistic or internal modes of proof available to deliberative speech, see Kennedy, *Classical Rhetoric*, 60–82.

18. Ibid., 159–60.

19. Augustine, *Teaching Christianity: De Doctrina Christiana*, ed. Edmund Hill and John E. Rotella (New York: New City Press, 1996), 239.

20. Brilioth, *A Brief History of Preaching*, 68.

21. Paul Scott Wilson, *A Concise History of Preaching* (Nashville, TN: Abingdon Press, 1992), 71.

22. See Thomas L. Amos, Eugene A. Green, and Beverly Mayne Kienzle, eds., *De Ore Domini: Preacher and Word in the Middle Ages* (Kalamazoo: Western Michigan Univ. Press, 1989).

23. Wilson, *A Concise History of Preaching*, 71.

24. Ibid., 81–85.

25. See, for example, Old, *The Reading and Preaching of Scripture*, vol. 4: *The Age of the Reformation* (Grand Rapids, MI: Eerdmans, 1998–); and Peter E. McCullough, *Sermons at Court: Politics and Religion in Elizabethan and Jacobean Preaching* (Cambridge, UK: Cambridge Univ. Press, 1998).

26. See Richard Whateley, "Elements of Rhetoric," in *The Rhetorical Tradition*, ed. Patricia Bizzell and Bruce Herzberg (Boston: Bedford, 1990), 828–58.

27. John A. Broadus, *On the Preparation and Delivery of Sermons*, 4th ed., rev. Vernon L. Stanfield (San Francisco: HarperCollins, 1979), 68–75. (Orig. pub. 1870.)

28. T. A. Campbell, *The Religion of the Heart*, 177, quoted in Willimon and Lischer, *Concise Encyclopedia of Preaching*, 214.

29. O. C. Edwards, "History," in Willimon and Lischer, *Concise Encyclopedia of Preaching*, 214.

30. For a detailed account of the significance of *ethos* in the history of classical rhetoric and its impact on Pauline preaching and contemporary homiletics, see Andrē Resner Jr., *Preacher and Cross: Person and Message in Theology and Rhetoric* (Grand Rapids, MI: Eerdmans, 1999).

31. Kennedy, *Classical Rhetoric*, 68.

32. Wilson, *A Concise History of Preaching*, 136–37. See also the entry on John Wesley and George Whitefield in the same volume.

33. Ibid., 134.

34. Waznak, *Introduction to the Homily*, 32–40.

35. See, for example, Keith W. Clements, *Friedrich Schleiermacher: Pioneer of Modern Theology* (Philadelphia: Fortress Press, 1997), esp. 124–71.

36. Augustine, *Teaching Christianity*, 212.

37. Friedrich Schleiermacher, *Hermeneutics and Criticism*, ed. Andrew Bowie (Cambridge, UK: Cambridge Univ. Press, 1998), 227.

38. Friedrich Schleiermacher, "Praktische Theologie," in *The Company of Preachers: Wisdom on Preaching, Augustine to the Present*, ed. Richard Lischer (Grand Rapids, MI: Eerdmans, 2002), 8.

39. Karl Barth, *Homiletics*, trans. Geoffrey W. Bromiley and Donald E. Daniels (Louisville, KY: Westminster John Knox, 1991), 22–23. (Orig. pub. 1966.)

40. Schleiermacher, in Lischer, *The Company of Preachers*, 13.

41. Ibid.

42. Kennedy, *Classical Rhetoric*, 68.

43. Augustine, *On Christian Doctrine*, trans. D. W. Robertson Jr. (Upper Saddle River, NJ: Prentice Hall, 1953), 134.

44. Charles L. Campbell reminds us that, beside Aristotle's invention of the method long ago, the inductive movement has found a place in early eighteenth-century France, where François Fenelon proposed a homiletic style similar to induction. See Charles Campbell, ed., "Inductive Preaching," in Willimon and Lischer, *Concise Encyclopedia of Preaching*, 270–72.

45. C. H. Dodd, quoted in Lischer, *The Company of Preachers*, 23.

46. Ibid., 28.

47. See Sidney Greidanus, *The Modern Preacher and the Ancient Text: Interpreting and Preaching Biblical Literature* (Grand Rapids, MI: Eerdmans, 1988).

48. *The Documents of Vatican II*, ed. Walter Abbott, SJ (New Brunswick: New Century Press, 1966), 127. Quoting Saint Augustine, *Dei Verbum* says that "the cultivation of Scripture is required lest any of them become 'an empty preacher of the word of God outwardly, who is not a listener to it inwardly.'"

49. See Hans Frei, *The Eclipse of Biblical Narrative* (New Haven, CT: Yale Univ. Press, 1980).

50. Bernard Brandon Scott, *Jesus, Symbol-Maker for the Kingdom* (Philadelphia: Fortress Press, 1981). Also see idem, *Hear Then the Parable: A Commentary on the Parables of Jesus* (Minneapolis: Augsburg Fortress Press, 1989).

51. The study of how and why American audiences heard and received cinematic texts constitutes a significant area in film studies today. See, for instance, Janet Staiger, *Interpreting Films: Studies in the Historical Reception of American Cinema* (Princeton, NJ: Princeton Univ. Press, 1992); and Barbara Klinger, "Digressions at the Cinema:

Commodification and Reception in Mass Culture," in *Modernity and Mass Culture*, ed. James Naremore and Patrick Brantlinger (Bloomington: Indiana Univ. Press, 1991), 117–34.

52. Claude Elwood Shannon and Warren Weaver, quoted in Willimon and Lischer, *Concise Encyclopedia of Preaching*, 84. The six principles are listed and well glossed by J. Randall Nichols, "Communication," in ibid., 85–87.

53. Nichols, "Communication," 85.

54. See Richard C. Stern, "Communication Perspectives in Teaching Preaching," (Ed.D. diss., Northern Illinois Univ., 1990), 41.

55. Ibid.

56. D. C. Barlund, quoted in Stern, "Communication Perspectives in Teaching Preaching," 46.

57. Leonora Tubs Tisdale, *Preaching as Local Theology and Folk Art* (Minneapolis: Fortress Press, 1997), 45.

58. Ibid., 49

59. Ibid., 51.

60. See John McClure, *The Round-Table Pulpit* (Nashville, TN: Abingdon Press, 1995).

2
THE NEW HOMILETIC

So faith comes from what is heard, and what is heard comes through the word of Christ.

—Romans 10:17

Inductive preaching did not occur overnight but emerged out of a complicated and intricate web of theological and cultural circumstances. With the attention to audience reception given by multiple forms of technology in the twentieth century, some form of inductive preaching was practically inevitable. Preaching by induction was meant for a culture like ours, one that thrives on *experience.* Inductive homiletics begins with the concrete circumstances and realities of human life and perception and moves toward and into the contours of the gospel. The gospel's Good News becomes the light poured out upon that experience. Conclusions are drawn not by logical (deductive) propositions presented in the homily but by narrational movement. Like the great media tools of the last hundred years, induction encourages the audience to participate actively in the process of understanding, allowing listeners or viewers to come to their own decisions. In a certain sense, the democratic, pluralistic structure of American culture itself has enabled the inductive process to take hold. And indeed, as we will see shortly, underlying preaching by induction remains an authority issue, which perhaps explains why this style of preaching took shape first in liberal Protestant denominations.

Fred Craddock did not introduce a new idea into homiletics so much as initiate a shift in thinking about preaching. His books, *As One Without Authority* (1971) and *Overhearing the Gospel* (1978), are mandates for preachers to bring the pulpit "out of the shadows" and "into the spotlight" through holistic, indirect discourse. When he speaks of deductive sermons, Craddock echoes those who were troubled by "actional" communication, saying that "the sermon carried the entire burden; the listener accepted or rejected the conclusions"; these sermons "spoke but they did not listen; they were completed at the mouth and not at the ear.[1] Craddock's inductive homiletic was inspired by a changing cultural milieu and shaped around "the rapidly shifting nature of public language, the new biblical studies and contemporary hermeneutics."[2] Yet, while Craddock's contributions are significant in and of themselves, there is more to this imaginative man than an overview of his work would suggest. This chapter will deal first with Fred Craddock, one of the founders of what has been called the New Homiletics and then go on to examine some methods for preaching inductively he helped to inspire.

The Story

Most accounts of Fred Craddock would probably begin with an account of his most influential book, *As One Without Authority*, which laid bare the problem of deductive homiletics at a critical juncture in American history. Yet for our purposes here, I think that a most telling case for inductive preaching occurs somewhat later, when he records his encounter with the writings of Søren Kierkegaard in the late 1970s.[3] Craddock found Kierkegaard's lifelong question of "how to be a Christian, here and now" very compelling, especially in respect to the dynamic life of faith. Kierkegaard faces Craddock with a mirror image of the crisis in homiletics, a gap between cognition and experience: "there is no lack of information in a Christian land; something else is lacking."[4] For Craddock, the Bible experienced precisely as a human story will figure very significantly in its ability to confront the "how" of Christian existence, not only by virtue of the scripture's theological content, but because its *form* continually stretches the hearer into the middle of the fateful question of faith—the eternal "how." Craddock says that "a gospel is also a form as well as a message; it is a narrative conveying a sense of historical chronology and continuity, naming places and times and characters."[5] Craddock's assertion extends even further: the goal of scripture is to interpret *us* (and not the other way around), a long legacy rooted in apostolic preaching. "Paul understood the word was not just a certain content of meaning but an act, from person to person, that did something, that effected change."[6] Certainly, the long history of *lectio divina* in the monastic Middle Ages also suggests a tradition in which the Word both inspires and convicts a reader. As Richard C. Stern has remarked, "Although preaching is often referred to as 'breaking open the Word,' that is only half of the task. The other half is allowing ourselves to be broken open by the Word, letting scripture expose our weaknesses, our inadequacies, our need for grace, as well as the love of God that is already present in our midst."[7] With his reading of Kierkegaard, Craddock is initiating a powerful textual dynamic for Christian preaching. We are not only encouraged to listen to the text, but the faithful listening to scripture becomes the very essence of living the gospel.

If preaching is meant to change people, then, for Craddock, that transformation occurs not through a text that is *message centered* but by way of *experience*—induction. The inductive sermon organized around narrative logic reaches out and grabs the congregation, compelling them into the "how" of Christian existence, a question posed by the scriptures themselves, especially evident in the parables of Jesus. In a sermon Craddock preached called "But What About the Weeds?" he tries to get the congregation into the disposition of Jesus's listeners in Matthew 13:24–30:

> It is also quite natural that the servants would say, "Master, do you want us to take the weeds out?" It is a natural impulse. Pull out the weeds, get rid of the weeds. Out in the world there are all kinds of groups dedicated to doing just that, to getting rid of what is undesirable. "Put them on a boat and send them back where they came from."…But the difficult part of this parable is the fact that the boss said, "Leave the weeds alone." What? Just leave the weeds in there with the wheat? Have wheat and weeds together? Isn't there any such thing as right and wrong, good and evil, true and false? We need to take a stand. We need to draw the line.[8]

To preach inductively is to preach so that the possibility of conversion blossoms fully as the Word is broken open for all; it is a sermon that is informed both by life and biblical discourse itself, an inductive process that identifies with the listener, and uses analogy.[9] This inductive method follows a general pattern of movement from the specific avenues of experience toward a concluding inference. As Ronald Allen says: *[handwritten: inductive = tension]*

> The inductive sermon creates tension: the congregation recognizes unresolved qualities in understanding a biblical text, doctrine, practice, or situation and seeks to know how those tensions can be resolved. Inductive preaching is itself an experience of discovery. In this respect, inductive movement reflects the movement of many human experiences.[10]

Some Implications

The ramifications of Craddock's homiletic enterprise are clear. It is useful to point out here the underlying politics of inductive preaching as Craddock has framed the method: it wants to allow for an utterly democratic process, to de-center the authority of a single voice controlling a perspective on a "message." The overall fluidity of the text is crucial, because the congregation will be unpacking the sermonic text at various levels, depending on the hearers' individual dispositions at the moment. Any preconceived "outline" of the text is always subordinate to its "movement," which "is so vital to its effectiveness that a structure should be provided that facilitates rather than hinders that movement."[11] Craddock maintains that the motion of the homily is not something extraneous to the world of faith but its very substance. True faith is never static but dynamic. Indeed, the scriptures themselves demonstrate ways of preaching and, because these texts are foundational in the life of the church, their essential structure can begin to suggest a contemporary language that ought to embody and empower the church. The Bible is normative as much as it is formative. As Gail R. O'Day says, "Preachers readily turn to Scripture for the subject of sermons, but that is not enough. The Bible offers much more than the subject matter for preaching....That does not mean simply that the words of Scripture should pepper one's sermons, but that the preacher embrace the entire *language world* of Scripture."[12] The preacher extends the formal dynamics of scripture into the sermon itself.

Scripture offers the reader a process of conversion by virtue of its very *form*, placing the reader on the growing edge of faith, as Jesus did in his own use of the parabolic form when he preached. The scripture text is shaped as a biblical narrative, remembering that story is used not just as an episode to illustrate but precisely as a form to convert. Jesus certainly deployed the immediate experiences of agrarian people in the Galilee region to construct his parables. And it was important that the content of these stories was shaped in parabolic form. Jesus often provided his hearers with stories with which they were very familiar but then added an unexpected twist. Jesus brings the hearers into the brink of a "how" moment, often confounding their expectations with a surprise ending or shift in traditional characterization. As Craddock makes clear in his interpretation of Lukan parables, the unique contours of parabolic narrative provide the inductive discourse that allows the hearer to engage and, as it were, to unwrap the text with other listeners—sometimes with a severe "jolt."[13] This crucial moment of revelation also occurs in the process of interpretation itself, where there is a certain tension between the text and the preacher.[14] The congregation interprets the texts of scripture, guided by the homily that fosters, engenders, and enlivens the hearers' collective interpretive powers.

Organic Unity

Craddock returns again and again to Jesus as his model for preaching. Like Jesus, "we are seeking to communicate with people whose experiences are concrete. Everyone lives inductively, not deductively. No farmer deals with the problem of calfhood, only with the calf."[15] Indeed, as Craddock continues his theological thoughts on the process of preaching he says that "the

Incarnation itself is the inductive method."[16] Since Craddock abandons any hope for a deductive sermon's success, he really has no hard-and-fast rules about establishing unity in the inductive process. At the same time, unity in the sermon is important to him. Craddock believes that the unity that comes to a sermon is actually shaped as a story is created, not by a series of points but organically and by an interaction between the congregation and the text. It is impossible to fabricate an external, preconceived structure on a text that becomes organized around a congregational interface.

Again, we can see that Kierkegaard's existential "how" occurs for Craddock in a dynamism, an event that Martin Heidegger, another influential figure, would call *Dasein* or "Being-in-Time." From a theological perspective, unity in a sermon is what happens in the *now* of God's kingdom. There is, then, no such thing as a written "*design* for preaching" (to quote the title of one of the most popular books in the late 1950s for producing sermons), only a *Dasein* for preaching.[17] "Unity does to the sermon what a frame does for a picture. The hearer, as with the viewer of a picture, has the edges of his attention gathered up and focused by the clear sense of being personally addressed with a definite expectation of some kind of response."[18] For Craddock, preaching is not about speaking a static text; it is about living dynamically within a graced event.

Narrative Preaching

Preaching by induction uses the techniques often associated with narrative and is therefore closely entwined with "narrative preaching." In fact, as Eugene Lowry has pointed out, narrative preaching is sometimes nearly identical to inductive preaching, although narrative preaching usually offers a tighter structure and will quite often have an arrangement of ideas that "takes the form of a plot involving a strategic delay of the preacher's meaning."[19] Whether or not the preacher chooses to plot the sermon as a series of episodes, along a specific plot or story line, or as David Buttrick will do, as a series of plotted "moves" ending in a conclusion, depends on the preacher and the text from which the preacher is preaching.[20] It seems to me that Craddock often chooses a somewhat loose narrational form in order to engage the congregation in provocative, gospel-inspired questions. If Craddock found himself preoccupied with the question of "how" in Christian existence, the narrational sermon would be a way to keep that deep question alive. The sermonic text that is narrational for Craddock occurs in the organic "how"—the very Spirit-driven flux of Christian faith—much like our encounter with the living Word itself. Above all, narrational form "determines the degree of participation demanded of the hearers."[21] Here, Craddock is guiding the homiletic process along the lines of the narrative tradition that has shaped so much of our modern media environment. Indeed, with his emphasis on experience and induction, Craddock seems to anticipate the interactive, virtual world of technology few people could have imagined in the 1970s. A good illustration for the way in which narrational form continually asks the participation of the viewers is the Hollywood detective film of the 1940s. Consider John Huston's *The Maltese Falcon* (1941), usually reckoned to be the primary example of such films. The movie's plot is configured around the whereabouts of a precious statue of a jewel-encrusted, golden falcon, once the treasure of the Knights Templar of Malta in the sixteenth century, and now lost. The film leads the viewer in a labyrinth of clues, through the help of Sam Spade, the detective who guides the viewer through the process. From the very start the audience is asked to unravel questions, one after the other, in order to discover the whereabouts of the mysterious falcon and who has it. Such is the process of narrative spectatorship at the cinema; it takes us through a series of unstated questions until we arrive at the final answer. Such narrative questions are posed at the beginning of most conventional narrations and are woven throughout; we are engaged in a process in which, in a certain sense, we all become detectives, no matter what the story. Narrative texts are questions waiting to be answered. And through a process of induction, the audience is invited to solve the problem.

The action of engaging in narrative occurs, as it were, between the lines. Preaching initiates a manner of congregational engagement in which listeners become shrewd detectives, moving along a narrative edge and guided by underlying questions. We sustain the deeper question of the "how" of Christian existence by being led through smaller, narrational clues. Dr. John N. Gladstone begins his sermon, "What's in a Nickname?" (Mark 3:17; John 1:42; Acts 4:36) like this: "I will never forget the day when I ceased to be known only by my name and I acquired a number."[22] We can just imagine the "suspense" mildly rippling through the congregation: What happened to him? How did it happen? Where? These are the kinds of clues that bring preaching into a narrational form and sustain the congregation as they ponder the "how" of Christian faith. Ultimately, Gladstone will guide us to more seminal questions: What is the real identity of the Christian community as named by Jesus? Why should we hold fast to attributes? Such questions are usually unstated in narrational preaching but lurk beneath the surface begging to be encountered, helping the listeners make connections with the text and their own lives.

Narrational preaching is always inductive, but not all inductive preaching is narrative. Preaching as a narrative, then, is notable for the way it engages the congregation in plot and intention; it is a *happening:* an oral, communicative event-in-time, which cannot be reduced to the stasis of writing. Inductive preaching is something like a contract between the preaching and the congregation, in which they agree to make meaning together; this making of meaning may or may not happen in the context of a narrative strategy. Narrative preaching follows the plot design of human experience that is always in motion, makes connections, and moves toward a final ending. Using the formal devices of narrative shows us the quality of the inductive process, which literally occurs in thin air. As one person said of the act of writing a sermon: "There is the sermon you write and then there is the one that you preach." There is a marked difference between a fixed "speech" and the process of "speaking." Furthermore, for Barbara Brown Taylor, "the language of faith is fluid, not solid. Words like grace, judgment, and redemption are not abstract ideas but names for certain experiences."[23] It is worth pointing out, though, that Craddock's loose structure of movement in narrative form does not necessarily guarantee coherence. In fact, the sermon may suffer from a lack of structure.

Craddock's inductive, narrational method appears less concerned with textual coherence than with engaging the congregation in a primal level of religious experience; the sermon is supposed to be provocative, which may lead to a lack of internal structure. Critics may say, though, that a lack of coherence may cause more confusion than conversion. That kind of confusion may very well appeal to Craddock, since it would not be the first time that dissonance led a listener to an act of faith. As we will see later, Craddock's students and successors will tighten up the narrational form in order to engage the congregation more directly with much more attention to the specific dynamics of plot and story.

The Teller

Craddock is very interested in the *ethos* of the preacher. What the preacher reveals in the act of preaching becomes part of the sermon itself. The text of the sermon and its unity are generated because of the unique relationship of the teller with the hearer, one who "speaks *for* them as well as *to* them."[24] The preacher ought to be a Christian whose belief is clearly vibrant and visible. Yet Craddock's recommendation for the one who preaches not only includes a life of "faith, passion, authority and grace" but an intense interest in study as well.[25] Aristotle certainly would have included these as impeccable attributes for the virtuous orator whose *ethos* or character in the speech-act was of great importance. But Craddock also details a prescription for a certain amount of self-disclosure by the preacher for the purpose of intimacy and vulnerability with the congregation.[26] This attribute of personal transparency is undoubtedly linked to Craddock's interest in the oral communicative process of preaching, which must be "transactional" if it is to be effectively engaging: a mutual, intimate sharing of the faith experience in the context of worship. Also, in recognizing the importance of self-revelation, Craddock is recalling an attribute that we know is extant in the early tradition of the *homilia*, which took the shape of an expository discourse in the midst of fellow Christian travelers.

In his own sermons Craddock often gives a personal illustration that serves as a reflection on a particular aspect of the biblical text. But the self-revelation also creates a feeling of shared history with the congregation:

> I recall how difficult school was for me. Even after all these years, the experience is still very vivid. My brother and I rode Bess, our family mare, five miles from the country into town to school. We were sort of laughed at, riding a horse to school. I was poorly clothed and suffered from chronic malaria. I was not very well, not very strong, and not very big. That was before I achieved the stature that you are admiring before you now.[27]

Such personal disclosure on the part of the preacher not only allows the congregation to realize that this sermon is in everyday language, but that the preacher has emerged from the midst of the assembly. This level of self-disclosure increases the dynamic "how" of Christian faith, since many in the assembly will find themselves identifying with the preacher's childhood. "Unlike textuality, orality generates intimacy, in that speaker and listener experience a sense of being on the 'inside' of something very important."[28] Barbara Brown Taylor begins her homily on the Ten Lepers (Luke 17:12–17) with a personal reference that draws us directly into the gospel:

> Lepers became part of my nightmare repertoire at an early age, after I went with my parents to a film directed by Federico Fellini. I don't remember what town we lived in then, or what the movie was about, but I do remember the lepers. They lived in caves, out of which they crept like vampires, shielding themselves from the light, their heads hooded, their whole bodies hidden under tattered shrouds....That is, thank God, the extent of my acquaintance with lepers, but not so for the people of the Bible.[29]

Taylor's personal references and vivid recollections of a film at an early age are for the sake of an introduction, focused sharply on the gospel. The preacher is not there in a confessional mode or engaging in the kind of therapeutic homiletic of the kind advised by Harry Emerson Fosdick some years before.[30] "We do preach Christ and not ourselves," Craddock says, "but the one who speaks the gospel does so from faith to faith, never in any sense exempt for its promise or judgment....The communicator is striving to become while urging others to become."[31] The preacher helps to build up the community through language. As O'Day puts it, "The challenge to the church to know and speak its own language rests acutely on the preacher, because the preacher's work depends on language."[32] Ultimately, the teller risks a personal encounter in the preaching event. That experience with the congregation may not always guarantee a pleasant intimacy, as Craddock suggests, but an angry antipathy. Stephen's moment of self-revelation in Acts was also the occasion of his martyrdom.

The Imaginative Interpreter

Along with narrative movement and unity, Richard Eslinger identifies imagination as one of the principal qualities of an inductive preacher for Craddock:[33] "The galleries of the mind are filled with images that have been hung there casually or deliberately by parents, writers, artists, teachers, speakers, and combinations of many forces....By means of images the preaching occasion will be a re-creation of the way life is experienced now held under the light of the gospel."[34] Craddock pays careful attention to the power of what he calls "generative language," the kind that evokes concrete feelings, memory, or experience for the hearer.[35] Language ought to be as specific and economical as possible, using images and metaphors that generate the concrete world of brick and mortar, the skin and bones where men and women work and love. Such concrete language is deployed also for descriptions and illustrations. These are, however, not tales told as glosses for an abstract point but the very matter of the sermon. "The story is it."[36] In his sermon on the Woman at the Well (John 4:5–29),

Craddock has a little story to illustrate the scene between Jesus and the Samaritan woman:

> Do you understand why she was so defensive?
>   I asked a woman in the Winn-Dixie grocery store one day, "Could you tell me where I can find the peanut butter?"
>   She turned around, looked at me, and said, "Are you trying to hit on me?"
>   I said, "Lady, I'm looking for the peanut butter."
>   Later when I found it over on aisle five, there she was. She said, "Oh, you were looking for the peanut butter."
>   "I told you I was looking for the peanut butter."
>   She said, "Nowadays you can't be too careful."
>   I said to her, "Yes, you can."
>   But I understand the Samaritan woman's defensiveness.[37]

Avoiding abstract language helps the preacher to incarnate the Word, to give it flesh and blood. Preachers should be always reading, not only scripture, good literature, and newspapers, but attending to goings-on in their environment as well. What about that image of the old woman waiting at a bus stop in the rain? Or a child tossed in the air by an adoring father? These small snapshots of daily living might become ways of making the gospel more real to the assembly. In *Writing Down the Bones* (1986), writer and poet Natalie Goldberg says that it is important to use "original detail" in writing and to write from what you know and see:

> Life is so rich, if you can write down the real details of the way things were and are, you hardly need anything else. Even if you transplant the beveled windows, slow-rotating Rheingold sign, Wise potato chip rack, and tall red stools from the Areo tavern that you drank in in New York into a bar in a story in another state and time, the story will have authenticity and groundedness....The imagination is capable of detail transplants, but using the

details you actually know and have seen will give your writing believability and truthfulness. It creates a good solid foundation from which you can build.[38]

The preacher brings hermeneutic skills to almost everything, but most important, to the scriptures themselves. Craddock sees the role of the preacher above all as a well-prepared interpreter of scripture by necessity. Why? For five reasons:

> 1) the church spends its time collectively in front of texts; 2) they are authoritative; 3) they are also on-going and serve a living God; 4) they need to be interpreted precisely as Church; 5) the Scriptures themselves testify to the necessity of interpretation by those who figure prominently in them.[39]

There will be a variety of interpretations open to the teller, because the teller, like the congregation, is a full participant in the life of faith. "To the extent that the speaker's struggle is Everyman's, the listener can be brought thereby to clarity and to hope."[40] The congregation participates in the preacher's own life of faith and, in so doing, is moved to more wondrous, active participation.

The Listener

It should be clear by now that the listener plays a primary role in Craddock's plan for effective preaching. Craddock takes his cue, of course, from the preaching of Jesus when he says, "It is with his burden I identify; to enable a new hearing and, quite possibly, a hearing for the very first time."[41] Jesus faced a more or less calcified institutional religion, which he attempted to radicalize. In his preaching the kingdom of God, Jesus allowed his hearers to listen to the good news as Word becoming incarnate, breaking into their midst. In our day, says Craddock, that momentous, kerygmatic hearing has been lost because "the clergy predigests every morsel offered through lesson and sermon. The path of discipleship, lest it prove too difficult, is made monotonously smooth....The message no longer carries the paradox of God in the flesh, placing the hearer in the position of risk and decision."[42] In a word, religion has taken the edge out of Christian preaching. Craddock likens the condition of the hearer to Kierkegaard's analogy of "the children of well-to-do parents who never stopped to realize that their daily food is a gift. In fact, they refuse wholesome food because they have never been hungry, preferring sweets instead." Rather, "those who hunger and thirst shall be filled."[43] Faith is fed by hearing the Word, not in a "predigested" rhetorical discourse, but with what Saint Benedict calls "the ears of the heart."

The Pastoral Imperative

Craddock's attention to the hearer has its foundation in pastoral care. The sermon exists for the sake of the gathered assembly. When Cardinal Newman was asked what he thought of the laity, he wondered where the church would be without them. So it is with the preaching of the gospel. What is the sermon if it does not find its final destiny in the hearts, minds, and ears of the people of God? The listeners' function in the sermon is obviously as crucial as it is indispensable. From Craddock's perspective, the sermon does not even exist without them; the hearer together with the preacher and the text form integral parts, none of which can be separated from the others. The implication here, of course, is that the listener is not only central to the message but that these hearers will condition both the teller and the story by virtue of their own vital and particular circumstance. Craddock is aware that the typical listener in a religious congregation needs a "new hearing." The sheep are in danger, "because they too are victims, not of darkness, but of constant exposure to the same kind of light."[44] If Craddock fears that religion makes people too complacent, or overexposed "to the same kind of light," then inductive preaching can serve as a wake-up call to a kind of defamiliarization. Jesus defamiliarized his own hearers in Galilee by rendering strange that which was taken for granted. The kingdom of God, traditionally likened to a great cedar of Lebanon, becomes akin to a tiny mustard seed. For Craddock, changing language transforms lives.

In order to serve the listeners as well as challenge them, it is the primary pastoral responsibility of the minister to know his congregation, and Craddock offers three very practical suggestions. The first way to know an assembly is formal. Movies, television, newspapers, radios, all shape people's perceptions. The pastor as preacher should interview funeral directors, fellow clergy, police, key parishioners.[45] It is not enough simply to look at the assembly as a group, a collective. There are individuals in the pews, with hopes and dreams, disappointments and tragedies. Second, there is an informal way to understand a congregation as well, through hospital visits, recreational events, and so on. This pastoral work never suggests the preacher is a sponge, soaking up the details of peoples' lives in order to glean homily material. Rather, "to be a minister in a community is to be a resident, a citizen, a responsible leader, and one who shares the blame and the credit for the quality of life in that place. One preaches *in* and *out of* as well as *to* that community.[46] Certainly, the sermon improves exponentially to the degree that the preacher is in touch with the daily pastoral struggle of the congregation. Indeed, the scripture passage for Sunday ought to be informed by the circumstances of the previous week. Finally, the preacher must cultivate an empathetic imagination, or "the capacity to achieve a large measure of understanding of another person without having had that person's experiences."[47] The ability to develop empathic skills breathes life into the sermon, making the experiences real and compelling.

Craddock insists on the specific historical and pastoral circumstances of human living, not the abstract concepts of problems for which there are equally opaque answers. The sermon cannot be deductive, not only because the method fails, but because such an outline never attends to the God who lives in the depth of the human subject, from which the preacher intuits the very matter of his or her communication. "Effective preaching reflects the open receptivity to those life scenes that are noticeably emotional...that constitute memorable and important stations along the way most people travel."[48] Craddock shapes his homiletics along the disposition and flux of living and breathing hearers— where they are and where they are going. Therefore, the sermon is always skating on the edge of at least two important qualities for

Craddock: freedom and experience. "Let the preacher, then, first of all know where he and the congregation are going, whether this be in the proper sense a conclusion or whether this be a point at which he stops, leaving each person to draw his own conclusion, as Jesus often did in the parables."[49]

Eugene Lowry and the Homiletic Plot

With Craddock's work in the 1970s the inductive process in homiletics was only beginning.[50] Craddock introduced what Eugene Lowry has called a "revolution of sermonic shape" into homiletics.[51] Following Craddock's lead, Lowry wants to take his teacher's invitation to inductive and narrative preaching very seriously; he does so by suggesting a specific narrative method that will adhere to the formal structures of Western plot. Lowry wants to define narrative preaching in a very cohesive way, not by a somewhat loosely plotted process of engagement. To this end, Lowry offers homiletics a Craddock-inspired shift from a deductive, "spatial-oriented rationalistic" method to one that is "time-based" and organized by the specifics of plot dynamics as we have come to appropriate them.[52] Here is how Lowry describes the process:

> You begin sermon preparation on an Old Testament narrative. You already know what you're going to say—sort of. But then the passage begins leading you down a new road. Perhaps you are paraphrasing a scene out loud to yourself, and then you begin saying things and seeing things you'd never thought before. You are utterly surprised with it all and suddenly...your new homiletical question is: How can I relive the experience in the pulpit in such a way that they can see and hear what I just heard?[53]

Lowry's version of narrative preaching becomes one that progresses by stages, tensions and relaxations. Craddock allowed his congregation to move along freely in a series of unstated questions, always attempting to confront a central one: the "how" of

Christian belief. Craddock's sermons usually have some loose narrative plot structure, if only that of suspense and waiting for narrative closure. Lowry, on the other hand, has a very identifiable structure in mind: he wants to encompass the dynamics of a story with a mechanism drawn from a traditional *plot structure*, since it moves "from opening conflict, though complication, toward a *peripeteia* or reversal or decisive turn, resulting in a denouement or resolution of thought and experience."[54] We can see that Lowry is evolving a more particular kind of narrative preaching than Craddock, whose inductive homiletics can more generally be called narrational, even if the congregation members bring the sermon to an ending by their own individual engagement toward closure. In his book-length treatment of preaching parables, Lowry is able to clarify what he means by narrative preaching: "The term *narrative* (or *story*) may mean a particular story…or the term *narrative* (or *story*) may mean the underlying thread or plot line typical of oral narration."[55] Where Craddock's plot thread is a brightly colored strand of yarn moving from beginning to end, Lowry's takes many threads and weaves a complete tapestry.

Lowry's study of the parable form becomes a blueprint for preaching both biblically and narratively. Parables form a core strategy for narrative preaching, which Lowry himself describes as a plot "involving a strategic delay of the preacher's meaning"[56] or sometimes, "suspending the story." As Lowry describes his own sermon on the Parable of the Householder and the Laborers (Matt 20:1–16), he says that he "will begin inside the text, run into a problem, and hence require the telling of that story to be suspended while another text provides a way out of the dilemma. Once accomplished, the sermonic process moves back to the central text for the completion of the message."[57]

The Internal Expansive Force

Unlike Craddock, Lowry is not much concerned with existentialism or the preoccupations of Kierkegaard. Lowry is much too practical to be drawn into philosophical discourse at any length but rather intends to give explicit shape to the "how" of the sermon: unity, movement, and imagination fashioned along a creative axis of formal plot dynamics. Somewhat differently from Craddock on this strategy, as well, Lowry prefers to give the sermon "some kind of internal expansive force."[58] Lowry says that he sees "every sermon as an event-in-time...from opening disequilibrium through escalation of conflict to surprising reversal to closing denouement (in which the table of life gets set for us in a new way by the gospel)."[59] In his attempt to organize the mechanics of the sermon around a cohesive center, however, Lowry has also been criticized for centering most of the control of the sermonic text on the preacher and not the listener; this fault became especially clear when focus groups were sampled for "receiver involvement" in Lowry's method and "the receiver was not seen as a co-participant."[60] Indeed, Lowry's emphasis on a Western-style plot typically relies on the way in which these narratives have been shaped by an author, unfolding particular elements of story to a reader or audience.

Nevertheless, Lowry offers a congregation a way to participate in the biblical and theological action of the text through a well-wrought, long-tested Aristotelian poetic. It may well be that the preacher/author holds most of the narrative control in a Lowry sermon, but such a narrative armature exists precisely for the pleasure and edification of the congregation. Moreover, it may well be that in a media-driven culture there needs to be a kind of homiletic apparatus in order to allow the congregation to participate in the most engaging way possible—even if it is a heavily plotted formula. After all, so much of media culture uses such devices in much the same way. So saying, Lowry identifies five stages in the homiletic plot, popularly called the Lowry Loop. These are (1) upsetting the equilibrium, (2) analyzing the discrepancy, (3) disclosing the clue to resolution, (4) experiencing the gospel, and (5) anticipating the consequences.[61] Lowry says that sermon plots always move from itch to scratch, but he will admit to some variations along the way.[62] He is clear that these are stages and that they are variable; it is more important that they are viewed as "events-in-time." His students popularized these plot movements as, "Oops, Ugh, Aha, Whee, and Yeah."[63] The following schema is how he imagines a typical homiletic plot moving as an event-in-time.

Upsetting the Equilibrium (Oops)

We know instinctively that Western narratives engage our attention by introducing a startling moment of imbalance early on. The short story has only a precious little time to engage the reader, so the first sentence is crucial. The opening sentence of Dorothy Parkers' short story "A Telephone Call" begins like this: "Please God, let him telephone me now."[64] Such a startling opening suggests that the central voice of the narration is in jeopardy, in a bind. Or again, consider mainstream Hollywood films that, because of time limitations and commercial interests, must necessarily hook and engage the audience within the first several minutes of the feature. The opening shot of *The Wizard of Oz* (1939) finds Dorothy Gale running with her dog, Toto, from Elmira Gulch, who wants to restrain the little pet for biting her. Some scenes later we find out that Miss Gulch takes the dog away. Shortly thereafter, Toto escapes, only to force Dorothy to run away from her beloved family. And as everyone knows, she finds herself further away than she bargained for, trekking off across the rainbow to Oz. The moment of disequilibrium functions very deliberately to move the plot along. In "A Telephone Call" we sense the agitation of the main character and want to keep reading to find out what is happening. Dorothy's actions similarly place the audience in a state of "oops," an ambiguous situation: we want her to escape the wicked woman's influence, but we don't want her to run away from home to do it. Things get worse when the girl is further alienated from her family by a twister that carries her away to Munchkinland.

Lowry says that in order for the sermon to work at this level of disequilibrium, the ambiguity or upset must really be felt and experienced not only by the preacher but also by the listeners. With the opening of the sermon, then, "there is always one major discrepancy, bind or problem which is the issue. The central task of any sermon, therefore, is the resolution of that particular central ambiguity."[65] The initial bind having been felt, very deeply and sympathetically, we want to return to balance. Dorothy has to get home to her family because "there's no place like home."

Analyzing the Discrepancy (Ugh)

This stage is a diagnosis that attempts to sustain the initial bind created in the first movement. Lowry regards this analysis as a most crucial phase because "the ultimate form of presentation of the gospel is directly dependent upon it."[66] The "why" that is posed here remains consistent with New Testament theologizing and anthropology, although Lowry admits that this stage also deliberately keeps people in suspense, like a good detective story.[67] Such mystery is often difficult to sustain, and at this point the sermon should be suspended through a process of *diagnosis*. But unfortunately, that challenging and complicated task is often "exchanged for description or illustration."[68] If the diagnosis is shallow (premature closure) or lacking in sufficient theological depth, then the ambiguity has been shattered and the Loop will fail. The mystery will be given away too early and the congregation will lose interest.

The key to the diagnosis in the "ugh" section is the ability to draw out the initial rupture creatively. A distillation of one of Lowry's own sermons demonstrates the "ugh" moment following an initial "bind" with the two friends on the way to Emmaus:

> *(Oops):* They seem "to be running away—away from the action."
> *(Ugh):* "Could they be afraid that there might be new victims in this story? Or in confusion did they want to take a long walk? We don't know. I can't help but wonder if they knew. For whatever reason, they are walking to Emmaus—Cleopas and another never named."[69]

Lowry is drawing us into the experience of the disciples on the road, asking us to participate in their own difficulties. The discrepancy is analyzed by the congregation's own imaginative powers, which re-create a scene of frustration and loss.

Disclosing the Clue to the Resolution (Aha)

In this stage the key lies in the twist, or the *principle of reversal*. "It turns things upside down. In the visualized plot line shown, the radical change of direction is intended to suggest how the sermonic idea is turned inescapably by the clue; things can never again be seen in the same old way."[70] All good narratives have a turning point, as critics since Aristotle have pointed out. In classical dramatic formulation this occurrence of the unexpected is called the *peripetia*. In *Oedipus the King* the protagonist is set on a certain course that eventually has tragic consequences. Aristotle identifies the appearance of a messenger to cheer Oedipus and dispel his fears about his mother, but this information has the very reverse effect. He learns that he has been sleeping with his own mother and that he (unknowingly) killed his father. His downward spiral begins. In the tragic play, of course, it is the protagonist himself who has brought this upon his head.[71]

This reversal stage parallels the gospel in its most radical form. The reversal is part of the twist in Jesus' parables in which the hearers' expectations are confounded and become our own. As Craddock says to his contemporary reader about a well-known parable, "Are you *really* in favor of parties for prodigals?"[72] I don't think that it is coincidental that in order to facilitate the reversal, Lowry's sermons often introduce a vivid story at this point in the Loop's configuration precisely in order to grapple more deeply with the experience of the text on the emotions of the congregation. More often than not, it is a story that the preacher himself has encountered.[73] I think that such a reflection in a story also allows for the principle of reversal to occur somewhat seamlessly, as it does in Lowry's Emmaus sermon. This story will set up the next stage of his sermon on the Emmaus passage:

> Somehow it was beyond my capacity to believe that Peggy would have painted my likeness—so I didn't. I remember the face looking familiar. But it was just too much to perceive—to recognize.
>
> Well, so it was for them. Too incredible, no matter what the women had reported earlier in the day. Way too much to imagine. And so they didn't, and, instead, proceeded to "instruct him" about the events of the last few days.[74]

This stage is a genuine moment of illumination. "Consequently, the new and revelatory clue is received as an intuitive leap, turning normal expectations, and the sermon, upside down."[75] Shrewdly, Lowry achieves this reversal with the congregation by *showing*, not *telling*; we participate in the reversal as we see someone else come to an illumination. He then comes to a conclusion about the dramatic episode in the gospel based on the insights he has gained from his own story about encountering his likeness in a painting.

Experiencing the Gospel (Whee)

As crucial as these previous steps are, the Lowry Loop exists at the pleasure and service of stage four, where the gospel will shed its light. The preacher must be careful to give only a clue in the previous step, thereby allowing the gospel to be *experienced* in full. Sometimes, however, the eager preacher deploys the scripture text as a kind of anecdote or remedy, and that is hardly the world of experience required for inductive preaching. The result of simply telling and not showing the gospel in full robs the text of its power. Timing is everything in Lowry's homiletic plot. "The actual content of the proclamation of the good news must be consistent with the diagnosis which precedes it."[76] Hence, the difficulty for preaching up until this point is really the struggles in the previous stages. "If the diagnostic process of stages two and three results in the clue to resolution, the matter will be illumined and the hearing context prepared for the receipt of the gospel of Jesus Christ."[77] At this stage there is a dissipation of the tension that has been building in the narrative. In a way, the gospel is relaxed into, "listened into" more deeply. The mind and ears expand. Clearly, Lowry has in mind here a space that will open up the text to a new hearing in the way that Craddock has imagined it. We can see at this point, however, that the "internal expansive force" that Lowry created does not constrain but rather liberates the hearer, as it does in the "whee" section of the sermon on Emmaus:

> And as the bread was broken so was the veil of their ignorance. They recognized it was Jesus. It was Jesus who had been walking with them, explaining the scriptures to

49

them all along the road. And the moment they recognized who he was, he disappeared, vanished from their sight. Poof. Just like that. Seems like divine humor to me. Just when we think we can get our hands on the holy—poof, it is gone, beyond our grasp. We should never imagine any capacity ever to survive more than a glimpse. Not here.[78]

The experience of the gospel allows Lowry to draw some conclusions about how its dramatic function is instructive to our daily living. The "new hearing" is there for a purpose: to broaden the experience of the risen Lord for the people of God.

Anticipating the Consequences (Yeah)

Although Lowry regretted using the term *consequences*, this stage implies closure and follows naturally from the entire process. This is by far the most practical section in the Lowry Loop, the one that attempts to apply the experience of the gospel to Christian living. The "yeah" stage is pragmatic and integrative. And while this step offers closure to the Lowry Loop, it functions mostly to anticipate the future.[79] This step also answers the question "So now what?" or, in a more Pauline sense, "What shall we say to this?"[80] As Lowry points out, there are obvious analogies to literary plots that transition in a similar manner. "Perry Mason always had a visit with his secretary or client."[81] Yet we might say, in addition, that it is here that the preacher makes a practical closure with the community. It is not that the problems of the congregation have been solved; rather, the possibility for faith has been widened from the dynamics of another kind of listening, or what Luther called an "acoustical affair."[82] If the five stages have been worked out well, the resolution is really the kind of closure that brings new possibilities. Ultimately, the Lowry Loop ushers the congregation through a narrative process that causes its members to think differently, not come away with new cognitive information. After experiencing the story of Emmaus, the congregation is waiting to face the challenge of living it out:

Well, I'll tell you, it gripped their bodies, too, and literally turned them around—one hundred eighty
degrees. The text says that within the hour, "they got
up and returned to Jerusalem." By this time, it must
have been dark. They had to walk back to Jerusalem in
the dark. Oh, no they didn't. Don't think it for a
moment. It was during the day—as they walked toward
Emmaus—that they walked in the dark. And now, at
night they started walking in the light.

    That's the way it can be for us all. If any of us ever
get a glimpse—you know, even just a fleeting, momen-
tary, fragmentary glimpse—well, it'll turn you around!
Yes, it will.[83]

Perhaps the best way to see a Lowry Loop at work is to see
the process in an entire homily. The following is a homily for the
Twenty-second Sunday in Ordinary Time (Cycle A, Isa 51:1–6;
Rom 12:1–8; Matt 16:21–27) by Dr. Richard Stern illustrating
Lowry's narrative plot:

During these many summer Sundays following
Pentecost, the broad theme of the Scripture texts has
been something around the quality or character of the
life in Christ: the risks, the dangers, the demands, the
freedoms of following Jesus.

    These last several weeks, in particular, the gospel
passages have been accounts, really demonstrations, of
how people's lives are changed by their encounter with
Jesus. Five thousand people were fed on a few loaves
and a couple of fish. The real *miracle* there or the point
of that miracle was not that Jesus could magically produce a mountain of food but that he used what little the
people had to offer—used it, transformed it, and made
it sufficient.

    Then Peter walked on water with Jesus' help. Peter
got his feet a little wet when he started to sink in doubt
and Jesus saved him. But Jesus did not completely
remove Peter from the risks and dangers of faith. Finally,

in last week's gospel, with the Canaanite woman, we heard a story of mutual ministry in which a bold woman verbally wrestled with Jesus to convince him to bless her daughter who was possessed by a demon.

In all these passages, the thing to note is the interaction that takes place between Jesus and his followers. They struggle and stumble, doubt and despair. And yet because of that faith develops and grows. Faith it seems comes in *living*, not just in assent to a certain set of beliefs. This morning's gospel falls in line, but with a twist. The message in today's gospel seems clear enough: the first and biggest step in faithful Christian living is proclaiming Jesus as the Messiah. Have to do that first. Can't take the next step until that one is done. Unfortunately, it is not a step we can take just once. It is a step we take, a commitment we make over and over and over again because we fall, doubt, betray that faith that Jesus is the Messiah. Jesus is *our* Messiah, *our* savior, *our* Lord. Again and again we say it—reminding ourselves and those around us.

If you need a model, an example, a demonstration of the *difficulty* of this important step, that is the need to make it over and over, the apostle Peter will do nicely. Think back to this morning's gospel passage. Isolated from its context in Matthew, this passage, this statement by Peter seems very perceptive, grand and profound. Yet Peter's response to Jesus' question is no great revelatory insight. After all, for the last several chapters in Matthew and for the last several weeks in church, we have heard how Jesus has fed 5,000 people with a few loaves of bread and a couple fish, walked on water and helped *Peter* to walk on water (probably the greater miracle), healed mute people, blind people, all other sorts of ailing people, fed 4,000 *more* people, and told a collection of mysterious parables. For Pete's sake, how much more evidence do you need? I mean really.

It might be something like the time you bought a new winter coat at the August pre-season coat sale.

When you got home, you took the package into the bedroom, put on the coat and then, while the rest of the family was watching the Simpsons on TV, you came parading through the living room in front of the family wearing the coat and then asked, "Notice anything?" How could anyone *help* but notice, it's 95 degrees out, and you are wearing a red, wool winter coat! But anyway, Peter, with all sincerity, grandly announces *he* believes Jesus *is* the Messiah. And he was right. Jesus has set Peter up here to make this proclamation after witnessing a whole string of miracles, healings, and divine pronouncements. Only then after all this, does he ask Peter and the others, "Who do people say that I am?" And then, "But who do you say that I am?" Who would miss it? "You are the Messiah, Jesus!

The truth, however, is that Peter really did not realize the depth of his own words, did not recognize what it meant for *Jesus* to be the Messiah, was not clueless, but a bit misguided. Nor did Peter know what it would mean for him to profess Jesus as the Messiah. Only three verses later, Peter rebukes Jesus when Jesus informs Peter that he, Jesus, would have to die as the Messiah. It was then that Jesus said to Peter, in what must have certainly been painful and shocking words for Peter to hear, "Get behind me Satan! You are a stumbling block to me; for you are setting your mind not on divine things but on human things." Peter did not really understand the fullness of what he was saying. He was mouthing familiar words, important words, but *filling* them with only half-baked meaning, *failing* to realize the full import of his words...*failing* to recognize the *impact* his words would have on his own life.

Not too many chapters later, Peter denied even knowing Jesus at all. Is it any wonder that Jesus refers to Peter and the other disciples as *oligoipistoi*, which is Greek for "people of little faith?" I am Peter. We are all Peter, people of little faith. Not no faith, but little

faith, not daring to see what we could do if we trusted
Jesus' promises completely, not wanting to see where
faith might take us and what faith might call us to do
or not do. Jesus knew and understood Peter's weakness. Even so, he chose Peter to be the rock on which
Jesus would build his Church. Just so, he chooses you
and me to be the bricks and mortar of this same
Church. He knows our weakness. He understands.
And he chooses us anyway.

To say "Jesus is the Messiah," is quite another
thing. It is a statement of faith about someone we have
never met, but claim to know personally, deeply, intimately. It is a statement that implies that you and I are
willing to put our lives and futures and our *complete trust*
in this same person. It is a statement that proclaims that
nothing, absolutely nothing, is more important than
our relationship, our obedience, our love for Jesus, the
one we call the Messiah. Not family, not friends, not
job. Not peace, not war. Not wealth, not poverty.
Nothing is more important than the Word and will of
Jesus. *His life* becomes a model for our lives.

Jesus talks about this as divine versus human
things. Paul talks about this as moving away from living
in the *flesh* to living in the Spirit. But what does such a
life look like? Well, what did Jesus' life look like? What
would you list as some of the principles, values, behaviors, or beliefs which characterize the life of Jesus?

One obvious quality for me is Jesus' willing to *listen*, even to the point of changing his mind as he seems
to have done with the Canaanite woman in last week's
gospel. How *often* the gospel authors note that Jesus
talked and even ate with sinners, tax collectors and others of questionable character. The same willingness to
listen should characterize our lives.

What else might be on the list? Certainly forgiveness—forgiving others because we have been forgiven.
Healing others from the sickness of hunger, loneliness,
despair, unresolved anger, prejudice, and so on. I think

of sacrifice for the sake of others—willingly, not grudgingly. You can add to the list as well as I can.

When you and I proclaim Jesus as the Messiah, we also proclaim his values as *our* values and his way of living as *our* way of living. Suddenly that first step in Christian discipleship becomes a whole lot bigger. And indeed, we should think twice before making it. Proclaiming Jesus as the Messiah could change our lives...forever.[84]

David Buttrick: Structures and Moves

For David Buttrick, a "new hearing" is not only a strategic idea, it is motivated by an epistemological change or a diversion in a way of knowing. He works out his phenomenological, narrative methodology most fully in *Homiletic: Moves and Structures* (1987), although his voluminous critical work and published homilies have continued to illustrate his theory. Like Craddock and Lowry, Buttrick assails deductive, rationalistic models of preaching of the past. Buttrick also analyzes the contemporary preaching scene, which he calls "pop-Schleiermacher." "Locating religious truth within human subjectivity, the preacher began to seek ideas derived from personal/pastoral experience, prior to searching Scripture for textual support of reproof."[85] Much of what Buttrick has to say will be in direct contrast to the preacher as witness. It is not that Buttrick does not trust the value of the witness of preaching, it is that attempting to discover truth in subjectivity is doomed to failure and incapable of communicating the radical truth of the gospel of peace and justice.

God-Toward-Us

Buttrick takes his homiletic mandate primarily from the narrative complexity of the scriptures. In the hands of the rationalist homileticians, preaching, he says, was reduced to a question of meaning, or a kind of post-Enlightenment "distillation" that becomes reductive and topical.[86] Buttrick, like his colleagues who preach narratively and inductively, recognizes the flight from biblical language that occurs especially with sermons that have separated scriptural content from form. As Richard Eslinger explains Buttrick's hermeneutics, "the issue for the interpreter is, therefore, not to ask first 'What did the passage mean?' but to inquire as to the logic of its plotted language."[87] As we have noted, plot is an event-in-time and never static, and really more like scripture texts themselves, which Buttrick is quick to point out. "Biblical language is intentional; a pericope will want to function in the consciousness of the hearer in some way. Therefore an interpreter is never finished with a text when a 'message' has been found. For Buttrick, the central question becomes, What does the passage want to do?"[88] Buttrick wishes to relieve the preacher of the naive question, What does this passage mean?, not only because it eschews the more pertinent issue of biblical form, but because questions of meaning quickly devolve into rationalistic, *deductive solutions*. On the other hand, structuring the homily around the biblical passage's intention propels the text into an inductive process ready for the consciousness of the congregation.

Textual, biblical intention is narration. Indeed, the very *act of narration* drives the biblical story because, just as the word transformed creation by God's utterance, so does language. The homiletic process replicates the textual intention of biblical narrative. Ultimately, Buttrick sees preaching as informed by narrative because "language constitutes our world by *naming*, and confers identity in the world by *story*....Preaching can rename the world 'God's world' with metaphorical power, and can change identity by incorporating our story into 'God's Story.' Preaching constructs in consciousness a 'faith-world' related to God."[89] What we hear can change our lives. Buttrick has in mind an audience who receives the Word like seed thrown on a fertile field. For Buttrick, current failures or collapses in the preaching event are most offensive when preaching fails to name God-with-us in the world.[90] On the other hand, in the preaching that Buttrick models, "Christ continues to speak to the church, and through the church to the world."[91] Obviously, preaching for Buttrick exists for the sake of the church and the world. And so Buttrick's homiletic intends to address not only a problem of preaching technique but also of the way in which we imagine God relating to the world, as the Word

56

made visible. "Preaching is Jesus Christ because it opens to us salvific new life and discloses the reality of God-toward-us."[92] That action of God is reconciliation, which is liberation. And therefore the purpose of preaching is "a conversation generated by the event of Jesus Christ which will continue until Christ's redemptive work is done, a consummation symbolized by second coming."[93]

Buttrick faces us less with communication skills than with ultimate concerns: the new and the now, characterized by Jesus' own preaching of the kingdom of God.[94] Still, he has a vital structure for transmitting God's redemptive, reconciliatory power revealed in Christ. Few homileticians are as serious about the power of language to transform as David Buttrick. Biblical narrative, theological reflection, images, metaphorical language—all of these constitute the pillars of David Buttrick's preaching, and all contribute to the way he structures his own version of a homiletic plot.[95] Yet Buttrick's plotting for sermons will not be shaped along the lines of Lowry's dramatic action. Rather, Buttrick turns to the scriptures and finds in them his blueprint for plot design.

Three Structures

Buttrick suggests three plot structures for the preacher, which will differ in degrees by the way that the preacher relates to the congregation. What these structures have in common is that they imagine an assembly with three different forms of consciousness that can be moved, converted, enlightened. The first is "preaching in the mode of immediacy." The preaching activity in this mode forms its structure of understanding in consciousness from the very text from which it emerges. Some texts will work better at this than others, but Buttrick says that all biblical texts will fit this paradigm. With narrative texts in scripture, the first step is to locate "a theological field" in the text. For Buttrick, scripture always carries theological meaning, and it therefore becomes a matter of discerning what way the biblical author is informing us of this meaning. This step is, of course, different from asking what a text means. The purpose of this stage is to engage the biblical text in a theological dialogue, to ask what it is intending, or wants to *do*. Following the immediacy of discerning what the text is intending, the narrative, homiletic plot ought to be rendered within a current cultural idiom, so the preacher "forms contemporary meaning by analogy." The text must speak to people in the world at a particular time and place. Buttrick's own homilies often confront the contemporary issues of race, unjust governmental practices, and broader issues of social sin. This stage ensures that preaching deals with the reality of God-in-the-world, that God's Word has something living and active to say to the world in which we live. Finally, the shape of the sermonic text is molded when the preacher "begins to spot intentional strategies with regard to a congregation."[96] Here again, the preacher takes a cue from the narrative intention of the biblical passage. This step brings out and stretches the scriptures into the very midst of the assembly; proclamation becomes actualized in their midst. Noting the way narrative passages function is the way the homily itself will come to be fashioned. These narrative passages have their own peculiar logic. At the same time, however, non-narrative passages in scripture "will operate with other kinds of logic and form in consciousness quite differently."[97] As Richard Eslinger summarizes preaching in the mode of immediacy:

> What occurs when preaching in the mode of immediacy, then, is that the intentional force of the biblical text is replicated in the consciousness of the hearers. Essential to the achievement is a keen assessment of the text's plot and intending to go along with a skill in shaping a homiletic plot that will travel in consciousness and imitate the text's intentionality.[98]

Eslinger suggests a helpful example when preaching on the Parable of the Barren Fig Tree. Each of these sentences forms homiletic blocks or fields that follow the parable's intention:

A. There is a barrenness in the vineyard. God's people are bearing little in the way of fruitfulness...etc.

B. Faced with all this lack of fruit, it is natural to hear the words, "Cut it down!"...We do it with each other; do it with ourselves.

C. Then comes the surprise—a word of grace comes on God's people...."Let it stand," the voice insists....A new season for becoming faithful.

D. Now comes the conditions of this new season—caring, encouraging, disciplined love—all designed to build us up in Christ.

E. Still, there is an end to this new season of grace. God will have a people of fruitfulness.[99]

Preaching in the mode of immediacy mirrors a sequential plot development and intention of the biblical text; it forms in the consciousness directly. But the second kind of preaching that settles in the assembly's consciousness, the reflective mode, takes one step back and draws from a passage that is "moving around within a field of meaning"...a moving from one contemporary meaning to another."[100] With the reflective mode Buttrick has in mind something of what the category suggests: a kind of mirror of human thinking, rather less structured than preaching from the intentions of a biblical passage. Buttrick senses that in the reflective mode meanings are collected in a way that can be followed by a congregation, according to its field of reception. The preacher gathers this language together in such a way that preaching in the reflective mode appears natural and easy to follow yet challenging. "Generally, the logic of sermon design will be a logic natural to the way in which contemporary human beings put meanings together....What matters in constructing a sermon is that logic of movement be natural to human consciousness and, at the same time, appropriate to the kind of meaning that is structured in consciousness, foreground and background."[101]

Some texts will be more appropriate for preaching in a reflective mode than others. Again, Richard Eslinger gives us a fine example of what a potential homily might look like, this time based on Mark 9:33–37. Here, there is really a dramatic scene (as opposed to a parable) in which a philosophical issue is being raised about being great in the kingdom of heaven. Jesus deploys the image of the child to make his point, and preaching in the reflective mode of consciousness accesses this reality:

A. "Who is the greatest," the argument goes....God's people strive for position, with one another and with the world.

B. And the rule of the game is this: You know when you're at the top when you hang around with all the other VIPs, the in-crowd.

C. Now listen to Jesus' word—"last of all," "servant of all."...What a strange way to become great—become a servant and welcome those who are least!

D. Just who, now, is Jesus going to take and embrace and put in our midst and say, "Whoever welcomes this one welcomes me"? We should know by now that it will certainly not be one of the in-crowd.

E. So maybe it's time to put away this arguing, and bickering about greatness. Servants, that's who we are.[102]

The reflective mode reaches out to the consciousness of a variety of listeners. Thus Eslinger wisely brackets this strategy in the homily to what he says is "reserved for the hearer," and not "most favored victims."[103] Buttrick's tactic of allowing this kind of homily to structure itself in consciousness is limited if the hearers are not free to parse precisely who those least in the kingdom of heaven are.

Last, Buttrick suggests that there is "preaching in the praxis mode," by which he means "a preaching that addresses persons in lived experiences and, therefore, starts with a hermeneutic of lived experience."[104] Buttrick is careful to distinguish this kind of preaching from the kind of topical sermons he finds so derivative and simplistic. The praxis mode of preaching asserts that Christian optimism is present in the existential moment, of situations of "being-in-the-world and being-in-history," despite indications to the contrary. Buttrick also finds in this mode of preaching "limit moments" in culture that are "characterized by a sudden awareness of transcendent mystery and, at the same time, acknowledgement of our human finitude."[105] These areas of preaching are informed by Christian consciousness and often provoked by a momentous cultural event, but they are always inspired by the gospel for the purpose of faith-consciousness, the realization of God-with-us. The praxis mode is sometimes an urgent call to action. It is a preaching that provokes us *now*, that makes the kingdom of God a reality *now*. By way of contrast, Buttrick has little use for "positive-thinking pulpit" that keeps the mysteries of transcendence and finitude at a safe distance.[106] And indeed, such therapeutic preaching also thwarts what he calls "Christian hermeneutical consciousness"[107] as well, because quick answers from the pulpit dulls the edge for the discovery of symbols and "our awareness of being-saved in the world."[108]

Here is a sketch for a preaching in the mode of praxis, a situational sermon that Buttrick wrote on the problem of theodicy. He notes that this structure is an alternative to another model he proposes. This one features the gospel first, followed by a situation:

1. The gospel announces that "God is Love."

2. But what then of terrible disasters?

3. Shall we say that nature is separate from God? Then, God not God.

4. Or claim tragedy is a learning experience? Then, God not good.

5. Only answer is to look at God disclosed on the cross!

6. In suffering, let us cling to God in faith, knowing that God is with us.[109]

Buttrick stresses that writing an outline in this mode is not a fixed form. He thinks of the outline as a "strategy." In a certain sense, all of Buttrick's modes of preaching are strategies, since they are efforts at targeting group consciousness.

Homiletic "Moves"

Perhaps the most influential of Buttrick's methodological structures is the deployment of building blocks of language, which he calls "moves"; he uses these to construct the consciousness of the congregation. Buttrick cleverly shifts the former language of preaching—ubiquitous in the deductive model—that was static and consisted of "points" to the more fluid term "move." We might notice from the start that the implication of a move is precisely that it is *intentional*. Moves are constructed to engage and change group consciousness. Throughout his work Buttrick is careful to keep in mind the important effect that language has on the gathered assembly. Too often privatized in a world of writing, Buttrick has elucidated the force preaching has to change the group mind. "One-to-one conversational language may involve a sequence of ideas, many in a brief moment, but public address can approach the simultaneity of human experience as it mingles meaning, image, and affect in unusual ways."[110]

The move is a module of language designed with the group consciousness in mind. "Every move has a shape, an internal design. The shape of a move is determined in an interaction of (1) theological understanding, (2) an eye for oppositions, and (3) actualities of lived experience."[111] The simplest move will contain an introductory statement; this will be developed and shaped along metaphorical and imagistic language. Then there will be closure, a rounding off of the move, which Buttrick regards as absolutely crucial not only for the individual unit, but for the overall working of the homily.[112] This closure is often a restatement of the initial, introductory observation. When the moves are taken together, narrative movement characterizes their linkage one to the other; they are sequentially and logically linked thoughts. Individually, each move is structured to transform the communal mind through a single idea, usually lasting about three to four minutes. "The unity is established by the statement and restatement at the start and finish of the move...and within the framework of the move, there is only one developmental system organized as a personal, temporal memory."[113] An overall unity is achieved in the sermon as a whole because, although each move is a discrete entity, each move is linked together by the one that it anticipates. Although the moves are distinct, they are logically connected.

How Moves Work

Ronald Allen has helpfully illustrated Buttrick's moves in a sermon on Jeremiah 24:4–9/Romans 8:35–39 by characterizing them in a series of single sentences like this:

> Move 1: The Church in the United States today is in exile in a culture that is becoming increasingly secular.
>
> Move 2: Many in the church long for the church to be rejuvenated and for its exile to end.
>
> Move 3: The church, however, should regard the exilic situation as home.
>
> Move 4: Moreover, God is involved in creating the exile. Exile liberates us from idolatries and other false loyalties.
>
> Move 5: The Church is called not to withdraw from the secular world, but to serve God in it.[114]

This structure would cover the entire sermon. It is characteristic that the moves, when taken together, behave almost as if they could form a kind of paragraph. The moves construct a logic that plots toward a consciousness in either the biblical, theologically reflective or praxis mode. At the same time, though, each of the moves has its own design and expresses a specific intention. For the sake of further clarification, the first move (above) might be summarized like this:

> *(Statement)* Exile: "Exile" does seem to be a metaphor for Christians in America these days. We live as exiles in a secular land. *(Development)* Oh, once upon a time America was settled by true believers—Puritans in New England and Catholics down in Spanish Florida. In between there were Dutch Reformed etc. *(Image)* So Tony Kushner on Broadway pictures American religion

as a crowd of old angels clutching a big Bible-sized book, wondering when and if God will come back to America any time soon. *(Closure)* Exile. "How can we live, Christian people in a secular land?" The question troubles us these days.[115]

The development of the move relies heavily on a focused image to bring historical detail into concrete reality. The closure "rounds out" the move by echoing the initial statement in some way. Moves can be more complex than this, of course, although Buttrick says that these building blocks of language may contain no more than three internal developmental systems; group consciousness cannot handle anything more than that.[116]

Because Buttrick is interested in the transformation of the collective conscious, he flexibly adapts to the contemporary congregational orientation and uses biblical imagery and literary devices to achieve those ends. He adopts the literary term *point of view* to suggest ways that the preacher might create perspective and attitude. It is essential that the homilist be aware of the perspective that each of the moves exhibit, Buttrick says, because "consciousness is so volatile."[117] In constructing a framework for the introduction to the sermon, Buttrick goes so far as to say that personal illustrations, especially when they occur in the beginning, are "devastating" for a congregation. Far from creating a relationship of empathy with the hearer, using subjective references generates numerous difficulties: "The problem is split focus....Personal narratives will always introduce a preacher, and the intended subject matter will not form in congregational consciousness in any satisfactory fashion."[118]

With its intricate structures and move systems, Buttrick's method appears to be designed for traditional Protestant sermons, but it can be adapted for use in writing liturgical homilies, just as the narrative designs of Craddock and Lowry can be. Buttrick himself worked to shrink the method to a smaller format when he taught for many years at Saint Meinrad School of Theology in Indiana. There may be less chance to develop the intricacies of the system of moves he suggests for longer sermons, but the logic of plotting a narrative piece of preaching with a textual intention is still possible in a liturgical homily of eight to ten minutes.

Here is an example of a homily in a Buttrick style that I preached for the Second Sunday of Advent Year A (Isa 11:1–10; Rom 15:4–9; Matt 3:1–12):

> Proclamations of peace are often found in the most unlikely of spaces.
>
> If you were to get on the Interstate and head south towards Memphis, you would eventually be faced with a number of options after arriving in that town. Mostly, it is the choice between two kings. Turn one way, and you would find yourself at the shrine of "the King," Graceland, the well-greened, well-adorned and well-known former mansion of Elvis Presley. Most out-of-towners go there at least for a peek. Turn another way, though, and you'd come upon a much impoverished part of that same city, and a very different sort of building. Another King stopped there several decades ago. The Lorraine Motel is a sad, dirty little building, made famous because it was the site of the last, fatal visit for Dr. Martin Luther King Jr. I don't know how many people see the Lorraine Motel in Memphis, Tennessee. But one distinguishing feature of this run-down place tells it all and justifies any visit. There is a small plaque which was installed after King's assassination, which is a quotation from Genesis and the story of Joseph and his jealous brothers: "Come, let us kill this dreamer and let us see what becomes of his dream."
>
> It has always been dangerous to be a dreamer, especially of peace. The prophets of Israel imagined a peaceable kingdom, a utopia where God alone would rule in justice. They announced a new order. They proclaimed an eschatological reign for the Lord. Many prophets in Israel were killed, which Jesus himself would acknowledge and later hold Jerusalem itself responsible. Indeed, Christ is the premiere example of the Messiah prophet who came to proclaim the reign of

God with a new order. "Blessed are the peacemakers for they shall be called the children of God." A kingdom not of the wise and the clever and the powerful, but of the guileless and the innocent. Jesus died for that kingdom. In our own day, we can consider the political murders in the last century, from Mahatma Gandhi to Oscar Romero and find a similar record: those who dream of a nonviolent world pay the ultimate price. So often we come close to the edge of peace and the scales are tipped again. These dreamers are like those brave soldiers who come running into the battle waving a white flag. But those intent on violence want no part of that truce, that peace. All that awaits those who run breathless for peace into the world of hate is the smoking gun. That is how treacherous dreams are: just thinking of peace can get you killed. Yes, it is always dangerous to be a dreamer.

Yet we still dream. Despite the outlandish improbability of the child making the cobra her playmate, the Christian community can feel very close to this Isaiah text on this Second Sunday of Advent. Here, we resemble those reformers of the past, as we continue to imagine the Great Society, free of poverty, crime, and racism. Rosa Parks didn't know she was a reformer, but she knew what it meant to work for civil rights. She had a dream, and it would not be pushed by any law on earth to the back of the bus. She sat there when everyone expected her to move, and she would not budge. Rosa Parks probably didn't know a lot about litigation, navy blue suits, and congressmen. All she knew was a dream of freedom. That's what the persistence of dreaming is: a quiet African American woman who refuses to be dominated by the crushing crowd that says, "Forget your dream. Move along or I am going to trample you." Dreams never give up, not if they are real. Dreams stay in the front of the bus glued to one of those hard vinyl seats and say, "I am not budging until I see justice." Like Dr. King and

Rosa Parks, we never stop dreaming. We remain in our seats dreaming of the kingdom that is to come. Dr. King said in his last great speech: "Well, I don't know what will happen now. We've got some difficult days ahead. But it doesn't matter with me now. Because I've been to the mountaintop. And I don't mind." Not even a rifleman's bullet can stop our dreams. We still dream. We cannot stop dreaming.

We keep dreaming because that is our vocation as God's people. As Christians, we may not all be called to be prophets or preachers or priests, but we are all called to dreams of sinless peace. That is, after all, the work of John the Baptist and Christian baptism: original evil obliterated and replaced with a divine dream. In baptism we are called to become what the Second Vatican Council's *Dogmatic Constitution on the Church (Lumen Gentium)* referred to as a "Pilgrim people." "The Church, to which we are all called in Christ Jesus, and in which by the grace of God we acquire holiness, will receive its perfection only in the glory of heaven, when will come the time of the renewal of all things" (no. 48). We are headed toward that Holy Mountain, which only a few prophets are fortunate enough to glimpse briefly. Paul's Letter to the Romans offers the rest of us an abiding hope, especially in regard to the symbol of hospitality. Here is where monastics have a special place and a unique commitment to peace. At every turn the Rule of Benedict urges us to be open, to listen, and to welcome one another, especially the guest. Think of the monk who opens the door, knowing full well who is on the other side: Christ the guest. Greeting the guest is like reading scripture: the page is turned and we wait for what is before us to speak as we listen with the ears of our heart. Hospitality is the greatest of dreams: it imagines only the door swung flung wide, welcoming the stranger. Perhaps monastic life is the only symbolic order in which the human subject engages the "other," the stranger as a true friend at first sight. This, too, is hope for the future, for there will always be a stranger before us, ready to be transformed, because we see that person as Christ. Our corporate and individual lives can be filled with places of welcome where barriers cease to matter. We are left only with promise, dreams on the edge of fulfillment, and the Holy Mountain stretched out before us. That is the peaceable kingdom, a dream for the future. It is, after all, our calling to dream.

So what do we do in the face of blatant injustice and violence in the world? We keep dreaming. The God of Peace and Justice is living and active in the world. We have before us that Holy Mountain that Advent has been preparing us to ascend. Once climbed, the Prince of Peace himself will stand before us, victorious. Even now we await his coming: God's Son, the dream all creation longs for.

Further Directions in Narrative Preaching

Like his contemporaries, with whom he shares similar views about the necessity of a renovation in preaching, Charles Rice finds the older, rationalistic, and discursive preaching evasive when it comes to the human condition. Even further, he says that "the preacher is apt to rely on canned illustrations; slices of human life are seen as lines for a performance rather than as the very locus of the incarnation—as if the purpose of living were to make sermons."[119] Understanding the *dynamics* of story—not as a tissue of illustrations in a homily—becomes a genuine hermeneutic for making sense of both the scripture and our lives. Nothing short of a complete overhaul will do when it comes to encountering the Word. So, for Rice, "the renewal of preaching, then, involves a reconsideration of the tradition, the contemporary world, the preacher' style and identity, and the quality of Christian community, all within the homiletical model of storytelling."[120] Story, then, has become the model for many contemporary homileticians, including the radio preacher Edmund A. Steimle.[121] Richard A. Jensen says that "thinking in story" is necessary for a preaching in a post-literate, electronic age.[122] And Jana Childers reminds us that the Word is performed in preaching and creates an analogy among the sermon, drama, and the theatrical arts.[123]

Preaching informed by narrative is undeniable. Paul Scott Wilson says that "plot is essential for contemporary preaching."[124] Wilson regards the major pitfall in preaching to be lack of unity, and his insights endorse the research of Bishop Kenneth Untener and others.[125] Although Wilson does not follow Lowry's method of story dynamics, he designs some principal parts of the sermon that he believes sculpt the text into a kind of organic unity. He suggests that the sermonic text might be crafted as four pages: page 1: trouble in the Bible; page 2: trouble in the world; page 3: God's action in the Bible; page 4: God's action in the world. Wilson says that these four pages occur in a sequence "that ensures, as much as this is humanly possible, that preaching fosters faith in God and joyful lives of service and mission."[126] Ultimately, Wilson's aim is biblical, imaginative, theological, and pastoral, very well integrated so that the process of writing the four pages occurs over the course of the week.[127]

Stephen Farris thinks that the movement of the biblical text makes an appropriate theological analogy for our lives. Farris desires a shift from the traditional locus of preaching by analogy to biblical characters into something more holistic and narrational, a complete apprehension of the way that character functions in the story for the listener. Farris plots the way the narrative action moves in the text, and he imagines that sermons could respond with insights drawn from these moments of discovery. In discussing the Parable of the Prodigal Son, for example, he says that "it may be that it is not merely the case that we are like (or unlike) characters in the story, but that the movements and transformations experienced in the text are somehow similar to our own life experience."[128] Farris's observations about narrative movement are especially useful for preaching on the Lectionary, since this strategy suggests that it is appropriate to preach on an entire book of scripture.[129] The overall movement in the book of Tobit, for example, takes us from lonely alienation to healing and covenant, which an isolated portion of the text in a Lectionary reading only hints at. The same is true for the various cycles in the Hebrew Bible, such as the Joseph story.[130]

Shifting Paradigms

Narrative preaching is still evolving as I write this—and changing its strategies, to be sure. When the door opened to inductive preaching, that new space disclosed to us once again that preaching was at the service of the gospel, but conditioned by the hermeneutics of culture. The kinds of narrative that thrive during one historical period may not do so in another. People will not always make meaning the same way, especially when faced with a cross-culturally diverse system of language and symbols that are rapidly shifting. In his invention of moves, Buttrick believes that sermonic structures must be constructed along phenomenological lines or else they will fail to communicate. Some, like Ronald Allen, disagree with Buttrick's assumption.[131]

Despite Buttrick's ground-breaking work, we might ask about the way in which the "congregation" has been objectified as a kind of timeless entity whose consciousness can be formed in predictable, paradigmatic ways. Like readers, not all assemblies behave in the same way, something that ecclesial ministers are all too aware of in a multicultural environment.[132] What about generational differences? Surely youth groups in an urban setting hear somewhat differently from retired people in the suburbs who have worshiped together for decades. If the sermon is supposed to change consciousness, then how does the preacher find a common language that might guide the images and metaphors of preaching in the era of such diversity? What about the very nature of a shared language in an age of rapidly expanding technology and cultural pluralism?

At the same time, some have wondered if the traditional Western plot as imagined by Lowry is applicable in twenty-first-century America. Perhaps this coherent and creative armature works well now, but what are the creative alternatives for the future of preaching the "homiletic plot." Are there other plot alternatives, based on what we know about other literatures?

Although the plot systems deployed by Lowry are literally as old as Aristotle, the faith communities involved in many parishes are mixed, ethnically and generationally. Some non-Western church-goers come from cultures where plots are not linear and teleological but circular and cyclic. Furthermore, most of the experimentation of narrative in the West in the past hundred years has been precisely in an anti-Aristotelian, non-mimetic modality—stream of consciousness, meta-narratives, nonlinear fiction, to name only the most well-known forms. People are learning from sound bytes, cinematic montage, rap music, and any number of variations in mass culture. The Lowry Loop may be a viable option, but it could also be an exclusive one, aimed at a particular Eurocentric congregation. As imaginative and interesting as Lowry's homiletic plot might be, some may find themselves outside the Loop. If narrative preaching is to be effective, its linguistic net must be cast as wide as possible. After all, that kind of broad pastoral and biblical communication is what gave rise to inductive preaching in the first place. I hope to address some of the questions raised here, as well as their implications, more specifically in the last two chapters.

Notes

1. Fred B. Craddock, *As One Without Authority*, 4th ed. (St. Louis: Chalice Press, 2001), 26. (Orig. pub. 1971.)

2. Richard L. Eslinger, *The Web of Preaching* (Nashville, TN: Abingdon Press, 2002), 17. See Eslinger's useful summary of Craddock's "new homiletic," 16–33. Also see Eslinger's *A New Hearing* (Nashville, TN: Abingdon Press, 1987), 95–132.

3. Craddock's lectures at Yale University during this period were assembled into a single volume, *Overhearing the Gospel* (Nashville, TN: Abingdon Press, 1978).

4. Ibid., 59.

5. Ibid., 17.

6. Craddock, *As One Without Authority*, 37. See also Thomas G. Long, *Preaching and the Literary Forms of the Bible* (Philadelphia: Fortress Press, 1989).

7. Richard C. Stern, "Preaching as Listening: Good Preachers Listen First," *Church* (Winter 1999), 24.

8. Fred Craddock, *The Cherry Log Sermons* (Louisville, KY: Westminster John Knox, 2001), 26–27. I use the word *sermon* in this chapter to describe the preaching in the New Homiletics but suggest that these longer preaching events could be used in liturgical homily as well.

9. Craddock, *As One Without Authority*, 49.

10. Ronald Allen, "Simple Inductive Preaching," in *Patterns of Preaching: A Sermon Sampler*, ed. Ronald Allen (St. Louis: Chalice Press, 1998), 64.

11. Craddock, *As One Without Authority*, 115.

12. Gail R. O'Day, "Toward a Biblical Theology of Preaching," in *Listening to the Word: Studies in Honor of Fred B. Craddock*, ed. Gail R. O'Day and Thomas G. Long (Nashville, TN: Abingdon Press, 1993), 18.

13. See, for example, Fred B. Craddock, *Luke* (Louisville, KY: Westminster John Knox, 1990). Craddock's interpretation of Luke 15:11–32 (The Parable of the Loving Father) provides a backdrop to what the text is intending: "The reader who expected (or wanted) the father to give the party for the son who stayed home and worked hard feels a jolt which the parable does not relieve with its simple declaration, 'It was fitting to make merry and be glad.' Grace seems to abrogate justice, and the parable, with the restraint vital to a parable, leaves the reader to struggle with the tension" (186–87).

14. Richard Eslinger identifies three levels of interpretation when the preacher approaches the text in Craddock's model: the preacher's posi-

tion in the text; discerning the theme; discerning the action (see Eslinger, *The Web of Preaching*, 21–28).

15. Craddock, *As One Without Authority*, 50–51.

16. Ibid., 52.

17. According to Morris J. Niedenthall (in his entry for Davis in the *Concise Encyclopedia of Preaching*, ed. William H. Willimon and Richard Lischer [Louisville, KY: Westminster John Knox, 1995], 97–98), H. Grady Davis's *Design for Preaching* (1958) was one of the most widely used textbooks in the previous thirty years by the archpriest of homiletic theorists. Although Davis had in mind an organic unity—"the sermon exists in the thought or idea as the plant exists in the germ, the seed"—the method clearly reflects a "sender orientation," much more interested in the "what" of preaching than the "how." See H. Grady Davis, *Design for Preaching* (Philadelphia: Fortress Press, 1958), 21. Also, however flexible, Davis's "design" revolves around "generative thoughts," still a defined, spatial modality. See Richard C. Stern, "Communication Perspectives in Teaching Preaching" (Ed.D. diss., Northern Illinois Univ., 1990), 164–170. Concerning Heidegger, Craddock says that the philosopher helped him to understand that Being itself comes to expression in language. "It is not a case of our understanding and then finding words; the words precede the understanding. Life for us is linguistically constituted; that one can hear and speak words is one's primary gift" (Craddock, *As One Without Authority*, 35).

18. Craddock, *As One Without Authority*, 82.

19. Eugene Lowry, "Narrative Preaching" in Willimon and Lischer, *Concise Encyclopedia of Preaching*, 342.

20. Ibid., 343.

21. Fred B. Craddock, *Preaching* (Nashville, TN: Abingdon Press, 1985), 174.

22. John N. Gladstone, "What's in a Nickname?" in *Best Sermons*, ed. James W. Cox (San Francisco: Harper & Row, 1988), 74.

23. Barbara Brown Taylor, "Preaching the Body," in O'Day and Long, *Listening to the Word*, 208.

24. Craddock, *Preaching*, 26.

25. Ibid., 24.

26. Ibid., 23.

27. Craddock, *The Cherry Log Sermons*, 36.

28. Ibid., 169.

29. Barbara Brown Taylor, *The Preaching Life* (Cambridge: Cowley, 1993), 107–8.

30. See Wilson, *A Concise History of Preaching*, 154–61.

31. Craddock, *Overhearing the Gospel*, 50.

32. O'Day, in O'Day and Long, *Listening to the Word*, 18.

33. Eslinger, *The Web of Preaching*, 28–33.

34. Craddock, *As One Without Authority*, 64–65.

35. Craddock, *Preaching*, 196–209.

36. Ibid., 204. See also Garrett Green, *Imagining God: Theology and the Religious Imagination* (San Francisco: Harper & Row, 1989); and Paul Ricoeur, *Figuring the Sacred: Religion, Narrative, and Imagination*, trans. David Pellauer, ed. Mark I. Wallace (Minneapolis: Fortress Press, 1995), esp. 48–72.

37. Craddock, *The Cherry Log Sermons*, 50.

38. Natalie Goldberg, *Writing Down the Bones* (Boston: Shambhala, 1986), 41.

39. Craddock, *Preaching*, 127–29.

40. Craddock, *Overhearing the Gospel*, 50–51.

41. Ibid., 26.

42. Ibid., 30.

43. Ibid., 33.

44. Ibid., 38.

45. Craddock, *Preaching*, 94.

46. Ibid., 94–95.

47. Ibid., 95.

48. Craddock, *As One Without Authority*, 70.

49. Ibid., 116. See also the collection of Craddock's homilies in Craddock, *The Cherry Log Sermons*.

50. For a more complete overview, see Eslinger, *The Web of Preaching*, 57–102.

51. See Eugene L. Lowry, "The Revolution of Sermonic Shape," in O'Day and Long, *Listening to the Word*, 93–112.

52. See Eslinger, *The Web of Preaching*, 50.

53. Eugene L. Lowry, *Doing Time in the Pulpit: The Relationship Between Narrative and Preaching* (Nashville, TN: Abingdon Press, 1985), 49.

54. Eugene L. Lowry, "Narrative Preaching," in Willimon and Lischer, *Concise Encyclopedia of Preaching*, 342. See also Guerric DeBona, OSB, "Preaching for the Plot," *New Theology Review* 14, no. 1 (February 2001): 14–22.

55. Eugene L. Lowry, *How to Preach a Parable* (Nashville, TN: Abingdon Press, 1989), 25. Lowry is responding some years after the introduction of narrative into homiletics.

56. Lowry, "Narrative Preaching," 345.

57. Lowry, *How to Preach a Parable*, 115.

58. Lowry quoted in Eslinger, *The Web of Preaching*, 51.

59. Ibid.

60. Stern, "Communication Perspectives," 183.

61. Eugene L. Lowry, *The Homiletic Plot*, rev. ed. (Louisville, KY: Westminster John Knox, 2001), 26. (Orig. pub. 1980.)

62. In his first edition of *The Homiletic Plot*, Lowry had these five stages in mind without much variation. In his revised edition, however, he admits to some alternatives, particularly in regard to stages three and four, which could potentially occur simultaneously (see Lowry, *The Homiletic Plot*, 118ff.).

63. Ibid.

64. Dorothy Parker, "A Telephone Call," in *Points of View: An Anthology of Short Stories*, ed. James Moffett and Kenneth R. McElheny (New York: Penguin, 1985), 15.

65. Lowry, *The Homiletic Plot*, 31.

66. Ibid., 39.

67. Ibid., 41.

68. Ibid., 42

69. Eugene L. Lowry, *"A Knowing Glimpse,"* in Allen, *Patterns of Preaching*, 95.

70. Lowry, *The Homiletic Plot*, 54.

71. See Aristotle, *Poetics*, trans. Leon Golden (Tallahassee, FL: Univ. Presses of Florida, 1981), 19.

72. Craddock, quoted in Lowry, *The Homiletic Plot*, 67.

73. See, for example, the "aha" stage in Allen, *Patterns of Preaching*, 96; and "Nick at Night," in Eslinger, *The Web of Preaching*, 52–56.

74. Lowry, *"A Knowing Glimpse,"* 96.

75. Eslinger, *A New Hearing*, 81.

76. Ibid., 77.

77. Ibid., 78.

78. Lowry, *"A Knowing Glance,"* 96.

79. Lowry, *The Homiletic Plot*, 120.

80. Ibid., 86.

81. Ibid., 80.

82. Ibid., 81.

83. Lowry, *"A Knowing Glance,"* 97.

84. Richard C. Stern, "Homily for the Twenty-second Sunday of Ordinary Time," August 25, 1996 (circulated privately). Used with permission of the author.

85. David Buttrick, quoted in Eslinger, *A New Hearing*, 134.

86. See Eslinger, *The Web of Preaching*, 153–154. Overall, Eslinger's chapter dealing with Buttrick is excellent (see esp. 151–200).

87. Ibid., 136.

88. Ibid., 139.

89. David Buttrick, *Homiletic: Moves and Structures* (Philadelphia: Fortress Press, 1987), 11. See also, Edmund A. Steimle, Morris J. Niedenthal, and Charles Rice, *Preaching the Story*, rev. ed. (Eugene, OR: Wipf and Stock, 2003) (Orig. pub. Philadelphia: Fortress Press, 1980.) The language of story is the language of the Bible, which is the world of human experience.

90. Ibid., 17.

91. Buttrick, *Homiletic*, 451.

92. Ibid.

93. Ibid., 452. See also, David Buttrick, *A Captive Voice: The Liberation of Preaching* (Louisville, KY: Westminster John Knox, 1994).

94. See David Buttrick, *Preaching the New and the Now* (Louisville, KY: Westminster John Knox, 1998).

95. The parables of Jesus inform much of Buttrick's methodology. See David Buttrick, *Speaking Parables: A Homiletic Guide* (Louisville, KY: Westminster John Knox, 2000).

96. Buttrick, *Homiletic*, 339. See Buttrick's extended analysis of this kind of structure in preaching on the Parable of the Ten Lepers in Luke's Gospel (335–47).

97. Ibid., 391.

98. Eslinger, *The Web of Preaching*, 161.

99. Ibid., 160.

100. Buttrick, *Homiletic*, 391, 395.

101. Ibid., 404.

102. Eslinger, *The Web of Preaching*, 162–63.

103. Ibid., 163.

104. Buttrick, *Homiletic*, 405.

105. Ibid., 408.

106. Ibid., 410.

107. Ibid., 327.

108. Ibid.

109. Ibid., 433.

110. Ibid., 26.

111. Ibid., 33.

112. Ibid., 50.

113. Ibid., 35, 45.

114. Allen, *Patterns of Preaching*, 88.

115. Ibid., 90.

116. Buttrick, *Homiletic*, 47.

117. Ibid., 68.

118. Ibid., 94.

119. Charles Rice, quoted in Eslinger, *A New Hearing*, 18.

120. Ibid., 25.

121. See Thomas Long, "Edmund Steimle and the Shape of Contemporary Homiletics," *The Princeton Seminary Bulletin* 11 (1990), 253–69.

122. See Richard A. Jensen, *Thinking in Story* (Lima, OH: CSS Press, 1993). For a more practical application of story in homily writing, see William J. Bausch, *Story Telling the Word: Homilies and How to Write Them* (Mystic, CT: John XXIII, 1996).

123. Jana Childers, *Performing the Word: Preaching as Theater* (Nashville, TN: Abingdon Press, 1998).

124. Paul Scott Wilson, *The Four Pages of the Sermon* (Nashville, TN: Abingdon Press, 1999), 41.

125. "Too many thoughts" was the most frequently voiced complaint on the part of parishioners surveyed by Untener (see Ken Untener, *Preaching Better* [Mahwah, NJ: Paulist Press, 1999], 42ff.).

126. Wilson, *The Four Pages of the Sermon*, 16.

127. Ibid., 17.

128. See Stephen Farris, *Preaching That Matters: The Bible in Our Lives* (Louisville, KY: Westminster John Knox, 1998), 107.

129. Ibid., 116.

130. Ibid., 117.

131. See Allen, *Patterns of Preaching*, 89; For other critiques of Buttrick's method, see Eslinger, *A New Hearing*, 159–65f.; and idem, *The Web of Preaching*, 193–97.

132. In a certain sense, Buttrick was criticized for a reductionist view of the congregation the way that the phenomenological or "reader-response" literary critics like Wayne Booth and Wolfgang Iser were for "objectifying" the reader. See Wayne C. Booth, *The Rhetoric of Fiction*, rev. ed. (Chicago: Univ. of Chicago Press, 1983) (orig. pub. 1961); and Wolfgang Iser, *The Act of Reading: A Theory of Aesthetic Response* (Baltimore: Johns Hopkins Univ. Press, 1980).

3

LITURGICAL PREACHING

We ponder your steadfast love, O God, in the midst of your temple.

—Psalm 48:9

David M. Greenhaw has suggested that the theology of preaching is linked to an expectation of what the church is *doing* when it preaches: "Although the range is broad, generally expectations for preaching fall into two major groupings: those that expect preaching principally to play a role in the sanctification of the people of faith and those that expect it principally to play a role in the justification of human beings before God."[1] For much of the church's history before the Reformation, the role of preaching was used chiefly to sanctify, the aim of which was to purify the faithful and to explicate some aspect of the scripture or tradition and bring it into practical usage.[2] But, as is well known, the emphasis on the Word by the major Protestant reformers focused new importance on scripture and its relationship to the one who proclaims it. No longer simply a teaching moment for moral edification, the sermon was a revelation of God's grace in the human community. The interpretation of the Word, the evolving discipline of hermeneutics, was given primacy of place.[3]

A moment of clarity for liturgical preaching occurred when the church reformed the Roman rite and specifically defined the purpose of the homily. Indeed, with Vatican Council II (1963–65), the Roman Catholic Church began to rediscover the importance of the Word of God, not only as it is linked to liturgical and homiletical expression, but as a world of grace. Moreover, distinguishing among the various types of preaching has strengthened some of the theology surrounding homiletics. John A. Melloh has reminded us of the various kinds of preaching that have been evident throughout the history of the church, some of which have been the source of great attention in the years following the council: *kerygmatic preaching*, which seeks to capture an evangelical spirit by proclaiming that the kingdom is here and it is time to repent; *catechetical preaching*, which is often doctrinal but based on the scripture; *mystagogical preaching*, which explicates the mysteries during Lent and Easter and uses images drawn from scripture; *theological argument*, which makes arguments about doctrine contained in scripture passages; and finally, *liturgical preaching*, which has its roots in scripture and the liturgy.[4]

The rediscovery of the ancient *homilia* has had a ripple effect on other theological disciplines. Since the council the homily has become more or less a locus of many other liturgical and biblical issues because proclamation was conceived as the bridge to other areas in theology that, in turn, were also being redefined and rediscovered. For the rest of this chapter I will briefly explore a contemporary theology of liturgical preaching from a Catholic perspective and suggest some implications for the future of the homily.

From Sanctification to Justification

The church's work of preaching for sanctification was linked to the purpose of rhetoric, Christian teaching, and the efficacy of the sacraments themselves. Until the liturgical reforms of the nineteenth and twentieth centuries, the place of preaching at the Eucharist and its proper function as a revelation of God's Word in the context of worship was not an issue. Generally speaking, although the homily was an ancient practice in the early church—with its roots in Jewish liturgical tradition—until fairly recently most preaching in the Catholic Church has been doctrinal, usually drawing in a central theme, perhaps from scripture. Joseph M. Connors has demonstrated that the work of "perennial rhetoric"—a legacy of Saint Augustine's *De Doctrina Christiana*—was "to teach, to please, and to move." These tasks for holy oration generally correspond to the three modes of persuasion: *ethos*, *pathos*, and *logos*.[5]

Clearly, the purpose of the thematic or doctrinal sermon was to bring a moment of enlightenment into an area of moral darkness. After all, Augustine had defined the end and purpose of preaching exactly this way: "that good habits be loved and evil avoided."[6] The medieval period is filled with sermons on how to fight the snares of evil and keep steadfastly virtuous. In his extremely influential *The Art of Preaching* (1199), Alan of Lille, for instance, recommended that the purpose of preaching is "the forming of men" and that the preacher "may also introduce moving words which soften hearts and encourage tears."[7] And beyond purgation, there were more spectacular endeavors to move congregations as well. Lawrence F. Hundersmarck details the dramatic preaching the lives of Christ as sermon vehicles in the late Middle Ages so that the audience might have a "spiritual stigmata."[8]

Tridentine Preaching

The Council of Trent (1545–63) reformed the practice of preaching simultaneously with the *Catechismus*. In fact, the two enterprises were closely linked, since teaching the people what they needed to know to be saved occurred most often from the pulpit. In Session V (June 17, 1546), the Council of Trent's *Decree Concerning Reform* said:

> All who in any manner have charge of parochial or other churches...shall at least on Sundays and solemn festivals, either personally or, if they are lawfully impeded, through others who are competent, feed the people committed to them with wholesome words in proportion to their own and their people's mental capacity, by teaching them those things that are necessary for all to know in order to be saved, and by impressing upon them with briefness and plainness of speech the vices that they must avoid and the virtues that they must cultivate, in order that they may escape eternal punishment and obtain the glory of heaven.[9]

There are numerous instances when the noble work of sanctification (read: persuasion) of souls was the clear purpose; these are evidenced not only in numerous *Ars Praedicandi*, but well inscribed in the constitutions of the major religious orders of the Counter-Reformation. "In the very years 1544 and 1545 during the reform of preaching, St. Ignatius of Loyola wrote at least the tentative drafts of the Jesuit Constitutions, in which he crystallized some of his homiletic ideals in *24 Rules for Preachers*."[10] Indeed, some religious orders, like the Congregation of the Most Holy Redeemer (founded in 1732 by Alphonsus Liguori), were founded and commissioned to give parish missions over a period of several weeks; these retreats often concerned the terrible price of sin and the punishment of hell. The purpose of this concentrated period of preaching was to effect a more concentrated period of moral persuasion. One of Saint Alphonsus's sermons (on Matthew 13:30) brings home the point quite well:

> The reprobate, then, shall be tormented in all the senses of the body. They shall be also tormented in all the powers of the soul....At the very time they are so much afflicted, the devils continually reproach them with the sins for which they are tormented, saying, suffer, burn, live forever in despair: you yourselves have been the cause of your destruction. And do not the saints, the divine mother, and God, who is called the Father of Mercies, take compassion of their miseries? No...[the guilty have] voluntarily brought themselves to perdition.[11]

Concerning the work of sanctification, Paul Hitz has written that the mission's "central vision is far too much man and what he does, not primarily and simultaneously God's action to save us in Christ."[12] Moreover, Paul Scott Wilson says that Saint Alphonsus was continuing the tradition of classical rhetoric and Scholastic theology and that, like evangelical revivals, he faced criticism that his preaching was disruptive and short-lived.[13] The entire process of the preached mission suggested that the beginning and the end of preaching was purification and sanctification. In the context of a mission for sanctification, then, the eucharistic liturgy functioned as a kind of reward for those who received the grace of purification. Historically, confessions and eucharistic adoration are close allies to the moralistic sermon, strengthening the ties that preaching as sanctification has with sacraments.

In preaching for sanctification, holy scripture tended to be used as a rhetorical device rather than as an experience of faith to be explicated and understood. Preaching for sanctification typically used scripture as a vehicle for an exhortation on moral behavior. "Once the 'particular proposition' was determined from Scripture, the text was left behind, and any text, ancient authority or saint might be cited."[14] Although the Fifth Lateran Council of 1516 and the Council of Trent sought to reform the sermon by suggesting that the preacher root out non-gospel material, such as esoteric stories of cures and so on, these councils reaffirmed that the gospel of Jesus Christ should be preached so that the faithful would understand the virtues and vices and "in order that they may escape eternal punishment and obtain the glory of heaven."[15]

Much of the tradition in preaching centering around purification endured until well into the twentieth century. Until the reforms of the Second Vatican Council—as late as the 1950s—Thomas V. Liske could write that the scriptures or liturgy are really quite irrelevant to preaching:

> The canonical idea of a sermon does not include the text as essential to the sermon, for a sermon is defined by Father James McVann in "The Canon Law of Sermon Preaching," as "a sacred public address, given by one duly empowered by the church, and intended to instruct its listeners in the Christian faith and move them to practice it." The sermon need not begin with a text then.[16]

The Reforms of Luther and Calvin

Not everyone subscribed to preaching sanctification, especially since it appeared that the Word of God was no longer a centerpiece for the sermon, as it had been in the early Christian homily. Martin Luther (1483–1546) attacked the question of preaching by sanctification directly. At the time of the Reformation, Luther's reform sought to insert a wedge between the law and the gospel, claiming scripture as a much more prominent feature in the liturgical life of the church. To Luther's way of thinking, scripture would not be used as exhortation but as an invitation to *faith*. Rather than using scripture as a vehicle for moral law—the result of which would introduce a process of sanctification—Luther dismissed a sermon that "puts all the responsibility upon us. The Gospel focuses on God's action, and how we are enabled to do what is required by the law. Our method…can be first to struggle with a text to convict us of sin, and then, in the second half of the sermon, to allow sufficient opportunity from the text for the Spirit to give life."[17] Crucially, for Luther, the sermon accomplished nothing if it did not "give life," that is, if it was not received by hearers first. As Saint Paul says, "faith comes from hearing" (Rom 10:17). The language of scripture, then, takes on a very different meaning when it is proclaimed as kerygma and then received by a listener:

> The preaching of the gospel is nothing else than Christ coming to us, or we being brought to him. When you see how he works, however, and how he helps everyone to whom he comes or who is brought to him, then rest assured that faith is accomplishing this in you and that he is offering your soul exactly the same sort of help and favor through the gospel. If you pause here and let him do you good, that is, if you believe that he benefits and helps you, then you really have it. Then Christ is yours, presented to you as a gift.[18]

Luther's comments here hint at his famous doctrine of justification; the Word of God enables faith to take shape *by hearing*. "With this assertion, the reformers elevated the status of preaching from an edifying discourse to a revealing word of grace. God, through the Holy Spirit, effects the salvation of Christ for the hearer of the word."[19]

John Calvin (1509–65) shaped his homiletics from a revisionist perspective on scripture, the Holy Spirit, and the function of grace. Calvin was known to be a clear orator, who acknowledged the authority of scripture and the Holy Spirit's activity in salvation history. In his *Institutes*, Calvin says that "those whom the Holy Spirit has inwardly taught truly rest upon Scripture, and that Scripture indeed is self-authenticated; hence, it is not right to subject it to proof and reasoning. And the certainty it deserves with us, it attains by the testimony of the Spirit."[20] For Calvin, the people of God are graced through the Holy Spirit's power to interpret the Word in their midst. Much depends on the ability of the hearer to be disposed and open to the workings of the Spirit in the scripture because "the word of God is like the sun, shining upon all those to whom it is proclaimed, but with no effect among the blind."[21] Real understanding of scripture and an authentic encounter with Christ can only be accomplished through the grace of the Holy Spirit. No human agency can presume to lead the heart without the guidance of the Spirit of God.

According to Hughes Oliphant Old, the reforms Calvin initiated, particularly on grace and the work of the Holy Spirit in scripture, were met with great approval in his day because the populace was tired of being cajoled into purification:

> The preaching of grace by the sixteenth century Reformers was received with joy and enthusiasm by those who heard them, because for generations they had been oppressed by the preaching of Pelagianism. The preachers of the late Middle Ages had put the emphasis on the outward forms of religious devotion, the disciplines of penance, the sacramental system, the correct performance of rites, and the techniques of mystical ascent. The elaborate homiletical forms of the late Middle Ages had become worn and tired. The Christians of Western Europe longed for something more than the routine piety they had been preached.[22]

Calvin's writings and sermons also reveal that the gathered assembly in worship is a locus for divine disclosure because such activity recalls the biblical covenant long ago given by God to God's people. The gathered assembly was not to be bullied into purification—such a process was not possible with any authenticity anyway—but simply enfolded as baptized Christians into the context of worship, enlightened by the work of the Spirit and God's saving power in human history. Old explains Calvin this way:

> It is in worship that the covenant is established, maintained, nourished, and renewed. In worship we experience God as our God and ourselves as his people. In baptism we are introduced into the covenant community. In the reading and preaching of the scriptures as well as in the Lord's Supper, we are nourished in the covenant relationship. In the sermon the word is proclaimed; in the supper it is signed and sealed.[23]

Liturgical Preaching Reimagined

The invigoration of Catholic liturgical preaching at the Eucharist began with a different perspective on the laity and its function as the gathered liturgical assembly. The origins of the Roman Catholic reinstitution of the ancient homily and defining its place in the liturgy began in the nineteenth century and would extend more concretely into the twentieth with the promulgation of the documents of the Second Vatican Council. In 1903 Pius X issued a *Motu Proprio*, a document on church music, which laid the groundwork for future participation of the laity, using the phrase *participatio actuosa*. Two years later the same pope encouraged more frequent reception of holy communion. At the Catholic Lay Congress held at Mont César Abbey in Malines, Belgium, in 1909, the visionary Benedictine Lambert Beauduin took a central role in addressing "the need for participation of the faithful in Christian worship in a lecture entitled 'The Full Prayer of the Church.'"[24] The congress gathered to itself a period of reform that had already begun in 1830, but that would now discover greater momentum in the liturgical movement that would last well into the 1960s.[25]

Over a century of liturgical reforms, particularly in regard to the participation of the faithful, influenced the activity of the Second Vatican Council and its perspectives on the participation of the congregation. It is well known that in *Sacrosanctum Concilium (SC)* the Second Vatican Council gave new life to the liturgy, the homily, and the special place of the Christian assembly. We might say that one of the most obvious reasons for the shift in thinking about the homily in the Roman Catholic tradition in the mid-twentieth century occurred not over any particular doctrine, but because of the reconsideration of the *hearer* at the eucharistic assembly. Also, the council clearly adjudicated among the kinds of preaching and gave special attention to the liturgical homily, which ultimately has precedence over pastoral and catechetical forms; it is an act of worship, integral to the liturgy itself, and accomplished in community together with the people of God (*SC*, nos. 35, 52). The liturgical homily finds itself quite separate from other forms of preaching because it lives in the "how" of Christian faith; "it is not about doctrines defended but saving acts announced."[26] Shortly after the council, Domenico Grasso, SJ, published *Proclaiming God's Message: A Study in the Theology of Preaching*, in which he admitted the long legacy of a problematic homiletics that acknowledged cognition before experience:

> Here is the true nature of the problem of preaching. If it were only a case of transmitting a system of ideas, like philosophy, or a complex of facts, which, though true in themselves, have no direct relation to life, preaching would be nothing other than teaching. It is through teaching that philosophic systems and historical facts are passed on to us....Not so with preaching. What is transmitted and what one seeks to have accepted is a person. And the goal to be obtained is adherence to a person....The object of preaching is Christ in His role as Savior of man or, what amounts to the same thing, Christ in the history of salvation.[27]

Active Participation

According to Annibale Bugnini's *The Reform of the Liturgy: 1948–1975*, "the participation and active involvement of the people of God in the liturgical celebration is the ultimate goal of the reform, just as it was the goal of the liturgical movement. This involvement and participation is not limited to externals but reaches to the very root of things: to the mystery being celebrated, to Christ himself who is present."[28] *Sacrosanctum Concilium* states clearly that the work of Christ is ongoing and that God's presence and action in the world disclose themselves in the liturgy through a fourfold presence of Christ: in the minister, in the elements, in the ritual proclamation of the Word, and in the gathered assembly when it prays and sings (*SC*, no. 7).[29] Paul Janowiak points out that

> this interrelated mode of presence was a bold departure from the common understanding and actual practice. True, Roman Catholic theology, through its history had investigated and appropriated the presence of Christ in the elements and in the priest acting *in persona Christi*. What had been and continues to remain ambiguous is how Christ is present in the gathered assembly and in the word proclaimed. These were the questions that Protestant theology had raised centuries earlier.[30]

The Constitution on the Sacred Liturgy was echoing the importance of the assembly as a constitutive and vital element in the way in which Christ is made manifest in the world, and, in so doing, reminds us that faith comes by hearing: "The Church, therefore, earnestly desires that Christ's faithful, when present at this mystery of faith, should not be there as strangers or silent spectators. On the contrary, through a proper appreciation of the rites and prayers they should participate knowingly, devoutly and actively" (*SC*, no. 48).

The council echoed the importance of the homily in its teaching on revelation (*Dei Verbum*) as well, saying that in the context of the celebration of the Word at the Eucharist, "the liturgical homily should have an exceptional place" (*DV*, no. 24). In its revisionist expression of the character of the Word of God and how it is to be understood, *Sacrosanctum Concilium*, like *Dei Verbum*, reaffirmed the place of the homily in Catholic Christian worship as an experience of grace enabling faith to be ignited in the context of worship: the homily "should draw its content mainly from scriptural and liturgical sources. Its character should be that of a proclamation of God's wonderful works in the history of salvation, that is, the mystery of Christ, which is ever made present and active within us, especially in the celebration of the liturgy" (*SC*, no. 35). The pioneering Dominican theologian Yves Congar comments on the integration of scripture into the liturgy of Christian worship:

> If it is true that the Word did not only become Word but flesh, and the sacramental signs are rooted in this *incarnation*, it is also true that (a) the biblical meaning of "word," *dabar,* embraces both the aspect of an effective action and that of presenting it to our knowledge, and (b) the word of God, as operative in the Church, is also an *opus Dei*, a work of God to the extent precisely that it is the word of God.[31]

The Constitution on the Sacred Liturgy does not deploy the language of purification and exhortation in connection with the homily, but rather the language of thanksgiving and faith. Here, the council was echoing an Old Testament tradition. After the people heard the reading recounted in the book of Nehemiah, they "went their way to eat and drink and to send portions and to make great rejoicing, because they had understood the words that were declared to them" (8:12). The people of God participate in God's saving work even as they hear and understand; they give praise and thanksgiving, and so at the Preface Dialogue in the eucharistic liturgy the president of the assembly invites the hearers to "lift up your hearts." That is what is "truly right" because "our desire to thank you is itself your gift." If the homily has been a life-giving bridge from Word into sacrament—naming the wonderful works of God—then the people of God have reason to rejoice. As Benedictine William Skudlarek says, "If people have come together to make Eucharist, the word addressed to them should have something to do with the 'why' and 'how' of giving thanks."[32] "Authentic praise and thanksgiving—that is, praise and thanksgiving flowing out of a recognition of the graciousness of God (faith) and propelling us to actions of love and justice (obedience)—is ultimately the mark of effective proclamation of the word of God."[33]

The Role of the *Homilia*

In its revitalization of the liturgical preaching, the council intended to clarify and revive the ancient practice of the *homilia*, the meaning of which is complex, as I suggested earlier, and even more so when it is parsed from the perspective of the council's return to this ancient form. *Sacrosanctum Concilium* and the post-conciliar documents endorsed not only the homily itself, but its function in the Roman rite and other liturgical preaching events.[34] Reclaiming the *homilia* also reminds us of the importance the council was placing on the early church practice of explicating the sacred scriptures, free from the elaborate rhetorical constrains that would later bind them. It is clear though, that *The Constitution on the Sacred Liturgy* was redefining something that continues to be refined among biblical and liturgical scholars. As diocesan priest Gerard Sloyan recommends, "The Eucharistic act praises God for the deed done on our behalf in Jesus Christ through the power of the Holy Spirit. The homily must do that as much as the biblical readings, the Eucharistic prayer (the 'canon' or '*anaphora*') and the communion rite."[35]

It is the text of scripture that allows the work of God in Christ to unfold in the people gathered to hear the Word; the homily becomes an integral part of the liturgy as a vehicle for revealing God's wonderful works:

> By means of the homily the mysteries of the faith and the guiding principles of the Christian life are expounded from the sacred text during the course of the liturgical year. The homily, therefore, is to be highly

esteemed as part of the liturgy itself; in fact, at those Masses which are celebrated with the assistance of the people on Sundays and feasts of obligations, it should not be omitted except for a serious reason. (*SC*, no. 51)

Sacrosanctum Concilium predicates the importance of the homily on the mystery of the Eucharist itself, in which "the treasures of the Bible are to be opened up more lavishly, so that richer fare may be provided for the faithful at the table of God's word. In this way a more representative portion of the holy Scriptures will be read to the people over a set of cycle of years" (*SC*, no. 51). The recommendations of the council on proclaiming the Word of God emphasize the divine activity in the world, which occurs in the context of the church's prayer of thanksgiving, the Eucharist. As the Lectionary says:

> Whether the homily explains the biblical word of God proclaimed in the readings or some other text of the liturgy, it must always lead the community of the faithful to celebrate the Eucharist wholeheartedly....But this demands that the homily be truly the fruit of meditation, carefully prepared, neither too long nor too short, and suited to all those present, even children and the uneducated.[36]

As the Council and post-conciliar documents redefined the homily and its various forms, particularly in reference to the liturgy, the ecclesial documents were careful to delineate preaching as offering a word of hope about the God already present in the lives of men and women. Robert Waznak comments:

> These church documents emphasized the biblical, liturgical, kerygmatic, conversational, and prophetic aspects of the homily. The prophetic aspect is not found in *Sacrosanctum concilium's* description of the homily. While the documents that followed *Sacrosanctum concilium* do not use the term "prophetic" to describe the homily, the prophetic aspect is present in such phrases as "concrete

circumstances of life," "needs proper to listeners," and "relevant for the present day."[37]

Fulfilled in Our Hearing

Fulfilled in Your Hearing (FIYH), written by a subcommittee of the National Catholic Conference of Bishops' Committee on Priestly Life and Ministry (1982), expanded the ecclesial statements previous to its publication and offers us further insight into the homily as a world of grace, a faith experience encountered by a listener in the liturgical assembly. *FIYH* is divided into three parts: the assembly, the preacher, and the homily. These three aspects of the speech-act correspond, of course, to the classical categories of *pathos, ethos* and *logos*. Significantly, though, the traditional order of these rhetorical parts of the speech-act is reversed, with the hearer addressed *first*. The authors of *FIYH* were undoubtedly aware of the rapid changes in communications and technological developments that were occurring in the twentieth century, as well as anecdotal evidence of the paucity of Catholic preaching during the liturgy. With some exceptions, generations of Catholic priests received little or no training in sermon preparation before the council. Now they were expected to preach a homily that would no longer conform to old rhetorical styles. Moreover, *FIYH* takes a decidedly post-conciliar position on the laity: there is no fixed place, moral or otherwise, that the people of God inhabit and from which they must be purified. Rather, "the community gathers to respond to this living and active God. They may also gather to question how and whether the God who once acted in human history is still present and acting today."[38]

FIYH recognizes that the work of sanctification is to be accomplished not so much by the will of the individual participants or the one who preaches to them, but by the grace-filled encounter among preacher, text, and the people of God. In a word, it is not just preaching but the *entire liturgy* that is meant to sanctify, since it is a remembering of God's activity in Christ in human history. If the homily establishes itself as an integrated part of the sacred mysteries, then the work of preaching also participates in sanctification.

That sanctification is accomplished not by our wills, but by God's—"through Him, with Him and in Him, in the unity *[koinonía/communitas]* of the Holy Spirit, all glory and honor is yours, Almighty Father, for ever and ever. Amen."

Preacher as Interpreter

According to *FIYH*, the primary function for the preacher is to *mediate meaning*. Although the emphasis on the mediating quality does not eclipse the preacher's pastoral role as catechetical leader or witness, this definition of the preacher is a radical shift from previous models—often singular in their emphasis—such as the "teacher" or the "herald." As we have seen, "the preacher as mediator" is not a role claimed by pre-conciliar, Catholic conceptions of the homilist. Through the strong influence of Augustine as *rhetor*, the role of the preacher was more or less confined to the persuasive teacher. Although the preacher performs some mediation function by virtue of knowledge of sacred texts and doctrines, the preacher-as-teacher stands apart from the community by definition, removed to impart knowledge to those who need it for salvation. *FIYH* does not deny the important component of teaching in preaching, which is both biblical and an essential to good homiletic strategy. But teaching alone is not enough to sustain the preaching event. As Robert Waznak has said, "What the preacher declares often calls for an explanation."[39]

FIYH wants to call forth an important identity for the preacher in contemporary society. The document is at pains to point out the kind of fluid relationship that exists between the preacher and the hearer; they are clearly acknowledged as persons who are participating in a homily as an event-in-time. The preacher is not there to solve problems or to purify the congregation, but to engage in the mystery of God's saving works, whether rationally understood or not. "There will be occasions when nothing we can say will do anything to change a situation....What our words can do is help people make connections between the realities of their lives and the realities of the Gospel."[40]

The role of the homilist in relation to the hearer is fundamentally *pastoral*. The preacher uses language to sustain a congregation whom the preacher knows intimately. Again, *FIYH* stresses
the prophetic aspect of the homily by making a strong connection
between the preacher's knowledge and intuiting the signs of the
times:

> Preachers need to devote some time and energy to
> understanding the complex social, political, and eco-
> nomic forces that are shaping the contemporary
> world....Without this kind of informed understanding
> of the complex world we live in, preaching too easily
> degenerates into platitudes of faith, meaningless broad-
> sides against the wickedness of the modern world.[41]

A revisionist view of the preacher-teacher can be especially helpful
in helping the congregation to understand contemporary society.
As Waznak reminds us, the preacher can provide preaching syllabi
that disseminate church teaching over the three-year period of the
liturgical cycle of scripture readings; and give an instruction following the prayer after communion, perhaps on some important
political or ecclesial topic that may concern the parish. Ultimately,
the preacher might let teaching simply emerge in the homily from
the biblical texts.[42] It seems to me that the *Catechism of the Catholic
Church* is an ideal resource to provide illustrations when preaching
from the scriptures, helping the assembly to see its role as God's
pilgrim people in an ecclesial context.

As the interpreter of culture, the preacher stands in a special
position, a mediator for the people he or she serves. *FIYH* acknowledges the insights of the Second Vatican Council that the world is
not something from which we must be purged, but an environment
with which all God's creatures are in dialogue. It would be difficult
to imagine a homilist who does not access the riches of human creativity, both past and present, since these resources "will enable
preachers to engage in a critical dialogue with contemporary culture, recognizing what is conformable with the Gospel, challenging
that which is not."[43] This recommendation for lifelong learning
suggests that the preacher not only understands with some degree

of appreciation the world of good books and "high art" but is in touch with popular culture as well, in order to comprehend what might be driving the contemporary American idiom, often surfacing in complicated and conflicted patterns across generations. All good preachers possess what David Tracy has called "an analogical imagination"—trained to encounter similarity-in-difference; "all good interpreters possess it."[44]

Through the Scriptures

FIYH makes a bold statement about the homiletic text: "The homily is not so much on the Scriptures as *from* and *through* them."[45] The focal point of the homily must not be exegetical, although researching the background of the scriptures is an important, indispensable component in preaching the homily. It is necessary to understand the setting of the biblical world and how these texts spoke to the church throughout the centuries. Patristic homilies are a marvelous resource, perhaps under-utilized by contemporary homilists as touchstones in preaching and interpreting biblical passages. A contemporary congregation would benefit greatly from knowing how a particular passage has been interpreted and preached over the years. But there is more: the scriptures become a lens "to help us to understand, to interpret our lives in such a way that we can turn to God with praise and thanksgiving."[46] The homilist also must be attentive to preaching from the Lectionary and be conscious of the liturgical year that forms its spine. Having adequate biblical knowledge is fundamental, so that the homily can make connections and understand the *lectio continua* principle and help others to do the same.[47] Obviously, the rhythm and harmony of the liturgical year, encompassing Advent, Lent, Easter, the great feasts of the Lord, Marian feasts, and saints' feast days, form a dynamic that continues to invigorate the assembly as it hears the Word proclaimed and preached throughout the year.

FIYH says that homilies ought to engage in a personal style, "more like a personal conversation," which finds its origins in the New Testament use of the homily, such as the way in which the two disciples encounter our Lord on the way to Emmaus (Luke 24), or the conversation Paul had with Felix, procurator of Judea, when the apostle was a prisoner in Caesarea (Acts 24).[48] *FIYH* expands on the work set forth in *Sacrosanctum Concilium* on the homily, but it goes further, recommending the inductive method as a way of preaching and deliberately contrasting it with deductive structure.

> Another way of structuring the homily, and one that is more in keeping with its function of enabling people to celebrate the liturgy with deepened faith, is to begin with a description of a contemporary human situation which is invoked by scriptural texts, rather than with an interpretation or reiteration of the text. After the human situation has been addressed, the homilist can turn to the Scriptures to interpret this situation, showing how the God described therein is also present and active in our lives today.[49]

It would seem unlikely that after the teaching of the Second Vatican Council authentic liturgical preaching could ever be deductive in twenty-first-century American culture, since, as we have seen, that method of argument tends to eclipse not only the listening assembly but the scriptures themselves. In honoring the assembly *FIYH* says that the homily should be more informal, even on matters of utmost importance, rather than "a speech or a classroom lecture."[50]

FIYH echoes contemporary, narrative preaching methodology when its says in regard to the homiletic text that "the form and style will be determined by the form and style of the Scriptures from which it flows, by the character of the liturgy of which it is a part, and by the composition and expectations of the congregation to which it is addressed, and not exclusively by the preference of the preacher."[51] This recommendation reminds us of David Buttrick's "preaching in the mode of immediacy which forms a direct relationship in the consciousness of the congregation."[52] And we might recall, again, that for Buttrick and Craddock in particular, movement and structure become key to creating an experience for the listener. Craddock is very much akin to the mind of *FIYH* when he instructs the preacher to attend to "the form of the text to discern what it achieves—praise, correction, judgment, encouragement, defense, reconciliation, instruction—and then asking if the sermon is designed with that end in mind."[53]

The Role of the Hearer

The priority of *FIYH* is the listener—the congregation and its needs; it is almost always speaking of the listener, even when its pages are referring to the preacher and the text. Ultimately, *FIYH* is a statement on the state of pastoral, liturgical theology with insights about scripture, rhetoric, and modern culture. In the mind of the document's authors, the community that hears the Word in the liturgical assembly becomes central to the graced, sacramental encounter with the God. "All who heard him were amazed" (Acts 9:21). The hearer must remain open as that Word unfolds. As David Power reminds us, "to hear the Word as it is given to us, with all its variety of meanings, requires open minds and open hearts. Once we lay aside the illusion that the sense and impact of a text are fixed for all time, we can listen with greater attention, with the desire to receive what is being offered, and with the will to respond."[54] As I have already implied, the revision of the way in which the hearer is engaged in listening to the Word and in the speech-act in *FIYH* owes a lot not only to the council and the theology that supported it, but "the new language" of the homily and the new image of the preacher as formally initiated by Fred Craddock.[55] Indeed, *FIYH* powerfully claims the "how" that remains so much a part of Craddock's own homiletic: "The preacher acts as a mediator; making connections between the real lives of people who believe in Jesus Christ but are not always sure what difference faith can make in their lives, and the God who calls us into ever deeper communion with himself and with one another."[56] *FIYH* positions the preacher as the one who proclaims a world of grace.

The listener is best approached in a colloquial, unpretentious style. *FIYH* acknowledges that the preacher alone does not have "access to the truth." Recalling the foundational images of the Second Vatican Council, *FIYH* says that "in a church that thinks and speaks of itself as a pilgrim people, gathered together for worship, witness and work, such preaching will be heard only with great difficulty, if at all.[57] *FIYH* trusts the lives of men and women to be hearers of the Word by induction and experience, moving them toward insight. And so *FIYH* echoes Craddock, who asks, "Why not re-create with the congregation the inductive experience of coming to an understanding of the message of the text?"[58] As the listener moves from description to interpretation, "the conclusion of the homily can then be an invitation to praise this God who wills to be lovingly and powerfully present in the lives of his people."[59] As we might imagine, the vision of the liturgical homily in *FIYH* is never static but is animated by a world of grace in the Christian assembly.

Far from being separate from the culture, the homilist addresses the eucharistic assembly as a fellow traveler on the road of faith. As Karl Rahner says, "The preacher should be able to hear his own sermon with the ears of his actual audience."[60] As interpreter, mediator of meaning, the function of the one who preaches is to name both the good and the evil manifested in the world. "The preacher represents this community by voicing its concerns, by naming its demons, and thus enabling it to gain some understanding and control of the evil which afflicts it. He represents the Lord by offering the community another word, a word of healing and pardon, of acceptance and love."[61] Finally, the homily is acknowledged precisely as *liturgical* homily when the authors remind us of the presence of the baptized and the importance and function of the Word in their midst. It is clear that *FIYH* has a deep appreciation of the church's liturgy and the place of the *homilia* as an integrative moment and the Eucharist. Indeed, the ecclesial environment that becomes the domain of the preacher, the text, and the hearers is highly constitutive for making meaning. "We can say, therefore, that the homily is a unifying moment in the celebration of the liturgy, deepening and giving expression to the unity that is already present through the sacrament of baptism."[62]

In regard to the liturgy itself, though, *FIYH* might lead us to some further insights, not emphasized specifically in the document. I am thinking here of preaching on the texts of the liturgical rites, the collects and prefaces of the great feasts of the Lord and Mary, and the lives of the saints. How do all of these moments in the liturgy provide the preacher with a Word for the homily?[63]

Naming Grace

FIYH helped to initiate us into a vital understanding of the homily that it calls "central" to the document: "a scriptural interpretation of human existence which enables a community to recognize God's active presence, to respond to that presence in faith through liturgical word and gesture, and beyond the liturgical assembly, through a life lived in conformity with the Gospel."[64] *FIYH* and its underlying theological anthropology informs Dominican Mary Catherine Hilkert's *Naming Grace* (1997), arguably the most significant theological synthesis on preaching from a Catholic perspective in years.

Hilkert uses the theology of Karl Rahner, Edward Schillebeeckx, and liberation theologians Gustavo Gutiérrez and Carlos Mesters to help us understand God's self-communication in active, graced love. These theologians become key to Hilkert's comprehension of the Catholic homiletic. She writes, "Human beings are structured from creation as 'hearers of the Word'; while sin has affected, it has not destroyed, the image of God within humanity," since there is "a continuity between creation and redemption and the openness of humanity to the divine."[65] Grace has been disclosed historically and definitively in the person of Jesus, yet it continues to be revealed in the depths of the human subject. For Rahner, Hilkert writes, "the role of the preacher is to bring the depth dimension of the mystery of human existence as God's self-offer of love to explicit expression through interpreting that experience in light of the scriptures, the liturgy, and the whole of the Christian tradition."[66] Interpreting experience is a key point in *FIYH*, of course; it positions the preacher as mediator. For Schillebeeckx, the preacher becomes an agent of grace as well, mediating the Holy in the concrete world of history. As Hilkert understands Schillebeeckx, the preacher opens up a world of mediated, graced possibility, albeit contingent and revised throughout history. "We are born into a world of language and culture that provides us with frameworks for interpreting our experience....The preacher is called to tell the Christian story in such a way that people can recognize the experience of grace— God's presence—in their everyday lives."[67]

Such recognition of the Holy in the context of the world in which we live surely recalls the active engagement of the assembly, precisely as those who hear the Word of God and keep it. The reality of concrete human existence becomes the locus of transformation, as God has become Incarnate Word, even in the midst of suffering. Indeed, the preachers who liberate stand in "solidarity with the poor and outcast of this world if they are to share the good news that Jesus promised would be heard by the poor."[68] Gutiérrez and Mesters, like Schillebeeckx, insist on the historical moment as the place where grace unfolds because human history always involves interpreted experience. We can see that Christian preaching is going to play a crucial part in liberating the human subject, perhaps naming the demons of structural sin that plague society and threaten to obscure the presence of grace.

The Sacramental Imagination

Hilkert, then, sees preaching as "the art of naming grace." Far from the work of the dialectical theologians such as Karl Barth, for whom the preacher is a herald in a world drenched in sin, Hilkert's task is to locate preaching inside a sacramental imagination, implicating the preacher as one who mediates, that is, names grace. Her model is biblical, citing Acts 3:12–26, where the "salvation that the preacher announces in word has already been made tangible and visible in deed....As preacher, Peter interprets what has been operative in the depths of the community's experience; he points to the power and presence of God. He names grace."[69] Naming grace does not mean, as is often popularly thought, finding the good in everything, or even worse, that "inside every cloud there is a silver lining." No, the sacramental imagination claims the good news of the passion, death, and resurrection of Jesus and the limitless horizon of God's mercy; the word of salvation has been made manifest in a *new* way and its moment is *now*. Preaching as naming grace is both resurrection and conversion. The preacher is a mediator of meaning, locating mystery, "speaking on the level of story, myth, image, and human experience." He or she moves beyond what Paul Ricoeur has called "the first naiveté," or the precritical and reflection stage that confronts us when we engage a text for interpretation.[70]

Preaching as naming grace has three qualifications: "(1) The experience to be named is human experience in its depth dimension; (2) in the contemporary world situation, most people's experience of God is in the face of, and in spite of, human suffering; and (3) the interpretative keys to identifying grace in human experience are located in the biblical story and the basic symbols of the Christian tradition."[71] These aspects of naming grace occur in the context of narrative preaching because "narrative is the most appropriate, even the necessary category for the holy within the limits of human experience....Narrative does not simply repeat history; it shifts its configuration, thus changing it fundamentally."[72]

The preacher as narrator can fundamentally reorient the perspective of the congregation the way the teller of any good story changes the listener's attitude or disposition. There is a long history in the church of *lectio divina*, in which the reader encounters the movements of grace in sacred scripture.[73] "A book must be an ax for the frozen sea within us," wrote Franz Kafka. The prophet Nathan confronted King David's adultery with a story in 2 Samuel (12:1–15) in which a rich man takes a poor man's most prized possession from him. Feeling sympathy for the poor man, David condemns the rich one. Then Nathan says, "You are the man." David convicts himself by his own reading. Beyond sacred reading, secular literature also repositions reader response as well. Consider, for instance, how novelist Muriel Spark as omniscient narrator handles time in order to shift the reader's point of view on a particular character in *The Prime of Miss Jean Brodie* (1961):

"Speech is silver but silence is golden. Mary, are you listening? What was I saying?"

Mary Macgregor, lumpy, with merely two eyes, a nose and a mouth like a snowman, who was later famous for being stupid and always to blame and who, at the age of twenty-three, lost her life in a hotel fire, ventured, "Golden."[74]

Spark's narrator races ahead of time and, in so doing, grants us a deeper insight into the liminality and contingency of the human person; our own judgments are altered, changed because of a narrational perspective on time. The narrator in Spark's novel is making sense of life by an omniscient sensibility that projects the life of a character into the future. The preacher as narrator of the human story does not claim an arrogant, all-knowing narration but puts things in perspective by some kind of story or pattern of events that (re)orders human experience. The parables of Jesus come to mind, to be sure, which consistently place the hearers in a narrative space other than the one they expected. The revelation of our own human story and journey and how we understand these unfolding in the larger narrative of time becomes an incisive, intrepid way into our lives and the hearts of those around us.

Although the liturgical homily is not the time for tedious personal revelations, the preacher's story is crucial to the shaping of the homiletic narrative. We might recall the emphasis that Fred Craddock placed on the intimate encounter between the preacher and the congregation. When a preacher engages a congregation authentically, an unwritten story emerges, a faith journey is witnessed. That personal pilgrimage may or may not find external expression in the homily itself. Personal stories of Christian witness find their roots in early apostolic witness: "I have seen the Lord." These accounts of personal conversion move others to consider their call; we are profoundly moved when others encounter the Holy, as Saint Augustine did when he wrote in the *Confessions*, "You have touched me, and I have burned for your peace." As Hilkert says:

Part of the power of narrative preaching derives from the insight that life's most powerful experiences can be shared only in and through personal testimony. Hearing the story of human pain or rejoicing gives access to an experience where abstract description and analysis fails. Precisely because of this ability of stories to communicate experiences that exceed the boundaries of other human language, many would claim today that narrative is the most appropriate, even the necessary, category for the holy within the limits of human experience.[75]

Yet, narrational preaching is not simply a matter of telling this story and that, although stories may well be part of the homily. Indeed, a loosely constructed linkage of stories in a homily that does not cohere around a focus statement or what Bishop Kenneth Untener calls a "pearl," can devolve into chatty folklore or homiletic dissipation.[76] "That was an interesting story," someone in the assembly may remark, "but I am not sure where he was going with it." Rather, a homily that weaves a narrative plot that exalts God's wonderful works in human history and connects this divine activity with everyday life already suggests that a story is at work in the lives of men and women. God's mysterious, divine narrative sets the stage for a graced encounter; Christ, the Word made visible, initiates a communal shift in congregational perspective. Here is how Walter Burghardt, SJ, frames his own witness in the context of the beginning of the liturgical year in a homily for the First Sunday of Advent (Year B). He began his preaching on Philippians 4:1–7 like this:

This first evening of Advent I am of two minds, two hearts. I believe I possess Paul's "peace of God, which surpasses all understanding" (Phil 4:7) and I do "rejoice in the Lord" (v. 4), perhaps not "always," still many an enchanted evening. At the same time I am troubled— troubled even though Paul tells me, "Don't worry about anything" (v. 6). In point of fact, I am profoundly worried. At peace and worried for the selfsame reason, Paul's declaration that "the Lord is near" (v. 5). To me, the Lord is near in three ways. Two of those ways bring me peace and joy; the third way causes me to worry. I owe you an explanation.[77]

Burghardt's self-disclosure engages us not so much in his autobiographical details but with a dialogue—even a little bind—he is having with scripture. The preacher leads us through a mediation process as a witness; Burghardt speaks from within the liturgical assembly, giving voice to concerns, worries, and contemporary problems. But in the course of the homily, he will name grace for the assembly.

Beyond *Fulfilled in Your Hearing*

Much of what Hilkert has to say about preaching is related to liturgical preaching but not exclusive to that enterprise. Her theological speculation leads her into helpful clarifications in related areas in homiletics that were not covered in *Fulfilled in Your Hearing*. She goes on to address other forms of preaching, and these distinctions help to establish a vital connection among biblical, liturgical, and doctrinal preaching; all three "are related to human life."[78] For Hilkert, catechetical or biblical preaching may not be liturgical, but liturgical preaching is always biblical and doctrinal.[79] Ultimately, the interconnections in these three areas are best evinced in the process of liturgical catechesis in the fourth and fifth centuries, because "the scriptures and the liturgy clearly formed the context for doctrinal instruction."[80]

When the Word of God is proclaimed in the liturgical assembly and sustained by rituals, it is an event-in-time. In her strong emphasis on the need to connect biblical and theological symbols to everyday life, Hilkert is obviously informed by Rahner's observations expressing the difficulty experienced today by men and women: "Theological expressions are not formulated in such a way that they can see how what is being said has any connection with their own understanding of themselves which they have derived from their experience."[81] And she reminds us of David Buttrick's radical observation that the preacher is a "reverse theologian," "discovering new images to point to the experience that the doctrine is intended to preserve."[82]

Finally, where Rahner and Schillebeeckx help us understand preaching as naming grace and community praxis, liberation theologians become a useful instrument for unlocking the kinds of listeners inside the homiletic event. "Using political and liberation hermeneutics to interpret the scripture, a preacher or faith community will ask specifically political questions: Who holds authority in the passage? Who are the outsiders and who are the insiders."[83] Often, liberation preaching does not mean promoting or condemning various groups, as if to catalogue a list of victims or perpetrators for the congregation. Instead, the preaching might explore a biblical text in which it seems a character has been marginalized and preach from that person's point of view. Giving voice to one who has none or a minor character who is often ignored can provide another example of a narrative shift in thinking. Tracy Chevalier's novel *The Girl with the Pearl Earring* (2001) is a first-person narration about a young servant in the household of seventeenth-century Dutch artist Johannes Vermeer. Griet tells her story, how she came to the Vermeer household, sat as a model for one of the artist's most recognizable paintings, and wound up with a pair of large pearl earrings.

I preached a homily on Genesis 19:15–29, which details the well-known episode of Abraham and Lot fleeing from Sodom and Gomorrah. I took the point of view of Lot's wife, who dared to be curious.

> I don't really have a name. They just call me Lot's wife. I don't even own a name among the rabbis in the Midrash; I am just referred to as "the wife of Lot." A wanderer through the stairways of salvation history, I have been consigned to the world of memory. Strange how people remember you for things done in an instant, a momentary slip, a glance backward to a beloved city. A home undone; a past erased. Odd to think that I am just like everyone else, only more so because I am now etched into a pillar of salt.

It was because of memory that I looked back. And how could I not? I grew up among the people of Mesopotamia, in the astonishing Fertile Crescent between the Tigris and Euphrates rivers. In those green days, we used to have frequent visitors from large cities far away. And while bringing cool water to our small sheep (my hair, burned as blond as a Canaanite basket from the sun), I used to dream endlessly of those exotic places. Then, I was given to Lot when I was just a girl, as young as my daughters were when we fled Sodom and Gomorrah. He took me with his Uncle Abraham through the gorgeous oaks of Mamre. At first Sarah and Abraham welcomed me as if I were their daughter. It was the only affection I knew, of course, having married a man addicted to bartering and selling. There was the inevitable rift with his uncle and the time to move on once again. And then when we had to move away, we traveled through the Negeb and finally, finally we reached what would be our home. I'll bet you would never think that anyone could call Sodom home, but it was the only place I knew as a refuge from the lonely desert and an empty marriage. It was a fair city, really, whose only flaw seemed to be that Wisdom had long left her gates.

I suppose I traded loneliness for a bad conscience, righteousness for an unreflective life. If the truth be told, I knew I had to make a clean break. Yet I knew nothing of eternity, nothing of endings.

It seemed my life was just beginning and would go on forever when, all at once, it was over. I hated the thought of disappearing into the desert night. Then again, there were the memories. All I could do was look back.

God of Abraham, severe actor in the human heart, why was I born in the habitation of the pre-sanctified, cut from the only real beauty of your Christ? How could I gaze upon your authorship when I was so anchored in the destiny of my own lonely heart? I know that I searched busily but was distracted by what I saw. I know too that all this happened because I regarded my memory and its attendant pleasures as more important than your creation. I learned too late that only your Wisdom, and not the shrine of my thoughts or affections, lasts forever. Sadly, now even the statue of salt that used to bear my image carries no trace of me. I dwell now with those who had no time for Wisdom to work its shrewd magic: Paolo and Francesca, aimlessly consumed by love of each other in the *Inferno;* Hamlet's father, caught dead without grace. Like them, I am endlessly blown to bits by the wind. Once a surveyor of a holocaust, I am now a spectator of eternity.

Now I can see the glorious Galilean before me, wrapped in light as in a robe, clothed in a mist, yes, of Wisdom. He is calling you beyond your cherished thoughts, your impoverished memories, even from what you think you hold most dear. Only God is eternal. He comes when you least expect it. Listen to what the Lord tells you. They call me Lot's wife. Remember me.

Claiming another character's point of view invites the congregation to participate imaginatively in that person's world view, one that Jesus might have emphasized for his own hearers as well. For example, the lovely episode in Luke 7:36–50, in which Jesus enters the house of Simon the Pharisee and receives true hospitality from the woman who anoints the Savior's feet, is another chance to tease out the drama and invite the congregation to participate in the perspective of the Pharisee. Richard C. Stern sees this passage as an opportunity to shift the perspective of the assembly to acknowledge the Pharisee in all of us, particularly those of us who are more comfortable with laws than love. In the beginning of this homily Stern shows the Pharisee addressing the congregation directly, using details and conversations that *might* have occurred in order to make a point. The homily gradually moves us into participation in the Pharisee's own point of view:

If you recall, she referred to me as "self-righteous." Oh, she said it in passing, maybe without really thinking. Just a word used in the emotion and fervor of the moment.

But I don't think it is true. Maybe she should think a little more carefully before making judgments about someone she doesn't even know, someone whose home she broke into uninvited, whose meal she interrupted. And she refers to me as self-righteous! Ironic. To say the least.

Throughout history, and long before history, there have been patterns, customs, rules, regulations, even laws that have provided guidance in how we are to relate to one another, how we are to interact with others; there are rules that govern or suggest those with whom we may associate, and, by implication, those with whom we should not associate. Jews and Samaritans, for example, do not associate. One should be certainly be cautious about associating with someone who has a "reputation."[84]

The advantages of taking another character's point of view in the scriptures are numerous and the technique is under-utilized, at least for something more than homiletic "skits." In addition to creating a sympathetic bond with an otherwise minor character or drawing a congregation into a perspective that may be an opportunity for conversion, first-person narration, or dramatic monologue, it discloses the cultural ambiance of contemporary biblical culture in an interesting, non-didactic way. In *Moses: A Memoir* (2003), Joel Cohen creates a sympathetic character and raises lively questions through the vantage point of one of the most important characters in the Old Testament. The method has found some admirers outside of preaching circles, particularly with narratives that emphasize the important (and neglected) role of women in ancient biblical culture. Anita Diamant's best-selling novel *The Red Tent* (1998) explores a woman barely acknowledged in the book of Genesis (Dinah, the daughter of Leah and Jacob), except for the story of her rape. Diamant takes her point of view as she talks about other women in Genesis. Finally, the deployment of another point of view can open the scriptural text up to explorations of various interpretations, enriching the depth of the homily.

New Directions for Liturgical Preaching

The legacy of the Second Vatican Council's teaching on the homily and its relationship with the liturgy continues to be strong, particularly in academic circles. The council's recognition of the fourfold presence of Christ in the minister, elements, Word, and assembly has opened up a major current of scholarship in liturgy, sacraments, and homiletics. Jesuit Paul Janowiak's *The Holy Preaching* (2000) has initiated a creative discussion linking some of the insights of New Historicism with sacramental theology:

> The multiplicity of discourses encompasses any sacramental celebration: the gathering of liturgical assembly in a common faith, symbolic gestures and actions, and a shared word and proclamation that is both sign and reality of the presence of Christ that binds them.... Consequently, one who preaches as if the texts were static and fixed, and whose words and actions appear oblivious of the congregation, acts against the ritual dynamics taking place.[85]

We know that the liturgical assembly comes to faith by hearing, but also because of the very nature of the liturgy as a *social* event. In a way, liturgical proclamation finds a salient analogy in the theater; both are "social texts," the product of "collective intentions." As Janowiak comments, "The faith of the Church, the liturgical cycle of feasts and biblical readings, the communal life of the assembly (the neglect of which enhances ritual dissonance), and the rubrical progression of proclamation/intercessions/sharing of the paschal feast are all a part of that shared cultural storehouse."[86] Through a dynamic of social energies the hearer is extrinsically linked to the dynamics of the text and the one who preaches, once again allowing the Christian assembly to live in the "how" of God's saving events proclaimed by the Word.

James Wallace, a Redemptorist who is very engaged in both preaching and scholarship, has introduced a practical way of thinking about images in homilies by considering archetypes. Using the work of Carl Jung and James Hillman, Wallace's *Imaginal Preaching* (1995) sees preachers as primarily the stewards of images in the Judeo-Christian tradition. Here, Wallace is very much of the same mind as David Buttrick and, indeed, *Lumen Gentium* itself, which sought to transform the way the church thought of itself by recalling foundational images like "the people of God." For Wallace, images are "soul-making." He says that "the preacher's responsible crafting of the images preserved in the biblical texts is one way to overturn the loss of soul found even in the world of religion. Through crafted images sown into the consciousness of a community, soul can be awakened, cultivated, and engaged."[87] Wallace wants to engage homiletics in a dialogue with the arts and even rethink the sources for preaching. He reminds us of Edward Foley's argument for a more conscious appropriation of the "liturgical bible," that is, "all of the sacred texts which constitute the liturgy for a given day."[88]

Wallace's vision of preaching is ultimately pastoral, guided by the teaching of the Council and *FIYH*. The liturgical homily can answer the "hungers of the heart." Wallace recognizes that the homily is, according to *Sacrosanctum Concilium* (no. 52), "highly esteemed as part of the liturgy itself," the result of which moves the hearer to praise, thanksgiving, and praxis. In order for the homily to be truly effective, however, it must respond to the "hungers" broadly facing the human condition. Wallace says that preaching encountered in the course of the liturgical year in particular can respond to three deep hungers. *Preaching to the Hungers of the Heart* (2002) deals with the hunger for *wholeness*, met on the great solemn feasts of the Lord; the hunger for *meaning* can be satisfied within various sacramental rites; and the hunger for *belonging and connectedness* is fed by the celebrations of the saints and Mary, the Mother of God.[89]

Much of this chapter has concerned itself with liturgical preaching. More work needs to be done to invigorate and clarify the homily in the liturgical assembly. At the same time other forms of preaching need to be strengthened. How, for example, can we claim the ancient tenants of catechetical preaching, particularly for the generations of people who need to be instructed on the elementary doctrines and teachings of the Christian faith? Recently some scholarly investigations have been done on the historical legacy of mystogogical preaching, and such explorations can only add to pastoral programs, such as the RCIA.[90]

Lay Preaching

The Appendix of the 1982 edition of *FIYH* recommended that doctoral programs be established for studies in Catholic homiletics. Organizations such as the Catholic Association for Teachers of Homiletics (CATH) continue to generate new ideas, while focusing attention on graduate schools, seminary education, and beyond. In 2002 CATH sent a white paper to all U.S. bishops and seminary rectors, recommending the number of hours for homiletics in preparation for ordained and non-ordained preaching ministry.[91]

All of these expansions in homiletics are quite rightly the province of men and women in the church, the people of God, according to the kind of ministry they have claimed. Perhaps the most exciting yet deeply complicated growth that has occurred in preaching over the last several decades has been the shear numbers of lay preachers who have been called "to preach the Gospel to all nations."[92] "For the Lord wishes to spread His kingdom by means of the laity also, a kingdom of truth and life, a kingdom of holiness and grace, a kingdom of justice, love, and peace" (*LG*, no. 36). There is a long and intricate history of lay preaching in the church, filled with the ups and downs dictated by cultural politics and ecclesiastical norms; the practice has made a significant return after the Second Vatican Council, based largely on the council's vision of the laity and the church as a pilgrim people of God, a mystical body, "and the growing need of ministry in a variety of areas."[93] Once again, preaching participates in a larger theological and social event. As the *Decree on the Apostolate of the Laity (Apostolicam Actuositatem)* puts it:

From the fact of their union with Christ the head flows the laymen's right and duty to be apostles. Inserted as they are in the Mystical Body of Christ by baptism and strengthened by the power of the Holy Spirit in confirmation, it is by the Lord himself that they are assigned to the apostolate. (*AA*, no. 3)

Hilkert writes: "The council asserted that all baptized persons participate directly in the common priesthood of Jesus Christ and share Christ's threefold priestly, prophetic, and ruling office."[94] Canon 759 in the Code of Canon Law also reinforces the baptismal event that mandates the witness of preaching when it says that, "by virtue of baptism and confirmation, lay members of the Christian faithful are witnesses of the gospel message by word and the example of a Christian life; they can also be called upon to cooperate with the bishop and presbyters in the exercise of the ministry of the word."[95] Finally, the Code recognizes the revitalized ecclesiology of *Lumen Gentium* when it says in Canon 766 that, "the laity may be allowed to preach in a church or oratory if, in certain circumstances, it is necessary, or, in particular cases, it would be advantageous." Precisely what *kind* of preaching might be done in the oratory is not specified here but will be clarified in a later canon.

Preaching emerges from the center of a faith-filled person in the context of baptism and confirmation. "If Love be Lord of heaven and earth, how can I keep from singing?" goes the old Quaker hymn. The laity who preach do so not on their own behalf but for the good of the church and the building up of the kingdom of God on earth; in this regard the lay preachers are also heralds. "The task of the herald is not to be somebody, but to do something on another's behalf and under another's authority."[96] Because of baptism, the laity are also called to witness in the world. Thomas Long says that "the witness of preaching" is a significant ministry, an essential ministry in the church. Witnesses go forth to tell the good news. In an address to the laity Paul VI said that "modern man listens more willingly to witnesses than to teachers, and if he does listen to teachers, it is because they are witnesses."[97] Strongly rooted in the biblical prophetic tradition, the claim here is that the joy of Christian living spills over to proclamation through witness. Like Mary Magdalene's testimony to the resurrection of the Lord, credible witness is capable of moving hearts and minds. Indeed, the post-conciliar document "Lay Catholics in Schools: Witnesses to Faith" (1982) also suggests that an integrated personal life of Christian witness is a far better instrument for catechesis than speech itself: "Conduct is always much more important than speech; this fact becomes especially important in the formation period of students" (no. 32). It is not only possible to preach without words, but effective preaching cannot occur in the absence of witness.

Although all Christians are called to witness in preaching—that is, to proclaim the truth of the gospel that Jesus is Lord and that the kingdom of God is upon us—the church as an institution qualifies its preaching witnesses. If all Christians are called to witness to the good news of God's saving actions in the world, then "preaching is witness in a more restricted sense; it is a specific kind of verbal witness. Because preaching is at the very foundation of the church and its mission, the church's ordained ministers are particularly responsible for its proper execution."[98] In a sense, if all Christians are called to proclaim the Word by virtue of their baptism, the church governs the speech-act itself as a public expression of faith. We might say, then, that through the faculties given to them by their local bishop ordinary, ordained ministers are the church's *official* witnesses.

Preaching at the Eucharist, then, is to be accomplished by ordained ministers, according to Canon 767: "The mysteries of faith and the norms of Christian life are to be explained from the sacred text during the course of the liturgical year" (no. 1). Therefore, "lay persons may not preach the homily in any of the sacramental liturgies except when the liturgical books explicitly allow it, as at baptismal services performed by catechists."[99] The U.S. bishops, in *Guidelines on Lay Preaching* (1988), viewed the homily as a way to instruct the faithful. As James Wallace has pointed out, because the homily has been linked to an "instructional moment," the preaching event is tied to those who have traditionally been teachers—bishops, priests and teachers.[100] Further clarification occurred in 2002, when the USCCB issued a decree (approved by the Holy See) reaffirming that the laity may not preach at the Eucharist "at the moment reserved for the homily."[101] Although there had been some confusion regarding Canon 761.1, the same teaching on the homily at the liturgy of the Eucharist in 1988 and 2002 was reinforced in the *New General Instruction on the Roman Missal.*[102]

Needless to say, the contemporary theological debate over lay preaching at the Eucharist has been very complicated. If it is the mission of the entire church to proclaim the Word, Sarah Ann Fairbanks sees the laity as severely restricted, referring to the lay liturgical preachers at the Eucharist as "displaced persons."[103] For pastoral reasons a short summary of the issue of preaching by lay persons might be useful here. Of course, it would be difficult to review the complex argumentation on lay preaching at the Eucharist in this short summary, much of which involves the relationship of priesthood to the Eucharist, the activity of the gathered liturgical assembly, and the homily itself.[104]

Briefly, the recent thought on the place of lay preaching during the Eucharist runs something like this. In addition to canonical restrictions, some say that there are liturgical justifications for restricting preaching at the Eucharist to ordained ministers. The argument here is that for the homily to be an integral part of the liturgy, the one who *presides* must also be the one who *preaches;* that is, the ordained minister provides a crucial link between Word and sacrament. Therefore, preaching is a "high priority" for the ordained; it should not be given over lightly, not only because of the duty to preach, but because of the essential and organic connection at the church's eucharistic liturgy. Additionally, there are numerous historical documents and apostolic exhortations that suggest preaching at the Eucharist should be performed by those ordained to do so. Karl Rahner says that "the Church ordains ministers that its necessary and constituent tasks may be accomplished."[105] As the "Decree on the Ministry and Life of Priests" *(Presbyterorum Ordinis)* states: The preaching of the Word is needed for the very administration of the sacraments. For these are sacraments of faith, and faith is born of the Word and nourished by it" *(PO,* no. 4). As Dominicans John Burke and Thomas Doyle put it, "God has chosen to preach his word on a regular, sustaining basis, through the men he has chosen to be pastors."[106] These and other observations maintain a theology that links holy orders necessarily with the work of evangelism. As Saint John Chrysostom said of the duties of the priest in his treatise *On Priesthood*, the ordained "have one goal in view—the glory of God and the upbuilding of the Church."[107]

The foundation for disallowing lay preaching at the Eucharist is grounded, then, not only in authority but in theological and liturgical interests. The issue remains organic unity for many liturgists and sacramental theologians: the one who presides must also preach. J. Frank Henderson says that this preaching should be "extraordinary," lest the good of the liturgical assembly be in jeopardy.[108] For others, like Frank Quinn, OP, this is simply good liturgical theology: "If the preacher is someone other than the presider, recognition of the priority, structure and character of the entire community action we call liturgy will prevent the minister of the word from treating preaching as if it is *the* event for which the worship of the assembly exists."[109]

Yet there are theological arguments against these objections to lay preaching at the liturgy as well. If organic unity is important, then does this reality prohibit permanent deacons from functioning at the eucharistic liturgy except as altar servers? Some of the theological observations surrounding the link between presider and preacher fail to account for the preaching function in the diaconate, an ancient order in the church; the number of deacons is growing rapidly in North America. Some do not see that organic unity is a real priority. Quinn argues, as do others, that accessing the non-ordained during the moment of the homily after the gospel will flaw "the character of the entire community action we call liturgy."[110] William Skudlarek suggests that "fresh voices will be heard" in allowing lay preaching at the Eucharist.[111] Noted liturgical and sacramental scholar David Power, OMI, sees no problem or conflict between the presider and the preacher. He says that "a firm presidency...through which the interpretation of the word carries over into the proclamation of the blessing and the offer of the sacrament to the community is quite compatible with a multiple exercise of charisms of proclamation and interpretation by other members of the community."[112] Seeking a compromise, many lay preachers function at another part of the eucharistic liturgy instead of the moment reserved for the homily—commonly after communion—or preach "reflections" after the priest or deacon has given a brief homily at the usual time.

One unusual and interesting exception in which the laity are permitted to preach is in liturgies for children, which require only the pastor's permission. The "Introduction" for the approved text of the *Lectionary for Mass with Children* (1994) cites the *Directory for Masses with Children:*

> Because the explanation of the Scripture readings is so important at Masses with children, a homily should always be given. However, in order that they may not be deprived of the riches of God's word, especially if the priest finds it difficult to adapt himself to the mentality of the children, and with the consent of the pastor or rector of the church, one of the adults participating in these celebrations may speak to the children after the gospel.[113]

Drawing some inferences from the *Directory*, some might claim that the real issue in preaching, based on a reading of *FIYH*, is the effective communication to God's people, which the presider may not be able to fulfill under certain circumstances. If that is so, special exceptions for the laity to preach, with appropriate permissions, might also be included for liturgies in languages other than English, where the presider is unable to preach effectively to a congregation in a tongue foreign to him.

Some of the interest in and theology of lay preaching has emerged from the theology of the Second Vatican Council *(Dei Verbum)*. Sarah Ann Fairbanks alludes to both *Dei Verbum* and *Lumen Gentium* when she says that these council documents envisioned the laity as having "a participation in the ongoing mediation of God's revelation, which includes the ministry of the word."[114] Moreover, the issue of lay preaching at the liturgy often becomes more entangled theologically because of an underlying ecclesiology revolving around the identity of the minister at the Eucharist. Mary Collins writes, "Perhaps the question is whether the presidency of the ordained minister in the liturgical assembly inevitably involves prelacy or may just as authentically manifest collaboration within the one Body."[115] Collins provokes many controversial questions, chief among them concerns about the theology of orders and the faculties for preaching in the context of collaborative ministry in the post-conciliar church. If Collins is correct, then what does it mean in the ordination rite to be ordained "to preach, to teach, and to sanctify"? The issue of lay preaching often carries with it huge theological and social implications involving ecclesiology and sacramental theology.

For those who are unpersuaded by canonical restrictions, Mary Catherine Hilkert makes a helpful distinction between authorization and charism: "Regardless of the reasons given for the authorization of preaching, the charism to preach is grounded in baptism and confirmation—the source of all ministry."[116] These qualifications go a long way in helping ministers to understand the public nature of the church's proclamation by ordained ministers. The invitation here may be to think creatively about the kinds of preaching available to the laity and to remember that the rich history of preaching is filled with many opportunities for preaching the gospel in ways that might complement liturgical preaching. One area that needs to be further explored is preaching at Sunday celebrations in the absence of a priest. As this approved rite grows in many areas, the need for qualified laity to preach will increase as well. Indeed, the 1996 *Directory for Sunday Celebrations in the Absence of a Priest* says that "by its very definition" the homily is reserved for the priest or deacon. But "the bishop may allow a layperson who is properly trained to explain the Word of God at Sunday celebrations in the absence of a priest or deacon and at other specified occasions."[117] Continuing education, cultivated reading in scripture and elsewhere, and certainly an awareness of the principles outlined in *FIYH* ought to be normative for those who are "properly trained" for these rites. Additionally, there is enormous need in the areas of catechesis, mystagogy, and apologetics that might be expanded and developed by lay preachers. Developing other areas of preaching besides liturgical preaching may seem to beg the question concerning lay preaching at the Eucharist. Yet who would argue that other kinds of preaching are not needed in all aspects of church ministry?

Who can preach? When? Where? All of these are important questions. Yet the most fundamental question may well be, Why preach? Clearly, Jesus' mandate holds sway for the Christian community; the faithful are to bring the gospel to all nations. In the last several years Raymond Kemp, SJ, and master preacher, Walter Burghardt, SJ, have pioneered a series of workshops entitled "Preaching the Just Word" designed to bring an awareness of biblical and social justice to homilists.[118] Evangelization takes many shapes, but it is clear that spreading the good news of Jesus Christ and the kingdom of peace and justice must happen under many different circumstances. Despite the theological differences that are occasionally at issue in lay preaching, the variety and plurality of many voices can only invigorate the church. There is a vast and diverse history of lay preaching outside the Eucharist in the tradition of the church; such preaching was accomplished by individuals gifted with that charism. They cannot keep from singing.

Notes

1. David M. Greenhaw, "Theology of Preaching," in *Concise Encyclopedia of Preaching*, ed. William H. Willimon and Richard Lischer (Louisville, KY: Westminster John Knox, 1995), 427.

2. Ibid. See also Joseph Connors, SVD, "Catholic Homiletic Theory in Historical Perspective" (Ph.D. diss., Northwestern Univ., 1962; Ann Arbor, MI: UMI).

3. Paul Scott Wilson, *A Concise History of Preaching* (Nashville, TN: Abingdon Press, 1999), 478–79.

4. Richard C. Stern, *Preaching for Today and Tomorrow* (St. Meinrad, IN: Abbey Press, 1996), 10–11 (Stern is referring here to Melloh's categories). Many of the kinds of preaching have been helped enormously by the work of biblical and liturgical scholars after the council.

5. Connors, "Catholic Homiletic Theory," 40

6. Augustine, quoted in Robert Waznak, *Introduction to the Homily* (Collegeville, MN: Liturgical Press, 1998), 8.

7. Alan of Lille, *The Art of Preaching*, in Richard Lischer, *The Company of Preachers: Wisdom on Preaching, Augustine to the Present* (Grand Rapids, MI: Eerdmans, 2002), 7.

8. Lawrence F. Hundersmarck, "Preaching the Passion: Late Medieval 'Lives of Christ' as Sermon Vehicles," in *De Ore Domini: Preacher and Word in the Middle Ages* (Kalamazoo: Western Michigan Univ. Press, 1989), 159.

9. Council of Trent, Session V (Paul III), *Decree Concerning Reform*, chap. 2. Available online.

10. Connors, "Catholic Homiletic Theory," 98.

11. Wilson, *A Concise History of Preaching*, 119–20.

12. Paul Hitz, CSsR, *To Preach the Gospel*, trans. Rosemary Sheed (New York: Sheed and Ward, 1963), 169.

13. Wilson, *A Concise History of Preaching*, 120. While the missions emphasized purification, it must be said that Alphonsus Liguori was also notable for his spiritual insights into the workings of grace in more subtle ways than the mission experience. *The Practice of the Love of Jesus Christ* (1768), structured around 1 Corinthians 13, seems to suggest that God's work is living and active with the renewal of spiritual gifts.

14. Wilson, *A Concise History of Preaching*, 118.

15. Quoted in Waznak, *Introduction to the Homily*, 22.

16. Thomas V. Liske, quoted in Waznak, *Introduction to the Homily*, 9.

17. Martin Luther, "Sermon I," quoted in Wilson, *A Concise History of Preaching*, 98.

18. Martin Luther, "What to Look for and Expect in the Gospels," in Lischer, *Company of Preachers*, 118.

19. Greenhaw, *"Theology of Preaching,"* 478.

20. John Calvin, "Internal Testimony of the Spirit," in Lischer, *The Company of Preachers*, 364–65.

21. Ibid., 367.

22. Hughes Oliphant Old, *The Reading and Preaching of the Scriptures in the Worship for the Christian Church*, vol 4, The Age of the Reformation (Grand Rapids, MI: Eerdmans, 2002), 130.

23. Ibid., 133–34.

24. Paul Janowiak, SJ, *The Holy Preaching: The Sacramentality of the Word in the Liturgical Assembly* (Collegeville, MN: Liturgical Press, 2000), 6. Janowiak has a brief but useful summary of the liturgical movement and its reform, 1909–69. See also Nathan D. Mitchell's reflections on the fortieth anniversary of *Sacrosanctum concilium*, which, he judges, was anticipated by various papal reforms, among them Leo XIII's affirmation of Eastern rites and the renovation of music in the context of liturgical diversity ("The Amen Corner," *Worship* 77/6 [November 2003], 553–65).

25. See Virgil C. Funk, "The Liturgical Movement," in *The New Dictionary of Sacramental Worship*, ed. Peter E. Fink (Collegeville, MN: Liturgical Press, 1990), 695–715. Beauduin's call for a democratization of the liturgical life of the church was based on Pius X's own call for "active participation in the sacred mysteries" in 1903 as well as other factors. Later, the movement would widen in official and popular circles, both in North America and in Europe.

26. Robert Waznak, SS, "Homily," in Fink, *The New Dictionary of Sacramental Worship*, 554.

27. Domenico Grasso, SJ, *Proclaiming God's Message: A Study in the Theology of Preaching* (Notre Dame, IN: Univ. of Notre Dame Press, 1965), 21.

28. Annibale Bugnini, *The Reform of the Liturgy, 1948–1975* (Collegeville, MN: Liturgical Press, 1990), cited in Janowiak, *The Holy Preaching*, 5.

29. See Janowiak, *The Holy Preaching*, 4.

30. Ibid. See also Janowiak's chapters on Luther and Calvin, 178–83.

31. Yves Congar, OP, "Sacramental Worship and Preaching," in *The Renewal of Preaching: Theory and Practice*, ed. Karl Rahner, SJ (New York: Paulist Press, 1968), 52. See also David Power, OMI, "The Word

of the Lord": *Liturgy's Use of Scripture* (Maryknoll, NY: Orbis Books, 2001).

32. William Skudlarek, *The Word in Worship: Preaching in a Liturgical Context* (Nashville, TN: Abingdon Press, 1981), 98.

33. Ibid., 69.

34. See, for example, O. C. Edwards Jr., *Elements of Homiletic: A Method for Preparing to Preach* (New York: Pueblo, 1982), 6–7. There are still a number of different takes on homily and sermon. The author suggests that simply because the etymology in the New Testament may suggest a "conversational tone" for the Greek verb *homilein*, it does not necessarily mean that this meaning in the lexicon indicates what our present-day usage should be. The Latin *sermo* and Greek *homilia* both have the same sense of conversation, talk, and discussion, according to Waznak (*Introduction to the Homily*, 11). At the same time, Gerard Sloyan says that the sermon is really a "discourse that develops a specific theme" ("Liturgical Homily," in Willimon and Lischer, *Concise Encyclopedia of Preaching*, 311–13).

35. Gerard Sloyan quoted in Waznak, *Introduction to the Homily*, 12. See also Gerard Sloyan, *Worshipful Preaching* (Philadelphia: Fortress Press, 1984); "Some Thoughts on Liturgical Preaching," *Worship* 71/5 (September 1997), 386–99; and "What Kind of Canon Do the Lectionaries Constitute?" *Biblical Theological Bulletin* 30 (Spring 2000), 27–35.

36. Quoted in Waznak, *Introduction to the Homily*, 10.

37. Waznak, *Introduction to the Homily*, 10–11.

38. National Council of Catholic Bishops, *Fulfilled in Your Hearing: The Homily in the Sunday Assembly* (Washington, DC: USCC, 1982), 7.

39. Waznak, *Introduction to the Homily*, 40.

40. *FIYH*, 10.

41. Ibid., 15.

42. Waznak, *Introduction to the Homily*, 44.

43. *FIYH*, 13.

44. David Tracy, *Plurality and Ambiguity* (Chicago: Univ. of Chicago Press, 1987), 20. See also idem, *The Analogical Imagination: Christian Theology in the Culture of Pluralism* (New York: Crossroad/Herder and Herder, 1998).

45. *FIYH*, 20.

46. Ibid., 21.

47. Ibid., 20.

48. Ibid., 24.

49. Ibid.

50. Ibid.

51. Ibid., 25.

52. See David Buttrick, *Homiletic: Moves and Structures* (Philadelphia: Fortress Press, 1987), 333–64.

53. Fred B. Craddock, *Preaching* (Nashville, TN: Abingdon Press, 1985), 178.

54. Power, *"The Word of the Lord,"* 14.

55. See Waznak, *Introduction to the Homily*, 53ff. Waznak also has some useful images of the preacher that help us to understand the preacher as mediator (interpreter), teacher, herald, and witness.

56. *FIYH*, 8.

57. *FIYH*, 5.

58. Fred B. Craddock, *As One Without Authority* (St. Louis: Chalice Press, 2001), 99.

59. *FIYH*, 24.

60. Karl Rahner, "Demythologization and the Sermon," in Rahner, *The Renewal of Preaching*, 26.

61. *FIYH*, 15.

62. *FIYH*, 6–7.

63. See Edward Foley, "The Homily Beyond Scripture: *Fulfilled in Your Hearing Revisited," Worship* 43/4 (July 1999), 351–58.

64. *FIYH*, 29.

65. Mary Catherine Hilkert, *Naming Grace: Preaching and the Sacramental Imagination* (New York: Continuum, 1997), 32–33.

66. Ibid., 34.

67. Ibid., 37.

68. Ibid., 53.

69. Ibid,, 43–44.

70. Paul Ricoeur, *The Symbolism of Evil*, trans. Emerson Buchanan (Boston: Beacon Press, 1967), 347–53, cited in Hilkert, *Naming Grace*, 142.

71. Hilkert, *Naming Grace*, 49.

72. Ibid., 97.

73. See, for example, Michael Casey, OCSO, *Sacred Reading* (Ligouri, MO: Triumph Books, 1996).

74. Cited in Shlomith Rimmon-Kenan, *Narrative Fiction: Contemporary Poetics* (New York: Methuen, 1983), 49.

75. Hilkert, *Naming Grace*, 96–97.

76. See Kenneth Untener, *Preaching Better: Practical Suggestions for Homilists* (Mahwah, NJ: Paulist Press, 1999), 42–47. Untener says that "too

many thoughts is the most frequently voiced complaint about homilies." Too many stories have the same effect.

77. Walter Burghardt, SJ, *Let Justice Roll Down like Waters: Biblical Justice Homilies Throughout the Year* (New York: Paulist Press, 1997), 5.

78. Hilkert, *Naming Grace*, 135.

79. Ibid., 134.

80. Ibid., 136.

81. Rahner, quoted in ibid., 136.

82. Buttrick, quoted in ibid., 136n32, 225.

83. Hilkert, *Naming Grace*, 176.

84. Richard C. Stern, "Homily on Luke 7:36–50," February 25, 1997.

85. Janowiak, *The Holy Preaching*, 100.

86. Ibid., 116.

87. James Wallace, CSsR, *Imaginal Preaching: An Archetypal Perspective* (Mahwah, NJ: Paulist Press, 1995), 34.

88. James Wallace, CSsR, *Preaching to the Hungers of the Heart: The Homily on the Feasts and Within the Rites* (Collegeville, MN: Liturgical Press, 2002), 20–21. See also Foley, "The Homily Beyond Scripture: Fulfilled in Your Hearing Revisited," 351–58; and Samuel Torvend, OP, "Preaching the Liturgy: A Social Mystagogy," in *In the Company of Preachers*, ed. Regina Siegfried and Edward Ruane (Collegeville, MN: Liturgical Press, 1993), 48–65.

89. Wallace, *Preaching to the Hunger of the Heart*, 27.

90. See, for example, Craig Alan Satterlee, *Ambrose of Milan's Method of Mystagogical Preaching* (Collegeville, MN: Liturgical Press, 2002).

91. Catholic Association of Teachers of Homiletics, "The State of Homiletics in Seminaries and Graduate School of Theology in the United States" (unpublished, 2002).

92. For a concise but thorough overview see James A. Wallace, CSsR, "Preaching by Lay Persons," in Fink, *The New Dictionary of Sacramental Worship*, 975–78.

93. See Patricia A. Parachini, *Lay Preaching: State of the Question* (Collegeville, MN: Liturgical Press, 1999), 9–19.

94. Hilkert, *Naming Grace*, 155.

95. *Code of Canon Law, English-Latin Edition* (Washington, D.C.: Canon Law Society of America, 1983).

96. Thomas G. Long, *The Witness of Preaching* (Louisville, KY: Westminster John Knox, 1989), 27.

97. Pope Paul VI, "Address to the Members of the Consilium de Laicis," quoted in John Allyn Melloh, SM, "On the Vocation of the Preacher," in *Ars Liturgiae: Worship, Aesthetics and Praxis*, ed. Claire V. Johnson (Chicago: Liturgy Training Publications, 2003), 177.

98. John Burke, OP, and Thomas P. Doyle, OP, *The Homilist's Guide to Scripture, Theology, and Canon Law* (New York: Pueblo, 1986), 57.

99. Burke and Doyle, *The Homilist's Guide*, 61. See also James H. Provost, "Lay Preaching and Canon Law in a Time of Transition," in *Preaching and the Non-Ordained: An Interdisciplinary Study*, ed. Nadine Foley, OP, 134–58 (Collegeville, MN: Liturgical Press, 1983).

100. James A. Wallace, CSsR, "Guidelines for Preaching by the Laity: Another Step Backward?" *America* 161/6 (September 9, 1989), 9–16. See also United States Conference of Catholic Bishops, "U.S. Bishops/ Guidelines for Lay Preaching," *Origins* 18/25 (December 1, 1988), 402–4.

101. United States Conference of Catholic Bishops, "Three Decrees of Promulgation on Lay Preaching and Radio, TV Teaching on Faith," *Origins* 31/33 (January 31, 2002), 551.

102. See United States Conference of Catholic Bishops, *General Instruction of the Roman Missal* (Washington, DC: USCCB, 2003), 35. The document intends to clarify the confusion about Canon 767.1, which was brought about by the interdicasteral Instruction "on certain questions regarding the collaboration of the non-ordained faithful in the sacred ministry of priests," *Ecclesiae de Mysterio*, August 15, 1997, art. 3: *AAS* 89 (1997), 864.

103. See Sarah Ann Fairbanks, "Displaced Persons: Lay Liturgical Preachers at the Eucharist," *Worship* 77/5 (September 2003), 439–57.

104. See Parachini's concise but useful treatment in *Lay Preaching*, 20–34.

105. Karl Rahner, quoted in Stephen Vincent DeLeers, "The Place of Preaching in the Ministry and Life of Priests," in *The Theology of Priesthood*, ed. Donald J. Goergen and Ann Carrido (Collegeville, MN: Liturgical Press, 2000), 93.

106. Burke and Doyle, *The Homilist's Guide*, 58.

107. See also DeLeers, "The Place of Preaching in the Ministry and Life of Priests," 87–103.

108. J. Frank Henderson, quoted in Parachini, *Lay Preaching*, 27.

109. Frank Quinn, OP, "Liturgy: Foundation and Context for Preaching," in Siegfried and Ruane, *In the Company of Preachers*, 11.

110. Ibid.

111. Skudlarek, *The Word in Worship*, 96–97.

112. David Power, quoted in Parachini, *Lay Preaching*, 28.

113. *Lectionary for Masses with Children: Study* Edition (Collegeville, MN: Liturgical Press, 1994), xv.

114. Fairbanks, "Displaced Persons," 444; see also *DV,* nos. 3–4, 14, 17, and *LG*, nos. 2–4, 9. An (imperfect) analogous theological parallel might be the understanding between the "priesthood of the baptized" and its relationship with ordained priesthood. See also Jack Risley, OP, "The Minister: Lay and Ordained," and Benedict Ashely, OP, "The Priesthood of Christ, the Baptized, and the Ordained," in Goergen and Carido, *The Theology of Priesthood*, 119–64; the essays collected in *Ordering the Baptismal Priesthood: Theologies of Lay and Ordained Ministry*, ed. Susan K. Wood (Collegeville, MN: Liturgical Press, 2003); and Nadine Foley, OP, ed., *Preaching and the Non-Ordained.*

115. Mary Collins, quoted in Parachini, *Lay Preaching*, 29.

116. Hilkert, *Naming Grace*, 157.

117. NCCB, *Sunday Celebration in the Absence of a Priest*, Liturgy Documentary Series 10 (Washington, DC: USCCB, 1996), 32.

118. For more information, search "Preaching the Just Word" online. Also see Walter Burghardt's widely available published homilies, many of which deal with biblical and social justice; they are an excellent resource for any preacher's library.

4
MULTICULTURAL PREACHING

Pero recibirán la fuerza del Espíritu Santo cuando venga
sobre ustedes, y serán mis testigos en Jerusalén, en toda
Judea, en Samaria y hasta los extremos de la tierra.
—Acts 1:8

Raymond Williams has reminded us that the word *culture* is "one of the two or three most complicated words in the English language."[1] In the nineteenth century, for instance, culture or being cultivated, was typically associated with high art or bookish learning. To read Shakespeare meant to be cultured. But the way in which we understand culture these days is less about something we need to acquire as much as the kinds of *differences* we come to experience and appreciate. We live inside culture. Over the last several years, curricula in elementary and secondary schools, together with institutions of higher learning, have made conscious efforts to include multiple forms of literature to reflect more accurately the diverse expressions of the human family. Cultural studies and folklore programs have flourished in the universities. Economic forces have made it clear that we are living in a kind of global village, with technology at our disposal to make communication instantaneous. The media in all forms have made us more conscious than ever before that there is not one dominant culture but many different anthropologies that contribute to the richness of experience. For our purposes here, I will use a working definition of culture espoused by Henry H. Mitchell, who has written extensively and most prolifically on black preaching. "Culture," he says, "is the accumulation over time of all the wisdom and methods of a given cultural group, for the purpose of ensuring its survival."[2] In this chapter I briefly discuss multiculturalism and its impact on preaching. Then I focus mostly on African American and Hispanic preaching and, in so doing, handle the various homiletic strategies that have emerged in each of these two cultural realities.

What Is Multiculturalism?

Multicultural is a complex word, owing in some degree to the greater understanding of *culture* in recent years.[3] For financial and personnel reasons, some dioceses have incorporated the work of ministering to non-native cultures under a single title. But these groups often take exception to the concept of a single hegemony encompassing so many differences. In fact, such a problem arose in *Encuentro 2000* in Los Angeles, at which the participants raised concern about a "one-size-fits-all" approach to ministry: "This model often dilutes the identity and vision of Hispanic ministry and those of other ethnic ministries."[4] And yet, there ought to be a term to address the way in which the dominant culture addresses and is challenged by the plurality and diversity of ministry. To recognize multicultural preaching is to stand apart from an evangelism and missiology that informed past centuries and was fueled by the economic, social, and theological interests embedded in Eurocentric colonialism. Our view of religious multiculturalism allows for different ethnicities to articulate their own language, in contrast to a former, imperialist perspective in which "religious belief provided a vocabulary of right—the right to know and to speak that knowledge, with the moral power that was attached to the speaking of God's word."[5]

Diversity continues to be complex and even upsetting for some. Over the last several years, though, Americans have begun to recognize that we do not live in a "melting pot" as much as in a "stew" containing many different offerings, each with its own distinct flavor. Hence, the literature on the subject of multiculturalism continues to grow and inspire change. Various authors from different cultural and ethnic origins continue to share their stories. More than fifty years have passed since the publication of Ralph Ellison's *The Invisible Man* (1952), which chronicles the story of a young, nameless African American. Now, although racism still continues in our culture, the multiple variety of ethnic groups in the country could be described as anything but silent. From hip-hop culture to independent Latino films to best-selling novels by Asian American women, the United States is populated by strong, diverse voices.

In their book *One Gospel, Many Ears* (2002), Joseph R. Jeter Jr. and Ronald J. Allen describe the benefits of multiculturalism in this way:

1. It broadens and deepens our own limited and circumscribed experience, as individuals and as community.

2. It prepares us for more effective and satisfying living in the real world of the new millennium as we better understand our own culture and better relate to others.

3. It moves us toward that time when we shall all gather before the throne of grace to share in the joys of God together.[6]

Similarly, the Pontifical Council for Culture's *Toward a Pastoral Approach to Culture* (1999) recognizes that we are living in a new age in human history, in which real inculturation carries no hint of syncretism.[7] As John Paul II has pointed out, the evangelization of culture allows Christ to be present within distinctive populations, where he penetrates "the very life of cultures, becomes incarnate in them, overcoming those cultural elements that are incompatible with the faith and Christian living."[8] With the bewildering complexity of a vast array of cultures unfolding before us, the church sees this multicultural experience as an opportunity and a challenge to evangelize, even when the division between the culture and the gospel is readily apparent: "The split between the Gospel and culture is without a doubt the drama of our time, just as it was of other times. Therefore, every effort must be made to ensure a full evangelization of culture, or more correctly of cultures. They have to be regenerated by an encounter with the Gospel. But this encounter will not take place if the Gospel is not proclaimed."[9]

That gospel must be preached with due attention to the listeners and the cultures from which they come. The way a culture interprets its inherited texts and tradition ought to be honored and treasured. The scriptures are interpreted according to the historical and social framework of a particular culture. As David Power reminds us: "The Word of God resonates within a social situation. It relates to a people's vision of life and to the values which they hold. These are inherited from culture but are always shifting with changes in living conditions and with the kind of relations one society has with another."[10] Power points out that when it comes to interpreting the gospel in our culture, we must shift not only our practices but the fundamental stance or horizon from which we act. A consideration of multicultural preaching is important, then, not only because of the reality of expanding diversity that continues to flourish in North America and elsewhere, but because taking into account the diversity of the human family causes us to be "other oriented" and to preach accordingly. Crucially, preaching to various cultures forces the homiletic model to inevitably turn toward the hearer. As Leonora Tubbs Tisdale tells us:

> In hearer-oriented communication...primary value is placed upon the ability of the hearer to understand the message in his or her own symbolic framework, and to relate it to his or her own world. The speaker varies the language and symbols used in communication in order to achieve maximum understanding and appropriation by the hearer, even if some peripheral aspects of content are lost or altered in transmission....Thus, the speaker seeks, as much as possible, to enter into the hearer's own world of symbolic understanding in the communication of the message.[11]

Our understanding about the diverse kinds of preaching has grown enormously over the last few decades, based largely on the changing characteristics of the hearers themselves. It is commonplace to observe the cultural, ethnic, and demographic shifts throughout North America that have affected worship across denominations. In 1950, for example, there were about 2.5 million Hispanics in the United States; this number has now swelled to over 36 million. The most recent documents on ministry to Latinos reflect a version of what Stephen Bevans calls contextual theology, which attempts to address not only the message of the gospel and the tradition, but also "the culture in which one is theologizing and social change in that culture."[12] The African American Catholic community is proportionately smaller than that of the Latinos, but it is still vibrant and expanding. As Benedictine Cyprian Davis has shown, in the last three decades of the twentieth century the black Catholic community expanded considerably.[13] Further, with the publication of *Lead Me, Guide Me: The African-American Catholic Hymnal* (1987), we have seen a marvelous inculturation of music from a rich and diverse heritage. The church must continue to respond to the needs of one of the earliest ethnic groups to hear the gospel.

Preaching must change its posture in order to accommodate the needs of the hearer if real evangelization is to take place. If, as studies in the 1950s demonstrated, an "actional" model has proven unproductive for middle-class white people, then we ought to assume that preaching that performs a "one-way" hermeneutic on African American or Hispanic congregations will be doubly ineffective. Adopting some of the terminology from cultural studies, we might say that preaching that fails to attend to the ethnic and cultural diversity of the listeners, not only does not evangelize, but also participates in a kind of "cultural imperialism," binding those hearing to a linguistic and symbolic system not their own, one alien to their God-given, graced experience.[14] As James R. Nieman and Thomas G. Rogers say in *Preaching to Every Pew* (2001), "Preaching that recognizes multicultural realities is, in some important respects, less a matter of the others we may hope to reach than of whether we make a serious engagement with our particular setting."[15]

African American Preaching

One of the great historical misunderstandings is the claim that white missionaries evangelized African Americans. Not so. The black nations had already received the gospel centuries before the great impulse to convert Africa took hold in the West. Indeed, as Cyprian Davis and others have demonstrated, the history of the early church has strong roots in Africa, particularly in Nubia and Ethiopia.[16] Henry Mitchell writes, "While there would have been no slave Christians without some form of exposure to white faith, the 'Invisible Institution' (underground church) of the South practiced its own African adaptation of that faith—both authentically Christian and unashamedly African-American."[17] African American Christianity emerges out of ancient Africa, to be sure, but William H. Pipes says that black preaching owes its style to a European encounter beginning in England in 1732:

> George Whitefield was the bridge between Black religious sentiments and the faith of the colonial White. Until the First Great Awakening (1726–1750), White religion had been formal, cold, and unattractive. Suddenly, with the preaching of Whitefield (as well as Jonathan Edwards, the Tennents and others), the response to preaching became very fervent and dramatic, with extreme physical manifestations.[18]

There is an important distinction to be made here. The enticement of African Americans into a model of preaching that broke away from more cognitive expressions of the Word was not a move toward excessively emotional, unthinking faith experiences. Rather, the move away from a rationalist homiletics toward an emotive experience signified an integration that would encompass not only the total human subject, but address class differences, especially for those, like the slaves, who lived in extreme poverty. Henry Mitchell says that the task of the African American preacher is precisely to confront the whole person: "This holistic approach includes high emotion, but not emotionalism. Faith, hope and love are primarily intuitive and emotive....The holistic approach also explains why this preaching tradition has served to empower an oppressed people."[19] Moreover, based on what we have seen in the history of preaching, the folks who were attractive to black Christians—Whitefield, Wesley, and their line of preachers—were also reshaping a sermonic moment that focused on the *preacher* as arbitrator of the Word. The *person* or *ethos* of the preacher, often very dramatic, like Whitefield himself, became very important to the African American community, since the preacher vitiates God's Word in a moment of needed, even prophetic urgency. Clearly, the preacher and the congregation together begin to shape a unique holistic homiletic experience.

Henry H. Mitchell and the New Hermeneutic

Henry Mitchell recounts that Martin Luther King Sr. publicly mused about why there were offerings in seminaries called black preaching. He goes on to say that "'Daddy' King failed to take into account the realities of culture. People hear the good news in their own mother tongue—their own idiom, images and cultural communication style."[20] Mitchell also claimed in the first edition of *Black Preaching* (1970) that an African American style of preaching might well be the New Hermeneutic advocated by Gerhard Ebeling and others. According to Ebeling, "The word of God must be left free to assert itself in an unflinchingly critical manner against distortions and fixations....Theology and preaching should be free to make a translation into whatever language is required at the moment and to refuse to be satisfied with correct, archaizing repetition of 'pure doctrine.'"[21] In a certain sense Ebeling was setting the stage for a hermeneutic of multicultural preaching.

Mitchell says that there are two fundamental hermeneutical principles that are rooted in the black tradition of preaching, an inheritance that counts its origins from the black fathers: "The first is that one must declare the gospel in the language and culture of the people—the vernacular."[22] The Bible is the cornerstone of the African American religious experience, and the sacred text must be "idiomized." In the best traditions, black preachers translate the scriptures in an imaginative way for the hearers, rendering it into a folk idiom. There is a rich history of African American preachers who were amazing in their ability to use English, despite being denied education.[23] "The second hermeneutic principle is that the gospel must speak to the contemporary man and his needs."[24] There is a stylistic urgency about African American preaching, obviously rooted in social and political oppression. Mitchell draws on an analogy between black people's spirituals and preaching: "When they say about 'stealing away,' they no doubt had some notion of the prayer closet, but there is strong reason to believe that to steal away to Jesus was to escape to freedom! Similarly, to sing 'I ain't got long to stay here' is not exclusively other-worldly escape. It is the code language of the gospel of self-liberation."[25] The ability to translate the complicated language of the sacred text into the pungent, ringing language of liberation remains an important object for the preacher in the African American community.

A small sample from a homily of Dr. Martin Luther King Jr. provides a nice illustration of Mitchell's idea of the New Hermeneutic, particularly its applicability to black preaching:

> On that day the question will be what did you do for others. Now I can hear somebody saying, "Lord, uh, I did a lot of things in life. I did my job well....I did a lot of things, Lord, I went to school and studied hard. I accumulated a lot of money, Lord, that's what I did." Seems as if I can hear the Lord of Light saying, "But I was hungry, and you fed me not. I was sick and ye visited me not. I was neck-id in the cold, and I was in prison and you weren't concerned about me, so get out of my face."[26]

King skillfully cites familiar *written* passages from Matthew 25:31–46, such as "I was sick and ye visited me not," and mixes these words with *oral, vernacular,* and *idiomatic* expressions, such as "neck-id in the cold" and "get out of my face." As the New Hermeneutic implies, African American preaching is intensely, emotionally pastoral and often marked by the distinctive ability to wrap complicated theological reflections in language that anyone can understand. "Although the great African-American preachers can present significant philosophical and theological arguments and cite the likes of Brunner, Barth, Bultmann and Bonhoeffer, black churchgoers prefer the word to be less discursive and more human. They want it to relate to life. They desire it to inspire and move them emotively."[27]

The role of the black preacher for African Americans is pivotal; a mystique surrounds the persona of the one who is able to "give a word" to the assembled congregation. The black community has a long history with the preacher, who has been more to it than a Sunday pastor. It was the preacher who took the black community through the unimaginable horrors of slavery to liberation. Mitchell concludes:

> Perhaps the greatest evidence of the power of Black preaching is that the Black belief system of folk Christianity has kept its believers alive and coping— even when in an oppressed condition that would have crushed many. Slave narratives by the dozens recall sermons stories and pictures with astounding accuracy. It is clear that these sermons were so meaningful because the storytelling and picture painting arts were excellent, because the issue at hand was so relevant, and because the hearers were not mere spectators, but were real participants in the experience.[28]

African American preachers were midwives for their people, bringing them out of the darkness of despair and death into light and freedom. Historically, then, the black congregation is poised to receive something very significant from the preacher. The New Hermeneutic in the black homiletic requires nothing less than full, active engagement on the part of both the preacher and the congregation; the preacher becomes a mediator of the gospel in the vernacular in response to urgent, contemporary needs. Scripture, as well as the theology that supports it, must have flesh and bones. "Black preachers weave the Word into the existential situations of the worshiping congregation. The Word must relate to their lives and needs and feelings. It must address the predicaments that constantly plague the black person and the larger

African-American society."[29] The legacy of the African American preacher has never lost its continuity, for the community still waits in hope for a liberating word, often in a troubled and difficult culture.

The Dialogical Moment: Amen!

One of the most recognizable features in black preaching is its conversational quality, or dialogical form. "The event of preaching is not hierarchical; it is a communal experience in which antiphony predominates. This is unlike most Eurocentric worship experiences which are spectator oriented, where the congregation sits and listens. In Afrocentric worship, the worshipers participate in the preaching."[30] It would be difficult to imagine an African American congregation that did not expect some kind of dialogical exchange between the assembly and the preacher. Moreover, there is a certain *ethos*, even an intimacy, that shapes the worship experience precisely because of the dialogue between the congregation and the preacher. Like any good pastor, the preacher addresses the needs of this congregation. The members respond: *"Amen!"* They respond: *"Preach it, Brother!"* They respond: *"You're getting into my pew!"* In any number of ways the congregation affirms the preacher in the midst of the homily itself. On the level of text, the encounter between preacher and congregation can only be called organic, spontaneous, even unpredictable. The homily is constructed in the midst of the present moment, not recited as a reflection of a past moment. While the preacher acknowledges the role of the Holy Spirit in the construction of the sermon, he or she becomes a listener as well, affirming the value and honor of the assembly as constitutive of the homily. The text of the homily is broadened from words on a page and even expanded from the words of the preacher. The boundaries of the homily are very fluid in African American preaching because of the dynamic of human exchange.

For Robin R. Meyers, the interaction that occurs during black preaching engenders "self-persuasion":

In African-American preaching, the sermon is not private property. The minister does not speak to the people but for them, and empathy need not be contrived, only embodied. The purpose of the sermon is to plead everyone's pleading, to exalt everyone's exaltation, and to talk so honestly about the life of faith that everyone's tongue is loosed. The preacher's compulsion to speak diminishes the congregation's hesitation to speak.[31]

The cry "Amen" from the congregation is not only an affirmation of the preacher's words but an acknowledgment of the faith of the believer for all to hear. Such an audible sign certainly reveals an aspect of Christ's presence in both the Word and the assembly that is so crucial to the insights of *Sacrosanctum Concilium* as well as *Fulfilled in Your Hearing.* "When one hears and accepts this vision of the world, this way of interpreting reality, a response is required. That response can take many forms."[32] Over the years, the response of the African American community has been a vibrant, life-giving homiletic text.

Black preaching, then, encourages immediate, spontaneous response. As Richard Eslinger writes: "The participation of the people is essential to the task of proclamation; there is a necessary 'word back' from the people that is crucial in proclaiming the Word. The priesthood of all believers is manifested in this dialogical character of the African-American sermon."[33] The "word back" is not unique to black preaching, although it is manifested in different, albeit more formal dialogue, such as the Preface/Dialogue in the eucharistic liturgy of the Roman rite, for instance. In a certain sense the traditional African American sermon we have been discussing parallels the liturgical homily and the ensuing dialogue of the Preface. When the congregation maintains its silence during the liturgical homily, affirmations (the "word back") are not eliminated altogether. The congregation is, in effect, electing to bracket its response until the point at which the presider asks it to "lift up your hearts." The people respond, "We have lifted them up to the Lord." The congregation reserves its response for that moment of transition, having been brought into the good news by joyful preaching and proclamation.

By some standards the people's response to the African American sermon and the enormous energy and spontaneity that surround that exchange cannot parallel the more pristine, reserved, and scripted Preface. At the same time, though, the liturgical homily wants to gather the assembly into a response; that exchange is poised at the edge of sacrament, where the "word back" is expressed in praise and thanksgiving. The emphasis in African American worship, on the other hand, is spontaneity at the moment of the sermon itself, what Mitchell describes as "the ability to respond to the movement of the Spirit among preacher and congregation and to express deep feeling without shame. Even when the preaching is done from manuscript, traditional freedom of expression prevails."[34] Perhaps that "word back" is also filled with centuries of gratitude for the preacher from the congregation, now liberated through a new hearing. Liturgical preaching might learn a great deal from African American sermons in Protestant churches. And, of course, there is nothing to prevent the liturgical homily from using the dynamics of black preaching at the Eucharist. In fact, such a practice is standard in Catholic parishes where large groups of African Americans gather for worship, such as St. Augustine's in Washington, D.C., and St. Sabina's in Chicago.

Celebration

It is impossible to overstate the charism of celebration in black preaching. African American worship is characterized by joyful celebration, and such activity remains the end or destiny of this genre of sermon. The celebratory aspect of African American preaching dominates any cognitive efforts at communication in the speech-act. With this celebratory aspect of black preaching in mind, Frank Thomas has explored the "principles of celebration design." He lists five guidelines: "avoidance of new concepts, contagious conviction, affirmative themes, focus on the theme, and timing of impact."[35] Moreover, the celebration of liberation has been historically a constitutive component in black preaching, with links to Israel's own movement from slavery to freedom. Mark Barger Elliot writes: "Arising from the history of slavery and discrimination, African-American preaching has persistently spoken a word of hope to African-Americans and to the world....The preacher's charge is to proclaim a message of hope by addressing how society can be transformed."[36]

Liberation leads to celebration. The preacher affirms the biblical connections between the African American people and the people of Israel; this recognition is a sign of God's activity in the world, not a self-congratulatory discourse. Carolyn Ann Knight's sermon on Joshua 17:13–18 masterfully links the historical linage of African Americans with God's design:

> Our Africanness is an instrumentality that God uses to enrich the world. God used Rosa Parks, Martin King, Adam Powell, Malcolm X, and Medgar Evers to remind the world that justice will well up like waters and righteousness like a mighty stream. God used Marcus Garvey to remind this world and us that we have one God, one aim, and one destiny. God used Randall Robinson to tell a U.S. President that your policy in Haiti is no good. God used Nelson Mandela to bring 350 years of apartheid to its knees and to tell Bill Clinton, "You run America, I run South Africa." And God wants to use us to make a contribution to this world. You see, we are a great people. This is our day. This is our time. This is our moment. This is our season.[37]

African American preaching is a language of *now*. Although there is a call to remember the past, memory serves to liberate the present. The celebration that results continues to drive the congregation into the realm of the immediate present, a further acknowledgment that the Lord remains present and risen in the gathered assembly.

The rhetoric of the sermon fundamentally speaks to celebration and opens a window for increasing the faith of the congregation, made visible to all. The "call and response" is a form of

137

"creative partnership" for Mitchell. For Richard Lischer, "the black preacher and audience...have at their disposal a second, non-discursive track on which the sermons proceeds. This is the sermon's *sound track*."[38] Indeed, black preaching is largely instrumental in facilitating a move away from cognitive, linguistic expressions and toward spontaneous, musical manifestations of the heart. "Rhetoric, repetition, rhythm, spontaneity, tone, chant, cadence, melody, drama, and epic are distinguishing elements in the African American preaching style."[39] One of the most distinctive features in black preaching is intonation, or "whooping" or "toning." This kind of musical tradition in preaching may be yet another legacy of the "musical sermons" of John Wesley or George Whitefield and the so-called First Great Awakening to black preaching. Yet, there is no universal status to "whooping" or "toning," according to Henry Mitchell. "There is a general consensus among thoughtful pastors, with and without formal training, that intonation or black-style chanting should be employed only where it is welcome and only by those who can do it with sincerity and cultural integrity. This communal code also requires that traditional chanting carry a vivid biblical message."[40]

The signature of most African American worship services remains the overall musicality, a quality that unites the head with the heart and involves the whole person. Consider the musicality of a sermon by Valerie Brown-Troutt on Esther 2:5–7:

> I want you all, especially the children and the young
> people, to meet Hadassah.
> Excuse me while I call Hadassah so you can meet her.
> Hadassah, Hadassah, Hadassah, where are you?
> Hadassah, don't you hear me calling you?
> Hadassah, where are you, girl?
> Get in here right now, so the people can see you and
> meet you.
> Hurry up girl, we can't keep them waiting.[41]

African American preachers creatively draw the congregation into dialogue, even provoking the assembly into response and excitement. The preacher becomes the mediator in a process where the listener is transformed into one who responds. Pedrito U. Maynard-Reid says that black preaching is a "kratophany": "As theophany is a manifestation of the deity in concrete objects, kratophany is the manifestation of power in preaching through the spoken word replete with drama and musicality. Kratophany is expected to move people and cause a reaction."[42] If the congregation does not seem to be celebrating, Mitchell believes that it is possible that the restraints too often apparent in the typical preacher are "contagious": "Thus the pastor dare not complain that the congregation simply does not loosen up, when in fact the main source of inhibition in worship may well be in the pulpit."[43] Here again, we see the great emphasis that black preaching places on the preacher's *ethos.*

When well executed, black preaching reflects a distinctive rhythm, and this technique may have historical roots developed as the early African church in America attempted to assimilate a new identity.[44] We know that timing and delivery are critical in any performance art; preaching is no exception. In some ways the preaching in African American worship finds one of its strongest contrasts with other churches simply in the way the preacher chooses to configure words. The cadences of black preaching are notably musical and rhythmic. Richard Eslinger suggests the following comparison:

> Majority culture preaching, for example, may lament that "persons simply do not come to church or Sunday school like they used to." A black preacher, though, may sing that "folk complain that Bible study on Sunday morning is too early, and Bible study on Wednesday evening is too late." Even a word itself may be chosen to exploit its inherent rhythmic character.[45]

Clearly, rhythm becomes one of the principle vehicles for the hearers' entry into the experience of the Word and, critically, with one another as well. Typically, the assembly gains momentum not only listening to the preacher but by hearing one another as the meter and rhythm of the homily increases. In *Sacred Symphony* (1987), Jon Michael Spencer writes: "It is evident that rhythm is not only heard, it is also observed as the momentum of preaching picks up."[46] Black preaching encourages listeners to broaden their ears to the Word and beyond—to the fellow Christians who rejoice with them. That acknowledgment of Christ in the assembly in the present is sufficient reason to rejoice and celebrate. Here we notice that the hermeneutics of black preaching echoes another fundamental teaching of the early church, even as it has affirmed the insights of *Sacrosanctum Concilium* and *Fulfilled in Your Hearing:* one of the significant pillars of the church, a locus of Christ in liturgical expression, is in the gathered assembly.

Structures for Black Preaching

African American preaching may be characterized by joyous, even ecstatic celebration, but the homiletic text is deliberately and carefully plotted and follows the scriptures very attentively. With such a radical attention to the listener, it is not unusual that some have compared the structures embedded in the texts of black preaching to Buttrick's phenomenological method. Both systems strive to move the congregation along in blocks of material in order to shape collective consciousness, not with abstract points, but inductively and narratively and based on scripture and congregational response. Mitchell says that "Buttrick has named the process and lifted it out of vague homiletic intuition, for the discipline and enrichment of preaching everywhere."[47] In fact, Mitchell insists on a behavior of purpose in the homiletic text, unified by one controlling idea in a narrative style that grows in stages.[48]

One of Mitchell's own sermons (on 2 Corinthians 3:1–4) illustrates the way in which the flow of the homily moves into celebration. He entitles the sermon "Living Epistles," in order to establish a central idea or theme, and then goes on to move the congregation through four blocks, which Ronald Allen summarizes as follows:

I. The text points to the necessity of being living epistles.

II. The letters that we write with our lives can manifest integrity between what we say and who we are and what we do, or they can show a contradiction in those arenas.

III. Showing love for all people is the acid test of whether our message and behavior are continuous.

IV. God's saving work in Christ empowers us to speak and live with integrity.[49]

The logic of the blocks of material resembles Buttrick's moves, and these systems create a cohesive unity. The bottom line in black preaching, though, is that the homily is plotted to move toward and end in celebration—thanks and praise. The last phase of Mitchell's sermon on 2 Corinthians, for instance, incorporates a poem that concludes:

Then the choir began a Hallelujah chorus
That resounded throughout the precincts of heaven.
Hallelujah, Forever and Ever!
And Ever and Ever, Hallelujah, Hallelujah!
HAL-LE-LU-JAH!! Amen.

Although the homily flows along a certain, determined logic, the very structure itself depends on a kind of climax or rush of emotion. In terms of plot, the experience of such celebratory activity is the affective equivalent of a resolution. Mitchell puts it this way:

No matter how misused by some or criticized by others, the celebration at its best is the goal to which all of the Black sermon is moving. In sermon preparation, it is often the celebration that is chosen right after a text and purpose have been selected. It is on the basis of the final celebration more than any other element that the sermon will be judged. If the sermon is remembered, then it will be because the text was etched by ecstasy on the heart of the hearer.[50]

As Maynard-Reid points out, the foundation of all black preaching is the Bible. The text and the celebration of God's work in the contours of salvation history that respond to its pages are chosen for the way that this particular episode or lesson in the Bible passage speaks to the real lives of people. "The biblical texts served as starting points for an interpretation relevant to the lives of the people."[51] To celebrate the Bible in worship recognizes how God has overcome the world—not the abstract universe, but the difficult muddy waters of daily existence.

The New Hermeneutic has provided the African American community with a unique voice—organic, biblical, and celebratory. Because its homiletic emerges from the interaction of the preacher, the congregation, and the scriptures, black preaching will never be silent or coopted. That said, an exploration of African American preaching as an aspect of multiculturalism can only inform the way in which the whole church evangelizes. At its best, multicultural preaching leads to revisionist histories and methodologies in majority preaching. In terms of liturgical preaching there are more than enough similarities between African American preaching and *Fulfilled in Your Hearing*, especially in regard to the integral position of the hearer in the assembly. Moreover, the emphasis on celebration in the sermon might also inform the liturgical homily, if only to suggest how the plot of a homily ought to move the assembly to rejoice at the altar of God, "the God who gives joy to our youth." Are we more inclined to deploy cognitive strategies in the homily, or do we urge the gathered assembly to approach God's table in a spirit of celebration and uplifted hearts?

Hispanic Preaching

There has been a massive amount of research in the last decade dedicated to investigating the mosaic of peoples called Hispanics or Latinos and their place in North America; these studies help us understand patterns and attitudes that shape this ever-changing population.[52] The U.S. bishops indicate that the presence of Hispanics in North America in recent years is bringing about another American Catholic Church, well beyond the European immigrant experience we have inherited. Jay P. Dolan says that Hispanics are changing the contemporary church as much as the Irish did in the nineteenth century.[53] "The numbers of Hispanics are increasing so rapidly that they can outpace the resources of the total Church."[54] From July 6 to July 9, 2000, the Hispanic Catholic Community of the United States hosted a National Celebration of Jubilee, *Encuentro 2000*, in Los Angeles, California. The function of the meeting was to affirm the growing Hispanic presence in North America and to "strengthen the unity of the Church in a cultural context."[55]

The result of the meeting was *Encuentro and Mission: A Renewed Pastoral Framework for Hispanic Ministry*, developed by the Committee on Hispanic Affairs of the United States Conference of Catholic Bishops. The document also served as an update for the guidelines initiated in the *National Pastoral Plan for Hispanic Ministry* (1987).[56] *Encuentro and Mission* is clearly informed by the most dramatic changes imaginable in Latino immigration to the United States, the pastoral response to that growth, and an overall awareness of the cultural diversity within the Hispanic community itself. Clearly, the U.S. bishops want to emphasize that the church in North America has much to gain from Hispanic presence:

> This pastoral statement, *Encuentro and Mission*, is our response to the voices of the leadership of Hispanic ministry about the Hispanic presence at the beginning of the new millennium. Hispanic Catholics are a blessing from God and a prophetic presence that has transformed many diocese and parishes into more welcoming, vibrant and evangelizing faith communities. We bishops see Hispanic ministry as an integral part of the life and mission of the Church.[57]

Yet, as Allan Figueroa Deck, SJ, has pointed out, "the cultural hegemony of the United States in the world makes it especially difficult for the Church and pastoral agents to develop the cultural critique needed if the evangelization of this powerful culture is to advance."[58] Moreover, the immigration experience of many Hispanics in this country continues to be their common denominator, although some Latinos experience their place in their new country in different ways. While some prefer to assimilate into the dominant Anglo culture, there are other Hispanics, as Deborah Organ has suggested, who would rather "function as much as possible with people who share their cultural framework."[59]

Ministry and preaching in a multicultural environment must involve the language of hospitality. Ministry to Latino peoples is not a crisis to be solved but a blessing to treasure. The open door is an effective and universal language without words. The church, its ministers, and its peoples welcome the Hispanic community with joy. Those who preach can extend the welcome of hospitality through God's Word, creating a safe shelter within an often discriminatory and racist culture. Radical hospitality is rooted in what the guest needs and who the guest is above all else. To be attentive to the congregation as guest means to recognize them as valuable listeners in the homiletic text. This kind of preaching welcomes the listener as one breaks open God's Word together with the preacher at the table of divine hospitality. A good host knows the language of the guest and does not dominate those who are welcomed; the host allows them to speak and even draws them out into good conversation. To be in the presence of the hearer is like approaching a bottle of fine red wine; it is not to be guzzled but opened and allowed to breathe so that its rich gifts might be savored more completely. What we taste may astonish us. All of God's children gather around a common table to be fed by Word and sacrament, together.

Preaching as Local Theology

One way of beginning to understand Hispanic preaching is to adopt a strategy of contextual, "local theology."[60] Leonora Tubbs Tisdale identifies six hallmarks of preaching as local theology:

1. "Preaching as *local* theology celebrates week-to-week congregational preaching, and the power of the particular in gospel proclamation."[61] The preacher welcomes these fellow

Christians into the house of God not as strangers but as those who are well-known and beloved. The familiar caregiver provides an occasion for hospitality. Certainly, language remains a fundamental issue in the pastoral care of Hispanic people. In a survey conducted by Thomas G. Rogers and Mauro B. de Souza, most of their Hispanic respondents said that what most attracts them to Protestant churches is worship services in Spanish.[62] With immigrants who are hungry for the Bread of Life and the Word of God, the host receiving them must be able to converse in a language that is as familiar as it is welcoming.

2. "Preaching as *local* theology is not only proclaimed 'to' but also 'out of the midst' and 'on behalf of' a local faith community."[63] There is no place for "actional," one-way communication in Hispanic preaching, or preaching that continually corrects and treats the congregation as uninformed, alien others. As we have seen, there is a long legacy in "preaching for sanctification" in the history of preaching, and it is far from finished. Yet in the tradition of Craddock, *Fulfilled in Your Hearing*, and many other sources, it is important to acknowledge that the assembly ought to experience the preacher as one who is a fellow traveler on the way to Emmaus. Moreover, Hispanic communities are typically turned off by dogmatic, speculative language and theological arguments that place a wall between the preacher and the congregation. Latinos prefer stories and a familial style of worship. Language and liturgical gestures either unite or divide, and this is most apparent when the dominant culture preaches to others. The ecclesiology can often be less important than the language of the familiar. One Lutheran pastor reported, according to Rogers and de Souza, "They come here because I preach in Spanish; they never heard of the Lutheran church."[64]

3. "Preaching as *local* theology seeks to be 'seriously imaginable' within a local community of faith."[65] It is a primary task of every preacher to make theology a concrete, serious reality for the people of God through the lens of scripture. That homiletic enterprise is especially important for those who minister and preach within Hispanic congregations, a population more often than not deprived of good catechesis for reasons of economic and cultural hardships. The preacher is what Tisdale calls a "local

theologian," parsing the complexities of the scriptures and dogmas. In so doing, though, the preacher acts as one of the faithful, a witness or mediator in the experience of a living faith tradition. The local theologian also deals with the practical theology of everyday life, bringing intellectual insights into pastoral situations. "Emotion is not seen as irrational but as complementary to the rational in the communication of the whole person. The Hispanic person is both emotional and rational and appreciates the necessity of an interplay of both in the totality of healthy life experience and communication."[66]

4. "Preaching as *local* theology is a 'hearer-oriented' event." Not only is "actional" communication ineffectual, but such speaker-oriented preaching treats mature adults as if they were children, according to Tisdale.[67] It is a serious challenge for ministers to help the Hispanic community develop a more mature ecclesiology. Often Latinos come from countries in which the division between laity and clergy is strikingly severe and where the normative posture at the liturgy is "actional" and speaker oriented. This model of communication will not fuel contextual theology. It might be the task of the preacher in a Latino parish to help the assembly claim its role as one who listens and responds to the Word of God in the process of the homily itself. Enabling the people to grow in faith by hearing is an acknowledgment of the assembly's gifts and presence at the Eucharist.

5. "Preaching as *local* theology has as a goal the transformation of the imaginations of the hearers in accordance with the message of the gospel."[68] It cannot be overemphasized that the Hispanic community thrives on images, not abstract ideas.[69] The language of the visual speaks to many people today, but Jaime Lara has written of the long history that the visual has had in preaching to Hispanic communities, as a form of popular religiosity (principally art and theater) used to convert them.[70] The visual speaks to the Latino community concretely and not rationalistically or deductively; it is the language of *now*, in which metaphors are derived from the midst of the community. The evangelical churches that have claimed the attention of many Latinos today have done so because their preaching has been vibrant, contemporary, and metaphorical. Deck writes, "Hispanic

exposure to powerful Protestant preaching that makes otherwise dead biblical images and stories come alive has added to the already vivid historical Catholic religious imagination."[71]

Evangelical preacher William A. Evertsburg recasts the portrait of Nicodemus and his meeting with Jesus in John 3:1–16 in contemporary images:

> Once a man came to Jesus under cover of darkness, because his friends would have scoffed at his search for a truth they were certain he already owned. His name was Nicodemus, which in Greek means "Conqueror of the People," and that is what he was....And so in my mind's eye I see a middle-aged man in a nine-hundred dollar suit, tastefully conservative, wingtips, and a cellular phone with the mysterious teacher he has come to quiz, for he has come to speak of nothing less than the meaning of existence.[72]

As one of its many gifts and blessings the Hispanic community reminds the whole church that God's Word is *living*. Preaching enkindles the Word into the *now* of human existence with the concrete language and contemporary idioms of our own cultural nexus.

6. "In preaching as *local* theology, exegesis of the congregation and its subcultures is not peripheral to proclamation, but central to its concerns."[73] Needless to say, the preacher in Latino communities must be familiar not only with the language but also with the many different cultural practices that inform the religious experience of the local church. It may be that the customs of the Hispanic community in a bilingual parish challenge the expectations of Anglos. How could the feast of Our Lady of Guadalupe take precedence over an otherwise simple Advent? Also, as Franciscan Kenneth G. Davis has pointed out, devotions differ within the Latino communities. "By heritage, they come from many different countries that do not always share the same vocabulary. Even their devotions are distinct. A Mexican may not want a Cristo Negro (black Christ) in the church, but a Guatemalan reveres that same image from Esquipulas."[74] Thus the language that

challenges the congregation may originate not from the preacher but from the non-dominant culture itself. What can the preacher do to foster the diversity of these images in the community while being inclusive and attentive to the needs of the whole body?

Skills for Preaching: Conversion, Analysis, Resolution

Preaching as local theology is fostered if the preacher is attentive to the specific dynamics of the congregation. But Anglo preachers in Hispanic parishes who are searching for strategies in cross-cultural homiletics would do well to attend to what Kenneth G. Davis identifies as three important skills of *self*-exploration: (1) the experience of what he calls incongruity (leading to conversion), (2) a perspicacious analysis of that experience, and (3) a resolution.[75] Davis and others are suggesting that effective multicultural preaching is rooted in a kind of hermeneutics of the self, without which effective evangelization cannot be achieved. This kind of preparation for preaching envisions a model in which the preacher is far from deploying an "actional" communicative tactic; quite the contrary, the preacher's homily is informed by dissonance and cultural incongruity that ultimately leads to transformation as the hearer becomes newly and readily available as a cultural conversation partner. Preaching has gained great insights from the reforms of previous practices of missiology. To attempt to "convert" without respect for the unique and gifted cultural orientation of the Other represents the most concrete, disastrous expression of the "actional" model. When two cultures meet in mutual dialogue and respect, on the other hand, transactional communication is bound to occur. Thus the dissonance for the preacher is the letting go of authority and preconceived notions about the position of the Other; indeed, true dissonance results in the conversion of the *preacher.*

According to most experts on Hispanic culture, the central factor contributing to incongruity among Latinos is social dislocation, and understanding this difficulty is essential to good preaching.[76] Davis writes:

Incongruity forces us to re-examine cultural and social presuppositions, once more to reflect critically upon and to re-appropriate affectively the Christian story in the never-ending process we call conversion. But we cannot converse as long as we all smugly share in the same assumptions. That is not conversation but shared rationalization. Any conversation with or about God must begin with a humble acceptance of the irony and ambiguity constitutive of the entire human situation.[77]

As we see once again, the vital skill of entering into incongruity is greatly helped by preaching that is driven by hospitality. To treat the guest not as a stranger but as Christ is deeply sown in the long tradition of monastic values. In *Welcoming the Stranger Among Us*, the U.S. Catholic bishops emphasize that all aspects of ministry ought to participate in hospitality:

> The welcome and hospitality that we ask our parishes to extend to newcomers must include active efforts on the part of the pastor and parish staff, individuals and families, parish councils, liturgy committees, social concern entities, youth groups, and other parish organizations to undertake the special effort necessary to learn about the cultures in their midst and to exchange visits with worship communities and parishes where different cultural groups make their homes.[78]

An open door signals the presence of an open mind. In a way, all hosts enter into dissonance the moment they open their quiet, stable home to friends, relatives, and, of course, strangers. As hosts are changed by the presence of their guests, Hispanic preaching ought to reflect the hermeneutics of transformation, not suspicion; the listener carries on a transactional relationship with the preacher that, in effect, brings about cultural conversion. What I am suggesting here is that Hispanic preaching becomes the test case for hearer-oriented preaching. The preacher is not only attentive to the congregation as a good component of classical *pathos*, but the preacher allows the experience of the listener to transform the homily. Hispanic preaching, then, requires the dismantling of the normative language and symbols of majority preaching and an appropriation of the culture of the Other. The Hispanic preacher is one who not only speaks the language of conversion but is in the process of conversion itself.

In terms of our discussion of the history of preaching, this kind of conversion-centered homiletic is radically disposed to the listeners, even at the sake of subordinating the text and the preacher. It urges us to engage listeners as active participants in the homily by speaking to their hearts and minds. Thomas Swears states, "Allowing the heart and the mind room to respond is as important as speaking to them both in the first place."[79] Finally, we might have to ask a dangerous question: Are we prepared for a response from the hearer that may be unsettling—incongruent— to our expectation?

The experience of allowing the heart of the Latino community to unfold before the preacher leads to a compassionate, preaching heart. It is the kind of preaching that may be informed by dogma but not driven and protected by treasured ideas; it is the kind of homily that moves in a familial, colloquial style amid the noise and confusion of children at the liturgy; it is the kind of speech that is one with the hearer because it is in the idiom of the people of God. Virgilio Elizondo writes, "Doctrine taught does not penetrate the minds of the needy, if a compassionate heart does not commend it to the hearts of the hearer."[80] Compassion requires an understanding and empathy only purchased at the price of dismantling the normative idioms that orient the preacher. The icon for such a profound transformation of the speaker might well be the story of Our Lady of Guadalupe, in which an Aztec woman of color appeared to correct the so-called first evangelization.[81] If good preachers do not practice the politics of assimilation, then the question rightly becomes one of disorientation, incongruity for the sake of the Other; that is, how much are we willing to allow the symbols and culture and language of immigrant Latinos to inform our (majority) practices? To a certain extent the Anglo preacher will always be at a disadvantage, since the language, the primary symbolic system, is a barrier. But sometimes even what seems an incredibly thick wall can be breached through good will, understanding, and allowing the Other to convert us.

The second skill Davis mentions, analysis, involves a public commitment to the explored areas of incongruity.[82] Davis suggests that there are some key questions that surface for the preacher in the context of doing such a post-incongruous stage of exploration in the context of community. "What are the causes underlying the conflicting problem of evil? Why is there poverty in our land of plenty? How might we look at the unequal distribution of wealth? How do we move beyond middle-class guilt? Are we as powerful as we think?"[83] It would not be unusual to find that the Latino community is already well versed in areas of social justice, based on their own experience.

Thomas Rogers and Mauro B. de Souza suggest that it is critical for the preacher to be aware of the high level of intensity that justice plays in the Latino world:

> U.S. Hispanic Americans are tired of living at the edge of dignity; they are tired of suffering discrimination; they are tired of having little or no share in the richness of the country that they help build. They want God's justice, and they want it now....Preaching justice to Hispanics is primarily a matter of dealing with the relationship between the powerful and the powerless. The preacher's task is to call those who abuse power into repentance and accountability and to strengthen the powerless.[84]

Preachers in Latino parishes might consider having scripture study with parish groups to engage them in interpreting the readings for the following Sunday. This practice is a marvelous idea for any parish, but Anglo ministers of the Word can only benefit from the shared opinion of their Hispanic parishioners, especially when it comes to issues of social justice, exile, and immigration. How can a native in this country hope to comprehend the Latino experience of political and social alienation? Also, preachers in Latino parishes might consider their own reading program on the Hebrew prophets, whose long relationship with the people of

God was fraught with such difficulties as estrangement and national exile.

The search for justice requires not only exploration but resolution, Davis's third and final stage. "The resolution through revelation will not simply appeal to the intellect, but will resonate with the whole person."[85] The strategy for finding resolution by way of revelation is discovering key biblical symbols in order to articulate a contemporary, necessary cultural idiom. The Bible becomes the language of now in the context of the present cultural moment for a particular people. In this regard Justo L. González's *Santa Biblia: The Bible Though Hispanic Eyes* (1996) is helpful to the preacher, since it attempts to read the scriptures from "the margins" and thereby provides useful metaphors for creating continuity between the Bible and lived experience.[86] Moreover, there are between three and five million undocumented immigrants in this country, a nation of exiles searching for a home. The preacher must understand that the homily, together with the scriptures and the liturgical year from which it emerges, provides a marvelous opportunity to make connections. Walter Brueggemann asserts: "As the preacher stands up to preach among the exiles, the primal task (given this metaphor) concerns the narration and nurture of a counter-identity, the enactment of the power of hope in a season of despair, and the assertion of a deep, definitional freedom from the pathologies, coercions, and seductions that govern our society."[87]

Discovering a resolution helps to settle the incongruity and dissonance recognized earlier. When the preacher finds a good symbol, it "resolves incongruity by showing that there is continuity (through Christ) between the mundane story of our banality and the sacred story of God's divinity."[88] The work defined in moving through incongruity, analysis, and resolution describes long-term pastoral care in the Hispanic community for preachers. But again, these three stages are somewhat loosely reminiscent of Lowry's homiletic plot, insofar as the pattern moves from a "bind" into a discovery of biblical language that might provide a clue for its solution, and then finally to the solution itself. Under this structure, though, an Hispanic "homiletic plot" will be remarkably cultural in its interests and seemingly establish *cultural* binds waiting to be resolved by God's justice. Whether or not this justice-as-ending provides resolution, or more specifically, homiletic closure, is an interesting question.[89] But even if the call for justice can never find closure, it must not fail to speak the truth.

Diverse Listeners

There are undoubtedly many communities that thrive on a single-language system. This situation is changing rapidly as more and more parishes find themselves with two, perhaps three distinct language groups. There are other, mostly urban parishes in which there is a mixture of Asians, African Americans, Hispanics and Pacific Islanders for whom English is a second language. Additionally, a generational divide separates congregations not only by age but by ideology. Seniors who were born and raised in the pre-conciliar church may have less in common with their children, raised in the 1960s, than they do with their grandchildren. Study after study reveals the gulf that contemporary young adults experience with past generations, and some are beginning to think of preaching strategies and tactic that might be used to reach out to several generations.[90] How is it possible to preach to all of these groups during a single liturgy?

We are only beginning to scratch the surface of the diverse-listeners issue facing the church. But Joseph R. Jeter Jr. and Ronald J. Allen have some practical suggestions for communication to listeners of different types. These authors take as a given the reality that those who preach treasure the diversity of the congregation. Jeter and Allen recommend one of the following four approaches, based on the assembly, the needs of the parish, and the preacher's proclivities and skills.

1. The preacher may prepare a homily aimed at the dominant group in the congregation.[91] Having one particular group in mind, the homily is geared toward the needs and the listening tendencies of that group. For example, a parish may be celebrating Eucharist on a Sunday when there is a large group of children present with their parents; the older children are ready to receive the sacrament of confirmation, perhaps within the next month or so. Or there may

a sizeable group of retired folks gathered to celebrate a class reunion at one of the masses. In each of these liturgies the preacher identifies key communication strategies aimed at the common denominator of those present. In the mass in which many older children are present, it is possible to draw on sports imagery or events from school, or the like, and then relate these illustrations to the readings and the youths' upcoming commitment to the church in confirmation. Or in the case of the seniors, drawing from a past event in history or the community could serve as common ground to guide them into the experience of the scriptures.

2. The preacher may try to blend the experiences of different groups into the homily, attempting to reach a wide range of listeners in the congregation. "The preacher would consciously include material that speaks to a range of groups."[92] Here, the obvious advantage is that the listeners can experience language that deliberately includes the many different types of people with whom they are worshiping. "The sermon might celebrate the divine movement through each culture, help the various groups recognize how they enrich one another, and address the tensions within the congregation (and in the larger culture) that configures around race and ethnicity."[93] Jeter and Allen advise the preacher to choose one of three modes of perception, visual, auditory, or kinesthetic (light, hearing, or feeling).[94] These modes are visceral and foundational ways that human beings experience the world. To access these avenues of human experience through metaphor and symbol and story allows the preacher to engage the whole congregation at least on a basic level.

3. This choice of preaching style takes place not on a single Sunday but over the course of the liturgical year, or at least several Sundays. The practice here is to combine the tactics in 1 and 2 above, while making sure that the diversity of the congregation has been attended to. "While no single sermon would include material designed to speak to all listeners in their various modes of perception, the whole listening community would be included over several Sundays."[95] With reference to the liturgical homily, the season of Lent could be a time when the preacher assembles many different groups into a particular hearing about their journey toward Easter. If there is a large RCIA group in the parish,

the homily could be addressed to their journey on certain Sundays. On other Sundays the young adults might find themselves challenged to move into a more ascetic space. If this strategy is adopted on the First Sunday of Lent, more traditional members of the community could find themselves renewed as never before as they approach Easter, simply because they "overheard the gospel invitation" to those in their midst. The liturgical year itself focuses the diverse congregation.

4. The last tactic takes into account the listeners more directly during the writing process. Typically, the homily will account for the biblical text and then craft a text around a single "pearl" that responds to these readings. But in the course of the homily the preacher imagines responses in a particular way. "How will the listening groups at the assembly hear (or not hear) this sermon? Are some groups excluded? Will some groups feel that they received too much attention? The preacher can then calibrate the material in the sermon to account for this aspect of pastoral analysis."[96]

It is a sobering reminder that a homily is never going to be 100 percent effective as a communication tool. Some will be excluded, either by virtue of their experience or disposition or numerous cultural factors. "Given the remarkable diversity of the listening community, a sermon never achieves complete communication with all members of the congregation. Nonetheless, a preacher can help the community have a good *opportunity* to enter into the world of the message."[97]

Homiletic Monologue and Bilingual Homilies

One of the most common situations in contemporary parishes is a combination of Hispanic and Anglo communities. The typical practice in many parishes is to have a mass only in Spanish, although some are recognizing the virtue of occasionally linking these two linguistic communities at a common liturgy, perhaps followed by a meal. Potentially, bilingual homilies could represent a wonderful, symbolic presence of the universal church, although there might also be frustration from the language group that feels either alienated or confused by such worship. Bishop Ricardo Ramirez, CSB, offers some practical advice for such homilies:

1. If the homily is short, it could be repeated.

2. A summary could be given at the end of the homily in the other language.

3. Consecutive interpretation without literal translation.

4. Simultaneous translation using portable earphones; however, those who have the earphones may feel like "second-class citizens."[98]

It is difficult to imagine that bilingual homilies, even in the best circumstances, could be all inclusive. In order to avoid replicating a kind of Tower of Babel event once again, Rosa Maria Icaza, CCVI, recommends that while the homily is given in one language, the other language group could be asked to reread the scripture passage with a specific question as a focus. After this session is completed, the roles would be reversed.[99]

Icaza's procedure may work under certain circumstances, but if the liturgical homily is intended to serve as a unifying element in the liturgy, bringing the people of God to the table of the Lord, asking one group to do one thing while the other members listen to the homily seems counterproductive. The homiletic strategy is for the benefit of the hearer, after all, not the text, and it may not be a useful symbol to engage the congregation in activities that accentuate difference. At the same time, Icaza's method is notable for its realistic approach and, although role reversal may seem awkward at a liturgical function, allowing two cultural groups to acknowledge their difference would be a crucial step under other social circumstances. Or an effort might be made to discover common words or patterns and use them together in order to form cohesive theological ideas and images that would suit both language groups (see the homily at the end of this chapter). Such a practice underlines our linguistic mobility and commonality. Along with bringing two language groups together, perhaps the preacher could deploy words or phrases that are immediately translated in order to sustain the attention of the mixed congregation.

Beyond the practical question concerning the mixture of language in a multicultural setting or a bilingual homily, there remains the issue of preaching *perspective*. What is the stance that I will take as a preacher of God's liberating Word for the marginalized? How can I free myself from an interpretation of the gospel that might be burdened with a very limited, middle-class, Anglo perspective on culture? Is there a certain point of view that the homily may take in order to present the good news in a wider horizon than either my own or that of the dominant culture? I might suggest a homiletic practice that uses a more subjective narrative technique that I explored briefly in an earlier chapter: the monologue. The monologue homily is shaped around the voice of one particular character, usually taken from the readings. In a multicultural setting this literary form has distinct advantages. This particular character—Lazarus, for instance—would simply speak and tell a story from his perspective or point of view. Lazarus never speaks in the gospel, and the monologue form enables us to uncover personal impressions of his world, of Jesus, of God working as he sees it. The monologue involves a historically limited character, which makes it a good and exciting narration for preaching in a multicultural environment, in which diverse peoples often find themselves excluded as minor characters in modern culture. When a biblical character speaks, the congregation is invited to participate in his or her world view. Or the monologue could take the shape of a less sympathetic character who undergoes a process of regret or conversion in the course of the monologue homily. There is no control or distance between the preacher and the assembly; the character's life simply unfolds before them, and the homiletic message is preached by a biblical witness, who, as it were, "comes back to life."

The monologue homily is also ideal for many multicultural preaching occasions, although perhaps not on a consistent basis. There are gospel stories that never quite tell the whole story, and the monologue could help listeners imagine what the "post-text" would look like. What would the younger son in the Parable of the Prodigal Son say after the party was over? Judas walking away from the Last Supper? Jairus's daughter? Although the roots of dramatic monologue are ancient, it is very contemporary in a culture that often finds itself captivated by personal stories and personal memoirs. Much of the great narrative innovation in the last century has been in the kinds of monologue written by James Joyce and T. S. Eliot, to name just the most famous. Additionally, there have been a number of recent Latino authors who have also made use of subjective narration in describing the experience of immigration or growing up as a minority in North America. Denise Chávez describes her playful, religious fantasy life as a young child in her short story "The Closet":

> When I close my eyes I can see Christ's eyes in the darkness. It's an early summer afternoon, and I should be sleeping. Instead, I'm standing in the silence of my mother's closet holding a luminescent sliding picture of the Shroud of Turin. One image reveals Christ as he might look fleshed out; the other shows shadows of skin pressed against white cloth. A slant of light filters through the closed door.[100]

The personal accounts of Latinos are very contemporary, vibrant and moving; they have a voice all their own in our American culture. From the point of view of preaching, subjective narration allows for a diverse community, a bilingual community, to participate in the homily without any group feeling excluded. Also, the experience of dissonance, as Kenneth G. Davis describes it, becomes much more real when the preacher adopts a subjective stance; the "teacher" model is abandoned in favor of historical witness.

It is especially important to be less doctrinal and more compassionate, to paraphrase Virgilio Elizondo, when preaching on the feast of Our Lady of Guadalupe. As many have suggested, that most important feast for the Hispanic community is precisely about cultural dissonance and the conversion of traditional European religiosity. The bishop's encounter with Juan Diego is an acknowledgment of the viability of Mexico itself—not as a conquered people but as a nation beloved by God and symbolized by the apparition of *la Morenita*, a pregnant Azteca. How best to preach this marvelous feast? From my perspective, engaging a narrative strategy that would allow for a shift in basic cultural orientation would be ideal. That literary tactic would not necessarily have to take the point of view of the marginalized (Juan Diego); it could focus on the one who was converted (the bishop) by encountering the culture of difference. The following is a homily I preached on the feast of Our Lady of Guadalupe, using a monologue and the kind of bilingual method that does not translate the English directly but keeps the text moving:

> Only a God who does new and wild things could dream up a meeting between a Spanish bishop and an impoverished Indian new Christian. Yet, that is how my name, Bishop Juan de Zumárraga, would be chiseled in stone for all eternity. I was sent by Emperor Charles V to teach the people of this New World about Christianity, the scriptures, and the church. Instead it was Juan Diego, *un indio pobre*, and the woman who appeared to him, who converted me.
>
> His story was incredible, *fantástica*. The first day, he came to me with a tale about a woman who said, "*Yo soy la Virgen María.*" Yet, something the man said did not make sense to me. He said she was dressed *como una mujer mexicana, una Azteca*. Although I am a poor Franciscan, I know how our Lady, *La Madre de Dios*, must look: a style that is *muy elegante*, royal apparel, as befits the court of heaven and the King of Kings himself. I thought of her portraits over the marble altars in the gold-leaf-decorated churches in the Basque region in Spain where I spent my life as a small boy. But Juan Diego talked of a brown-skinned woman, *la Morenita*, who was pregnant. She asked for a church to be built right here, *en la colina del Tepeyac*. It was all too much, so I sent him away. "Bring me proof," I said. My mother always told me that I was too cautious.
>
> Before he left my presence, I could see that poor Juan Diego's face was sinking under the weight of

disappointment like a stone. I am not cut out for this job, especially difficult after the surrender of Mexico City to the *conquistadores* ten years ago. *Soy un misionario pobre y no me gustan los asuntos políticos.* I don't like disappointing God's poor. What kind of proof would Juan Diego bring me, I thought to myself? The people said he had a sick uncle who was now cured. Perhaps he prays well, I thought. I just could not believe that the Virgin Mary would come the way Juan Diego described her. He said something else that disturbed me, which, if I repeated it to Señor Cortez, he would surely go crazy. *La Virgen de Guadalupe va a cuidar para siempre a los indios de México.* The Virgin would protect the Mexicans as *sus favoritos, sus preferidos.* But everyone knows that our Lady loves Spain before all countries on earth.

And yet, no matter how I thought of all this, nothing would convince me until Juan Diego came on that final day. It was only then that I realized that God had followed us into the New World, not as a king, but as an infant who brought his mother with him. *Un niño con su madre,* wrapped in poverty, like Juan Diego. I remember the exact *momento* I believed. Before me, like a river of our dear Savior's blood, *la Sangre de Cristo,* fell a cascade of roses. *Cuando Juan abrió su tilma, las rosas cayeron al suelo.* It was only then that I understood, not because the Lady provided the beautiful red flowers in winter from a cold hilltop, but because of what these blossoms revealed. She had left me her calling card, her portrait. Suddenly, all the depictions I knew of the Mother of God erased themselves. I was facing the vision of my own apocalypse on Juan's *tilma:* "*Una mujer, vestida del sol, con la luna bajo sus pies y una corona de doce estrellas sobre su cabeza. Ésta embarazada y grita de dolor, porque le ha llegado la hora de dar a luz*" (Rev 12:1b–2).

That is the moment for me too, *la revelación de Juan,* when I became a real *misionario.* The church would be built here in Mexico City, and so I promised. There, millions of every language will come to give thanks and praise and remember the works of the Lord from Mount Zion to Tepeyac Hill. God speaks to us with a Son about to be born who will transform our Towers of Babel into Pentecosts. This image of Our Lady of Guadalupe remains the sign of his care. O God, I love your house.

> *Que amables son tus moradas, Señor Sabaot.*

Finally, almost all studies of bilingual homilies and Hispanic preaching has been from the point of view of Anglo preaching. What about Latino preaching and evangelizing in a bilingual parish? A good first step to encourage both ordained and lay preaching in the Hispanic community would be a Spanish translation of *Fulfilled in Your Hearing*, which, as of this date, has not been published. Through language, the homilist might foster another Pentecost event leading to fellowship and insight instead of discord and confusion. That Pentecost is the goal of all multicultural witnesses:

> All the ends of the earth shall remember
> and turn to the LORD;
> and all the families of the nations
> shall worship before him.
> For dominion belongs to the LORD,
> and he rules over the nations. (Ps 22:27–28)

Notes

1. Raymond Williams, *Keywords: A Vocabulary of Culture and Society*, rev. ed. (New York: Oxford Univ. Press, 1983), 87. (Orig. pub. 1976.)

2. Henry H. Mitchell, *Black Preaching: The Recovery of a Powerful Art* (Nashville, TN: Abingdon Press, 1990), 12.

3. See, for example, Homi K. Bhabha, "Cultural Diversity and Cultural Differences," in *The Post-Colonial Studies Reader*, ed. Bill Ashcroft, Gareth Griffiths, and Helen Tiffin (New York: Routledge, 1995), 206–9. Bhabah writes: "Cultural diversity is the recognition of pre-given cultural 'contents' and customs, held in a time-frame of relativism; it gives rise to anodyne liberal notions of multiculturalism, cultural exchange, or the culture of humanity" (206). Then again, *multicultural* is occasionally used to signify the presence of a global society or a universal church, especially in ecclesial language and discussions. See the essays in Max L. Stackhouse, Tim Dearborn, and Scott Paeth, eds., *The Local Church in a Global Era: Reflections for a New Century* (Grand Rapids, MI: Eerdmans, 2000).

4. USCCB, *Encuentro and Mission: A Renewed Pastoral Framework for Hispanic Ministry*, bilingual ed. (Washington, DC: USCCB, 2002), 22.

5. Catherine Hall, "Missionary Stories: Gender and Ethnicity in England in the 1830's and 1840's," in *Cultural Studies*, ed. Lawrence Grossberg, Cary Nelson, and Paula Treichler (New York: Routledge, 1992), 241.

6. Joseph R. Jeter Jr. and Ronald J. Allen, *One Gospel, Many Ears: Preaching for Different Listeners in the Congregation* (St. Louis: Chalice Press, 2002), 109.

7. Pontifical Council for Culture, *Toward a Pastoral Approach to Culture*, no. 5 (Boston: Pauline Books, 1999), 20. See also these recent documents by the United States Catholic Bishops: *Welcoming the Stranger Among Us: Unity in Diversity* (2000) and *Strangers No Longer on the Journey of Hope* (2003).

8. John Paul II, *Pastores Dabo Vobis*, no. 55 (Washington, DC: USCCB, 1992), 151.

9. Paul VI, *Evangelii Nuntiandi*, nos. 18–20.

10. David Power, OMI, *"The Word of the Lord": Liturgy's Use of Scripture* (Maryknoll, NY: Orbis Books, 2001), 75. Power wants to broaden the concept of interpretation so that the role of the hearer and the hearer's response become a fundamental dynamic in liturgical preaching.

11. Leonora Tubs Tisdale, *Preaching as Local Theology and Folk Art* (Minneapolis: Fortress Press, 1997), 46.

12. Stephen Bevans, *Models of Contextual Theology* (Maryknoll, NY: Orbis Books, 1992), 1.

13. See Cyprian Davis, OSB, *The History of Black Catholics in the United States* (New York: Crossroad, 1990), 238–60.

14. See, for example, Edward Said, *Culture and Imperialism* (New York: Vintage, 1994).

15. James R. Nieman and Thomas G. Rogers, *Preaching to Every Pew: Cross-Cultural Strategies* (Minneapolis: Fortress Press, 2001), 14.

16. Cyprian Davis, *The History of Black Catholics in the United States*, 4–27.

17. Henry H. Mitchell, in *Concise Encyclopedia of Preaching*, ed. William H. Willimon and Richard Lischer (Louisville, KY: Westminster John Knox, 1995), 4. For an excellent discussion of African American preaching in the context of narrative, see Richard L. Eslinger, *The Web of Preaching* (Nashville, TN: Abingdon Press, 2002), 103–50. See also Cleophus James LaRue, *The Heart of Black Preaching* (Louisville, KY: Westminster John Knox, 1999).

18. William H. Pipes, quoted in Mitchell, *Black Preaching*, 32.

19. Mitchell, in Willimon and Lischer, *Concise Encyclopedia of Preaching*, 4.

20. Ibid., 2.

21. Gerhard Ebeling, quoted in Henry Mitchell, *Black Preaching* (San Francisco: Harper & Row, 1979), 25. See also Gerhard Ebeling, *Word and Faith*, trans. James W. Leitch (Philadelphia: Fortress Press, 1963).

22. Mitchell, *Black Preaching*, 29.

23. See ibid., 23–38.

24. Ibid., 29.

25. Ibid., 31.

26. Martin Luther King Jr., quoted in Paul Scott Wilson, *A Concise History of Preaching* (Nashville, TN: Abingdon Press, 1992), 174–75.

27. Pedrito U. Maynard-Reid, *Diverse Worship: African-American, Caribbean and Hispanic Perspectives* (Downers Grove, IL: InterVarsity Press, 2000), 89.

28. Mitchell, *Black Preaching*, 34.

29. Maynard-Reid, *Diverse Worship*, 92.

30. Ibid., 94. See also Evans E. Crawford and Thomas Troeger, eds., *The Hum: Call and Response in African American Preaching* (Nashville, TN: Abingdon Press, 1995).

31. Robin R. Meyers, *With Ears to Hear: Preaching as Self-Persuasion* (Cleveland: Pilgrim Press, 1993), 59.

32. *FIYH*, 19.

33. Eslinger, *The Web of Preaching*, 110.

34. Mitchell, in Willimon and Lischer, *Concise Encyclopedia of Preaching*, 3.

35. See Frank Thomas and Henry Mitchell, *They Like to Never Quit Praisin' God: The Role of Celebration in Preaching* (Cleveland: United Church Press, 1997), 90. For a concise summary of Thomas's points, see Eslinger, *The Web of Preaching*, 134.

36. Mark Barger Elliot, *Creative Styles of Preaching* (Louisville, KY: Westminster John Knox, 2000), 24.

37. Carolyn Ann Knight, "If Thou Be a Great People," in *Patterns of Preaching*, ed. Ronald J. Allen (St Louis: Chalice Press, 1998), 228.

38. Richard Lischer, quoted in ibid., 25.

39. Olin P. Moyd, *The Sacred Art: Preaching and Theology in the African-American Tradition* (Valley Forge, PA: Judson Press, 1995), 89.

40. Mitchell, in Willimon and Lischer, *Concise Encyclopedia of Preaching*, 3.

41. Valerie Brown-Troutt, "She Had Neither Father nor Mother," in Elliot, *Creative Styles of Preaching*, 26.

42. Maynard-Reid, *Diverse Worship*, 93.

43. Henry J. Mitchell, *Celebration and Experience in Preaching* (Nashville, TN: Abingdon Press, 1990), 26. Mitchell's antidote to the inhibited preacher is to become *intentional* about worship, deploying certain techniques in order to access the emotion of the congregation within the context of the liturgy as a whole. For Mitchell, genuine joy is always externalized. The difficulty with his position, in my estimation, is that the preacher must carry the whole burden of the liturgical service and thus become responsible for the lackluster condition of the assembly as well as its ecstatic quality. Also, it is not entirely clear to me that "genuine joy does not exist without some form of release of expression" (31).

44. See Eslinger, *The Web of Preaching*, 108. Eslinger quotes William Pannell, who believes that the distinctive rhythm in black preaching comes from a blended, new style of communication, a mixture of theology and scripture with African modal rhythms of speech.

45. Eslinger, *The Web of Preaching*, 108.

46. Jon Michael Spencer, quoted in ibid., 109.

47. Mitchell, *Celebration and Experience in Preaching*, 50.

48. Mitchell is interested in "experiential" motion of the homiletic flow in order to get the point across and "to beget trust and change behavior." Although he shares some similarities with Buttrick, *personal* narrative figures very importantly in Mitchell's work (see ibid., 53–56).

49. Allen, *Patterns of Preaching*, 17.

50. Mitchell, *Black Preaching*, 122.

51. Maynard-Reid, *Diverse Worship*, 91.

52. To name a few of these studies, see, for example, *United States Hispanic Catholics: Trends and Works, 1990–2000*, ed. Kenneth G. Davis, Eduardo C. Fernández, and Verónica Méndez (Scranton, PA: Univ. of Scranton Press, 2002), an exhaustive study of archives and resources; *Bridging Boundaries: The Pastoral Care of U.S. Hispanic Persons*, ed. Kenneth G. Davis and Yolanda Tarango (Scranton, PA: Univ. of Scranton Press, 2000), which investigates several different diversities within the Latino culture; *El Cuerpo de Cristo: The Hispanic Presence in the U.S. Catholic Church*, ed. Peter Casarella and Paul Gomez, SDS (New York: Crossroad, 1998), a valuable collection of essays investigating the symbols and beliefs in the Hispanic community; Allan Figueroa Deck, SJ, *The Second Wave: Hispanic Ministry and the Evangelization of Cultures* (New York: Paulist Press, 1989), which contains very valuable data (a large section on California) as well as practical strategies for evangelization.

53. Ana Maria Diaz-Stevens writes: "The distinguished Catholic historian Jay P. Dolan of Notre Dame University has suggested that Hispanics are changing the Catholic Church in the twentieth century as much as did the Irish in the nineteenth century. But while the Irish came at a time when the United States was still expanding, the Hispanics are coming when the only frontiers to conquer are out there in space. The numbers of Hispanics are increasing so rapidly that they can outpace the resources of the total Church" ("The Hispanic Challenge to U.S. Catholicism," in Casarella and Gomez, *El Cuerpo de Cristo*, 163).

54. Ibid.

55. USCCB, *Encuentro and Mission*, 26n2. There were also national meetings in 1972, 1977, and 1985.

56. See USCCB, *National Pastoral Plan for Hispanic Ministry*, in USCCB, *Hispanic Ministry: Three Major Documents* (Washington, DC: USCCB, 1995).

57. USCCB, *Encuentro and Mission*, 1.

58. Deck, *The Second Wave*, 98.

59. Deborah Organ, "Immigrants and Inculturation," *America* 189/15 (November 10, 2003), 12; see also, Gelasia Marquez Marinas, "Hispanic Family Life Ministry," in Casarella and Gomez, *El Cuerpo De Cristo*, 251–57.

60. See Tisdale, *Preaching as Local Theology and Folk Art*. Tisdale says that she borrows the category of local theology from Robert Schreiter's concept of contextual theology, which informs his missiology (see Robert

Schreiter, *Constructing Local Theologies* [Maryknoll, NY: Orbis Books, 1985]).

61. Tisdale, *Preaching as Local Theology and Folk Art*, 40.

62. Thomas G. Rogers and Mauro B. de Souza, "Preaching Cross-Culturally to Spanish-Speaking U.S. Hispanic Americans," *Homiletic*, 28/1 (Summer 2003), 5.

63. Tisdale, *Preaching as Local Theology and Folk Art*, 41.

64. Rogers and de Souza, *"Preaching Cross-Culturally,"* 5.

65. Tisdale, *Preaching as Local Theology and Folk Art*, 43.

66. Virgilio P. Elizondo, *Christianity and Culture: An Introduction to Pastoral Theology and Ministry for the Bicultural Community* (Huntington, IN: Our Sunday Visitor, 1975), 166. See also Maynard-Reid, *Diverse Worship*, 195–199.

67. Tisdale, *Preaching as Local Theology and Folk Art*, 45.

68. Ibid., 46.

69. Ibid.

70. Jaime Lara, "Visual Preaching: The Witness of Our Latin Eyes," in *Preaching and Culture in Latino Congregations*, ed. Kenneth G. Davis, OFMConv., and Jorge L. Presmanes (Chicago: Liturgy Training Publications, 2000), 75–92.

71. Allan Figueroa Deck, SJ, "Hispanic Catholic Prayer and Worship," in *Alabadle! Hispanic Christian Worship*, ed. Justo L. González (Nashville, TN: Abingdon Press, 1996), 24.

72. William A. Evertsburg, "A Lawyer Meets Jesus," in Elliot, *Creative Styles of Preaching*, 43.

73. Tisdale, *Preaching as Local Theology and Folk Art*, 46.

74. Kenneth G. Davis, OFMConv., "Cross-Cultural Preaching," in Davis and Presmanes, *Preaching and Culture in Latino Congregations*, 43.

75. Ibid., 57–61.

76. Ibid., 57.

77. Ibid., 58.

78. USCCB, *Welcoming the Stranger Among Us*, 33.

79. Thomas R. Swears, *Preaching to Head and Heart* (Nashville, TN: Abingdon Press, 2000), 61.

80. Virgilio Elizondo, quoted in ibid., 17.

81. For a very intriguing and thorough discussion along these lines, see Thomas J. Ascheman, SVD, "The Conversion of the Missionary: An Interpretation of the Guadalupan Narrative" (Ph.D. diss, Catholic University of America, 1991). Ascheman looks at the conversion in the narrative through the lens of Bernard Lonergan and the various levels of transformations (moral, intellectual, etc.). On the other hand, Juan Diego

is also converted, since he has a new understanding of himself as the bringer of the Word and no longer thinks of himself as "dung." See Roberto S. Goizueta, *Caminemos Con Jesús: Toward a Hispanic/Latino Theology of Accompaniment* (Maryknoll, NY: Orbis Books, 1995), 77.

82. Kenneth G. Davis, "Cross-Cultural Preaching," 58.

83. Ibid., 58–59.

84. Rogers and de Souza, "Preaching Cross-Culturally," 8.

85. Kenneth G. Davis, "Cross-Cultural Preaching," 60.

86. See Justo L. González, *Santa Biblia: The Bible Through Hispanic Eyes* (Nashville, TN: Abingdon Press, 1996).

87. Walter Brueggemann, *Cadences of Home: Preaching Among Exiles* (Louisville, KY: Westminster John Knox, 1997), 12.

88. Kenneth G. Davis, "Cross-Cultural Preaching," 60.

89. Frank A. Thomas and Henry Mitchell also suggest a similar "plot" to consider: (1) introduction to a problem; (2) resolution by the gospel; (3) celebration of resolution (see Frank Thomas and Henry Mitchell, *They Like to Never Quit Praisin' God: The Role of Celebration in Preaching* [Cleveland: United Church Press, 1997]). Thomas's and Mitchell's sermonic text always move toward celebration, but the weight of the resolution in Davis's configuration seems to be heavily in line with justice issues.

90. See, for instance, Colleen Carroll, *The New Faithful: Why Young Adults are Embracing Christian Orthodoxy* (Chicago: Loyola Univ. Press, 2002). See also Andrew Carl Wisdom, OP, *Preaching to a Multigenerational Assembly* (Collegeville, MN: Liturgical Press, 2004).

91. Jeter and Allen, *One Gospel, Many Ears*, 15.

92. Ibid., 16.

93. Ibid.

94. Ibid.

95. Ibid., 17.

96. Ibid.

97. Ibid., 20.

98. Bishop Ricardo Ramirez, quoted in Rosa Maria Icaza, CCVI, "Living and Sharing the Word Among Hispanics," in Davis and Presmanes, *Preaching and Culture in Latino Congregations*, 36.

99. Ibid., 37.

100. Denise Chávez, "The Closet," in *Growing Up Latino: Memoirs and Stories*, ed. Ilan Stavans and Harold Augenbraum (Boston: Houghton Mifflin, 1993), 85.

5
CONTEMPORARY PREACHING

You know how to interpret the appearance of earth and sky,
but why do you not know how to interpret the present time?
—Luke 12:56

The Reverend Timothy Lovejoy and the Springfield
Community Church are continually burlesqued on Fox's long-
running satire *The Simpsons.* According to Mark Pinsky, Lovejoy's
preaching is hypocritical while his ministry continuously faces the
problems of cults, New Age, and charismatic worship.

> The scripture passages he uses, when not mangled for
> comic effect, tend to be obscure, arcane, bloody, or sim-
> ply meaningless selections from the Old Testament, or
> depressing readings from Lamentations. To wake people,
> he sometimes resorts to desperate measures, including
> sound effects like ambulance sirens and birdcalls, and
> even his own rendition of the song, "The Entertainer."
> Once he offers a baby-sitting discount for anyone who
> can recall the theme of the sermon he had just finished
> preaching, but the congregation stares blankly and no
> one responds with the correct answer: "Love."[1]

Pinsky suggests that Lovejoy's frustration is emblematic of organized religion in our time; it struggles to make the gospel a reality,
to answer life's big questions.

How do we make sense of contemporary preaching? Even a
cursory reading of the history of preaching reminds us that the
practice of homiletics at a given time is shaped by a number of
influences. Some of these forces that have changed preaching over
the years are more often than not distributed across a vast cultural

web, some stronger than others. Hindsight necessarily grants us the privilege of reading the preachers of the past and their sermons in their historical context, which provides valuable clues in homiletic theory. The contemporary situation is another thing altogether, especially when it comes to assessing the revolution in communication that continues to evolve in our time. Although Fred Craddock was a massive force for altering the face of preaching in the United States, the cultural conditions that provoked him to deploy narrative homiletics were different than they are today. In a way Craddock and his colleagues anticipated a change in preaching that now may require alternative solutions. The New Homiletic not only offered a fresh method of preaching, but it was an indication that the line between written text and proclamation was becoming blurred. Popular culture and religion are not so easily distinguished. The Word may be disseminated in contexts other than liturgical space—the computer, the television, the cinema. With the slow erosion of the sermon as the perfectly crafted, written entity, the ambo now finds itself a place without constraints and even borders.

There have been a number of cultural movements over the last decades that have caused preaching to look at itself in another light; these movements are too numerous to investigate fully here. Perhaps most obviously, new ways of making sense of the world because of the rapid growth and distribution of technology in the post-industrial age has brought people into non-linear, non-narrative thinking since the 1970s. Much of what the New Homiletics relied on was a different understanding of communication, some of it already deployed in educational circles and elsewhere. Yet generations of children have been educated now in a manner that would have been unheard of in the 1960s. Rather than a paradigm that deploys once revolutionary, linear, "transactional" models, education systems now think much more intuitively; computers with endless menus provide students with links to ways to solve problems and to do so interactively. How can narrative, linear preaching that is plotted with a single focus leading toward a conclusion engage a youth culture that searches the Internet for hours at a time? Does the gospel truth become one of many options?

Put simply, communication systems now consider a wide range of factors when speaking about the transmission of information between sender and receiver.[2] Some communication models are not linear but triangular, such as Newcomb's paradigm, which introduced a social relationship into the equation.[3] Increasingly, the role of ideology in mass culture plays an important part in how information is received. How do these new models affect the communication techniques that were popular in the 1950s and the homiletic systems that were derived from them? Moreover, we know that visual information tends to dominate the everyday world in most places, providing a further challenge to the spoken word. What are we to make of the hearer who is mostly a watcher? We can communicate instantaneously around the world, so where does this place the local faith community in relationship to the many virtual communities that many have established? Finally, and more abstractly, is the homily capable of addressing the faith experience of listeners formed inside the nexus of postmodern culture?

I use the term *postmodernism* very broadly in this chapter to describe what some consider an enormous epistemological shift that has occurred in the West over the last fifty years or so. For the remainder of this chapter I focus my attention on how the condition of postmodernism has influenced preaching and what homiletics has done in response to this contemporary challenge. I first give some explanations of postmodernism and then go on to explain what some contemporary homileticians and liturgists suggest for preaching and worshiping in our present day. Then I give some suggestions for dealing with media in preaching.

The Problem of Postmodernism

The idea of the postmodern is not so much difficult to understand as it is slippery to identify or even define. In *Preaching to a Postmodern World* (2001) Graham Johnston writes: "In brief, postmodernism refers to a worldview, a way of perceiving the world, that is a backlash against the Enlightenment dream and dismisses any overarching set of ideas. Postmodernity is the worldview that says no worldview exists."⁴ To complicate matters, postmodernism should more properly be called postmodernisms, since the term covers an enormous range of topics, from artistic statements to political expressions, often interpreted by cultural critics working in academia.⁵ In their landmark book *Learning from Las Vegas* (1972), Robert Venturi and his co-authors suggest that Las Vegas is the premier postmodern city because it is a reaction against the universalist principles found in modern architecture.⁶ In fact, perhaps the most convenient way of looking at postmodernism is as a cultural formation distinct from and a reaction to modernism:

> Generally perceived as positivistic, technocentric, and rationalistic, universal modernism has been identified with the belief in linear progress, absolute truths, the rational planning of ideal social orders, and the standardization of knowledge and production. Post-modernism, by way of contrast, privileges heterogeneity and difference as liberative forces in the redefinition of cultural discourse. Fragmentation, indeterminacy, and intense distrust of all universal or "totalizing" discourses (to use the favored phrase) are the hallmark of postmodernist thought.⁷

Interestingly enough, fragmentation is precisely the problem with most homilies, according to the research of Kenneth Untener and others. "'Too many thoughts' is the most frequently voiced complaint about homilies, a runaway for first place."⁸ Postmodernism is more than just a style of architecture; it is a way of doing things and a way of knowing the world.

Beyond dispersion of thoughts and behaviors in contemporary society, theorists such as Fredric Jameson believe that the way that we make sense of our world separates the current age from any that has come before it. While observing some contemporary artistic formations, Jameson says, "The first and most evident is the emergence of a new kind of flatness or depthlessness, a new kind of superficiality in the most literal sense, perhaps the supreme formal feature of all the postmodernisms."⁹ What continues to surface as signs of postmodernism for Jameson is the evacuation of "authenticity," indeed, a disappearance of metaphysics, and more troubling, the erosion of a conscious, knowing human subject:

> The dissolution of an autonomous sphere of cultures rather to be imagined in terms of an explosion: a prodigious expansion of culture throughout the social realm, to the point at which everything in our social life— from economic value and state power to practices and to the very structure of the psyche itself—can be said to have become "cultural" in some original and yet untheorized sense.[10]

Religious experience, particularly the kind portrayed by traditional representatives of organized religion, often surfaces as ironic, inauthentic, or hypocritical (like the Reverend Lovejoy in *The Simpsons*). With religious institutions as de facto representatives of a "totalizing" ideology, can there be a representation of traditional religion that does not quickly devolve into satire or even camp? The fragmentation that signifies the culture of postmodernity faces people with an institution without a center; what is left is a cafeteria religion with endless choices, a "spirituality" without belief or adherence to dogma.

Jameson has not been alone in articulating the presence of a troubling voice inside contemporary culture, one that is incapable of grasping a traditional representation. Another substantial postmodern philosopher helpful to our understanding of what is at stake in Christian preaching is Jean-François Lyotard. Lyotard presupposes that the very condition of postmodernism requires that there is no claim to universal knowledge or even a legitimation of knowledge through narrative.[11] In short, there is no place in postmodernism for a meta-narrative. Meta-narratives have structured the way the dominant culture operates, but postmodernism opens up a window to diversity or the "micro-narrative." Postmodernism inhabits an atmosphere where all forms of meta-narratives, or any ideological claim to universal principles or metaphysics, are evacuated. No wonder that much of the debate on preaching today concerns a lack of integration of scripture and theology into the homiletic text. Salvation history is Christianity's greatest meta-narrative, and God's salvation in Christ for all humanity makes little sense without a fundamental grasp of this basic theological claim. Indeed, the Church's eucharistic liturgy is an *anamnesis*, a memorial; it is a new covenant that begins yet a new chapter in God's meta-narrative through Christ. Similarly, what can tradition possibly mean if there are only a series of micro-narratives, relativistic points of view to which one either adheres to or refrains from from one day to the next? Preaching seemingly must search for other methods for communication besides the ones proposed at an earlier time, when a culture gathered itself around a single, grand narrative.

To highlight the radical shift that postmodernism has introduced, Ihab Habib Hassan contrasts differences between modernity and postmodernism, some of which are paired below:

Modernism	**Postmodernism**
Form (conjunctive, closed)	Anti-form (disjunctive, open)
Purpose	Play
Design	Chance
Hierarchy	Anarchy
Mastery/*logos*	Exhaustion/silence
Art object/finished work	Process/performance/happening
Presence	Absence
Centering	Dispersal
Genre/boundary	Text/inter-text
Interpretation/reading	Against interpretation/misreading
Determinancy	Indeterminancy
Transcendence	Immanence[12]

I propose one illustration to clarify this contrast between modernism and postmodernism; it leaves us with a hint of the challenges we face in preaching the gospel in contemporary culture. The rise of photography occurred in the context of modernism, mostly because modernism would presume the integrity

of the photograph. The great photographers like Ansel Adams or
Walker Evans were presumably laying bare something hidden,
some essence, in the world of nature or humanity. Yet digital photography placed the integrity of the photograph in jeopardy. If
digital images can be manipulated, as they indeed can, then what
does this do to the status or the integrity of the photograph or,
more provocatively, to the idea of truth? What is on the page is
not necessarily what was present historically.

Similarly, the condition of postmodernism represents clear
challenges to the religious community now evolving within a culture that thrives on dispersion, irony, and diversity. The theological community has addressed Jameson's politicizing of culture and
Lyotard's report on contemporary epistemology in various ways,
which are too complicated to discuss at length here.[13] Yet, the challenges to preaching in the culture of postmodernism are obvious
enough. Even in this small sketch we are able to construe problems
facing the text, the preacher, and the listener. For example, if we
are to assume that there are no universal principles in this culture
of postmodernity, then whence does the textual authority come to
preach? Moreover, if any proposition is treated as ironic or super-
ficial, then how can the preacher attain credibility? Finally, if there
is no meta-narrative, how do the listeners make sense of their collective role in salvation history as God's people on pilgrimage? We
may disagree that we are operating under the conditions of postmodernity. On the other hand, there are enough symptoms present in our culture of the kind described by cultural theorists to
warrant an inquiry by those who preach the gospel.

John McClure and Postmodern Preaching

Professor John McClure frankly admits in *Other-wise
Preaching* (2001) that the postmodern condition has caused many
theological disciplines to rethink familiar terrain, especially in
regard to scripture, tradition, experience, and indeed, reason itself.
For McClure, "the grand narrative of a unified biblical text and a
unitary gospel to preach is fast disappearing. Preachers find themselves exiting the magisterial house of unitary and hegemonic

exegetical method, built more or less solidly on the foundation of historical-critical procedures."[14] McClure says that the New Homiletic of the 1970s and 1980s already sensed the fragmentation that was encroaching in postmodernity. But rather than embrace the fragile, deconstructive character of postmodernism, it "found support and insight in literary, rhetorical, and reader-response criticisms that were more concerned with the 'how' of the text, its focused relationship to interpretive communities, than with its 'what,' its referentiality or denotative meaning."[15] Indeed, McClure says that one of the reasons for the success of David Buttrick's method is "his underlying modernist commitment to a unifying consciousness and concomitant belief in the referential power of symbols."[16] By extension, we might make a similar modernist claim for Eugene Lowry, whose method also supports a modernist, literary armature as a way of guaranteeing the "how" of a text. Parenthetically, I wonder if McClure would place Fred Craddock in a modernist mode. As I have suggested earlier, Craddock's strategy from the start was to face the Christian community not so much with the "how" of a text but rather with the existential "how to be a Christian." In my view Craddock bracketed modernist alternatives precisely so that he could face us with referentiality or denotative meaning. Indeed, there was enough textual "slippage" that the assembly was expected to be jolted into a new hearing, and perhaps a new meaning as well.

McClure himself appropriates a great deal of dense philosophical material in evolving his homiletic theory. He anticipates a postmodernist, deconstructionist tendency in the homiletic use of scripture and wants to support a kind of defamiliarization that attends the reading process. "This basic premise is that biblical texts deconstruct themselves—that is, part of what these texts do is to reveal and thus undermine the metanarrative, theory, or philosophy on which they rely....For the deconstructive reader, therefore, the boundaries between writer and reader disappear, replaced by this womb of textuality in which writer and reader weave together 'yet more shimmering webs of undecidability stretching to the horizon.'"[17] Perhaps McClure complicates things a bit too much, especially in his adoption of postmodernist language. We have seen this "womb of textuality" before, a bit more frankly stated by Craddock in his discussions on the relationship between the preacher and the congregation. Craddock is also after a more egalitarian relationship between the speaker and the listener. Postmodernism wants to bring the question about the "one without authority" home in much more technical and philosophical terms, by a destabilization of the *logos*, the center and authority of the text as well as the preacher. In philosophical and literary circles the "de-centered" *logos*, the evacuation of "presence," has become associated with the work of deconstructive critic Jacques Derrida.[18]

McClure adopts a great deal of Derrida's language and theory to explain his own preaching methodology. McClure's version of postmodernism in preaching is best seen when he applies some of Derrida's insights to the specific tasks of reading and preaching scripture. I am thinking here of the way in which Derrida poses the opposition between speech and writing as determinative for metaphysics.[19] Along these lines, it is worth pointing out that McClure makes a careful distinction between the *Bible*, a written, linear text, and *scripture*, which is living, changing, and active. Indeed, McClure often seems to find himself in the same company as Derrida, especially when it comes to recognizing that our culture has prioritized linear forms of (historical) writing. The Bible as a text engages a center that cannot hold, according to McClure; it fixes meaning that no longer has any referents. McClure possibly has in mind here the fundamentalist who will go to any length to prove the stability of the *logos:* "It says right here that..." From the perspective of McClure, God's Word, the *logos*, is a defamiliarizing power. When the Bible is used as scripture, as revealed Word of God, it tends to destabilize our complacent identity, to shake us loose at our roots. The Bible does not give us answers, then, so much as questions. "Because of its centripetal quality as scripture, the Bible refuses over and over again to close itself as a book, to secure its connotations to a single self-referential tautology."[20]

The destabilized or open text creates a window for the preacher. McClure explains through the work of yet another postmodernist author, Roland Barthes:

Both preaching and the Bible as scripture are, in actuality, closer to what Barthes calls "writerly" texts. Operating within the centripetal force field of the Bible as scripture, preaching is the Bible "under the infinite paradigm of difference." Preachers are ultimately not readers or consumers of the biblical text, but producers of the Bible as scripture. Because the Bible opens itself towards an infinity of others, as a sign to and for the others, it exists for the preacher not as a "signified" but as a signifier of seeming endless signifieds.[21]

Under McClure's consideration, the postmodern reading of the Bible precisely as scripture is not subject to a particular hegemony but allows for a plurality of readings. He writes:

This is the experience of the Bible as a generative "word from the Lord," set into linguistic oscillation, involved in endless connotation and supplementation that denies a sustained and sustainable position from which to read. Because of this, readerly interpretations are unable to achieve full closure, and issues of identity and identification remain open-ended and unresolved.[22]

McClure advocates a deconstructive reading of the Bible, then, in order to experience what Derrida calls "shimmering webs of undecidability." McClure sees preaching not as a totalizing force or even a single perspective on an issue, but as a way to achieve a kind of non-hegemonic coherence in the Christian community. He is interested in affirming the diversity in the congregation in and of itself—its very "undecidablility," rather than the traditional voice of the preacher who speaks on behalf of the church. In other words, he does not think that preaching is supposed to galvanize the community around the Word or the tradition; as he puts it, it is *not* the job of the preacher to "negotiate an ancient canon and the lived experience of succeeding generations." Rather, McClure intends to see preaching as a pre-written event, a kerygmatic memory bequeathed to the church from pre-manuscript oral culture....Homiletic *anamnesis* begins, then, as invested, proclamatory (kerygmatic) remembering: a proclamation of a proclamation, the renomination of names. The preacher locates the sermon within the habits, customs, legends, and rituals that hovers around the biblical words and images preached and joins step with the centrifugal parade of *topoi* that constitutes the text's and larger tradition's denotative genius. The sermon speaks from the Bible in a way that accesses and regenerates the numinous power of kerygmatic memory in the church.[23]

McClure intends to reverse the priority that linear writing has historically had over speech; thus, preaching becomes a way into the contemporary psyche and a way of subverting linear history. In fact, this preaching is an erasure of writing and homiletic remembering that then becomes part of what McClure calls "countermemory," when "preachers allow their own well-formed memory, and the memories of their hearers, to dissolve into proximity to others, present and past, whose bodies begin to signify things unremembered. In this moment, memory is able to show itself to itself, contradicting the patterns and processes on which its own plausibility has relied for centuries."[24]

In his proposal for a counter-memory, McClure seems to address the issue of the loss of meta-narrative, or more specifically, salvation history or a "tradition." He goes on to deal with the problem that postmodernism raises in its critique of the human subject and proposes a homiletic alternative to traditional homiletics. McClure says that inductive preaching relies heavily on relational symmetry. "The fundamental premise behind relational symmetry is that preachers and hearers can and should identify with one another."[25] Still, McClure wants to support the vast array of subjectivities of those who experience themselves differently from the way in which the New Homiletic, humanist experience would have them do; these are those who, in the words of Sandra Harding, have to "struggle to name their own experience for themselves in order to claim the subjectivity, the possibility of historical agency."[26] Although not departing entirely from inductive homiletics, McClure sees himself alongside liberationist preachers and contextual theologians. "Homiletic models such as those by Tisdale, Rose, McClure, and Saunders and Campbell are designed to encourage preachers to make a mutual speaking-listening, face-to face encounter with others as an essential aspect of the preaching process."[27]

McClure's *Other-wise Preaching* is really a logical descendant of his radical "de-centering" of preaching, or what he has referred to in an earlier book as "the round-table pulpit."[28] There he called for a meeting between leadership and preaching, inviting the Other, the human stranger, into the preaching process. In so doing, preaching was de-centered, stripped of authority, and moved into a more public domain. "To ask these people what kinds of interpretive spins they put on the gospel of Jesus Christ is to embark on a homiletical adventure in the public realm."[29] Yet in *Other-wise Preaching* McClure is careful to point out the potential problems with "collaboration":

> Roundtable conversations can simply become a way of managing difference rather than allowing difference to transform homiletic practice. At its best, however, collaborative preaching offers one way to overcome the retreatist option. It has the potential to allow for the sermon expression of a variety of very particular struggles against hegemonic experience within a social and ecclesial context that recognizes that one's subjectivity is not just individual personal identity, but that all identity is, to some extent, socially constituted. It also ensures that preachers are confronted with some of the actual bodies of those whose experiences are addressed in their sermons.[30]

For McClure, these voices of diversity, "a web of conversations,"[31] are part of the emerging condition of postmodern, "other-wise" preaching that is ultimately rooted in a social gospel and an ethics of preaching. "The beginning of other-wise preaching is in the other-wise commitment: commitment to human others of all shapes and sizes and a personal and theological commitment to exiting the biblical, theological, social, experiential, and cultural hegemonies that exist within and beyond the churches."[32] Although some have advocated a somewhat different approach to the post-modern problem—Craig Loscalzo, for instance, advocates a program of "apologetic preaching"[33]—Lucy Atkinson Rose shares McClure's vision of gathered listeners around a table: "The experience of many of us in both the pulpit and the pew is that we are interdependent, not separated by a gap but joined in common discipleship and common tasks. For us the gap shifts. The preacher and the congregation stand together as explorers, while a text, meaning, or mystery lies on the other side or confronts us as Other."[34] Rose is interested in dismantling the traditional view of the preacher as the one with a particular message for those who listen. Here again, we are outside the linear model of communication: "We as preachers have no message, gospel, or experience for the congregation to receive. In the pulpit we are not senders, and in the pew we are not receivers. The fundamental experience of connectedness redescribes the roles of the preacher and the worshipers and demands new probes into preaching whys, whats and hows."[35]

McClure's rhetorical strategies for preaching are almost as complex as his postmodern theory of homiletics. Some find his assessments and methodology tough going. McClure's language is often dense and his philosophical references somewhat esoteric even for the educated reader. That problem of accessibility is accentuated when McClure endeavors to promulgate a "method" for preaching, which is by far the most sophisticated and intricate system of preaching that we have seen so far. His book *The Four Codes of Preaching* (1991) presents us with four systems of signs or words "that become a way of organizing a particular level of aspect of human interaction."[36] Ronald Allen summarizes these signs as scriptural ("what we remember as the foundation events of faith and how we remember them"), semantic ("what is Christian truth and how we hold it to be true"), theo-symbolic ("the theological world view that informs the community"), and cultural ("the experience of faith and how it is experienced").[37] McClure introduces these codes not as linear, static elements in a sermon but as *fields* that will have a number of sequences of movement. These codes play an important part in the composition and the transmission of the homily. Unlike his predecessors, McClure does not see the preacher directly relating to the congregation, even in so-called transactional ways of communication. For McClure, the necessity of the "roundtable" must hold sway. It is not just a discussion group, giving ideas to the preacher before Sunday; the group is absolutely essential to the process of creating and delivering a sermon. As his theory implies, the "roundtable" becomes an intermediary, collaborative module in the process.

Ronald Allen lays out a helpful schema for understanding McClure's strategy:

Sermon	Roundtable	Congregation
Theo-symbolic Code	➤ coming to terms with	➤ World view
Semantic Code	➤ coming to terms with	➤ Truth (meaning)
Cultural Code	➤ coming to terms with	➤ Experience
Scriptural Code	➤ coming to terms with	➤ Anamnesis (memory)[38]

These codes are meant to operate very fluidly. "Within a given sequence, each of the codes deals with the same subject matter but addresses a different communicative field. The preacher unfolds all four codes within each sequence....The goal is to complete each sequence by moving back and forth among the four codes.[39]

Allen uses an example of a roundtable discussion on a miracle story from the Synoptic Gospels. The sermon will want to account for the discussion between two students about the reality of the miracle. The preacher might record these interactions in the sermon, reporting the various points of view and so on for the purposes of engaging the scriptural code. The group might then go on to speak about the miracle story on the semantic level (or meaning) or how it is experienced in the life of faith (culture) and theological world view (theo-symbolic). Ultimately, "sermons in this mode will have several sequences of movement."[40]

McClure's positioning of the four modes of (postmodern) preaching is certainly thought provoking. The schema attends quite directly to his postmodern ecclesiology and roundtable homiletics. Yet, the system is perhaps best seen as a theoretical rather than a practical paradigm. Additionally, the lack of an "author" in the homily is somewhat troubling for hierarchical structures, like the Roman Catholic Church. And what does prophetic preaching look like in McClure's model? There seems to be very little biblical warrant for collaborative preaching, although the early church apparently reached consensus on some things, such as the choosing of deacons (see Acts). Finally, the collaborative strategy McClure suggests for homiletics may give an adequate reading of where the congregation is at present, but preaching ought to lead the assembly into the future, God's future. Can the intense collaboration and moving within codes represent "this community by voicing its concerns, by naming its demons, and thus enabling it to gain some understanding and control of the evil which afflicts it?"[41]

McClure perhaps is not giving his readers a usable method for preaching as much as systematizing the results of his philosophical speculations. The process, in my view, is far too complicated to engage all but a few courageous preachers in a strategic plan for preaching a homily. Perhaps McClure is really interested in the process more than the product, which would reflect, once again, his postmodern interests in "de-centering." His roundtable pulpit informs his homiletic strategy from the start, and that collaboration seems to be the fundamental issue McClure wants us to grapple with. Moreover, unlike the modernists Craddock, Lowry, and Buttrick, McClure's published homilies have been relatively few, so we lack practical examples of how his systems of codes play out when it comes to interpreting particular scripture passages. That does not matter if we take McClure for what he has offered contemporary homiletics; he is a philosopher of homiletic method in a difficult age and has offered challenging communication models to accomplish a collaborative, biblical sermon with a cultural and social conscience. His task is to come to terms with the challenge that the postmodern condition has brought to the twenty-first century and to help us to understand it. He has done an admirable job in confronting the problem of preaching in postmodernity, but whether or not the rest of us can preach out of this very intricate system may be another question altogether. Clearly, the preacher must account for collaboration in the preaching process, but how that transpires will probably depend on how one reads the culture of postmodernity and its ongoing challenge to ecclesial structures and teachings.

Feminist Preaching

Feminist homiletics might be viewed as part of the large postmodern condition itself, although there are a variety of feminist approaches to preaching. Lucy Rose prefers to see feminist scholarship's chief contribution as a revelation that "the primary mode of relating for many men is based on a sense of separation from others....Feminist scholarship also claims that the primary mode of relating for many women is based on a sense of connectedness."[42] Thus, Rose wants to fill the gap between the preacher and the congregation and uses feminism to underline the point. On the other hand, Elisabeth Schüssler Fiorenza proposes that the heart of the spiritual feminist quest is the search for woman's power, freedom, and independence. She then asks, "Is it possible to read the Bible in such a way that it becomes a historical source and theological symbol for such power, independence, and freedom?"[43] This is also the question of the alternative, subaltern, non-hegemonic "voice" of the Other raised by postmodern cultural critics. French feminists such as Hélène Cixous say that *l'écriture féminine* is unique and finds a voice in *différence:* "Woman must write her self: must write about women and bring women to writing, from which they have been driven away as violently as from their bodies— for the same reasons, by the same law, with the same fatal goal. Woman must put herself into the text—as into the world and into history—by her own movement."[44] So saying, the last several years have seen a remarkable rereading of biblical narratives from a non-patriarchal perspective gathered around a feminist hermeneutic.[45]

The implications for preaching in the context of feminism are still emerging. Christine Smith says that as women and men preach they must ask themselves several key questions in relationship to biblical hermeneutics:

What authority do I give the bible in my own life of faith and spirituality? What is the nature of this authority? How do the scriptures intersect with my own life as a contemporary woman, a contemporary man? How do the scriptures serve to perpetuate my own oppression and the oppression of the others? How do they serve as sources of liberation? Are there texts that simply should not be proclaimed or preached, texts that are not able to be redeemed in terms of feminist biblical critique?[46]

Smith has vital concerns over the presumed authority of preaching. Craddock had given his own view on the subject clearly enough: "Authority is that which gives one the right to speak. It is ecclesiastical by reason of ordination; it is charismatic by reason of a call; it is personal by reason of talent and education; it is democratic by reason of the willingness of the listeners to give their attention."[47] Smith's concern over the (male) authority of the preacher leads her to the metaphor of the weaver, which operates on a "loom of authority" and provides many different threads or variations rather than a single hegemony.[48] Here, as elsewhere, Smith configures herself to the postmodern suspicion of authority and the single voice. The weaver's loom she deploys to speak about the homiletic process is a variant on McClure's roundtable pulpit; both attempt to integrate voices of diversity and "de-center" the authority of a single, dominant point of view.

Smith finds that the homiletic profession in general has failed to address "issues of God language and Christology from a feminist perspective."[49] Since the publication of Smith's work, however, there have been some notable efforts in the area of feminism, preaching, and Christology.[50] Smith says that the difficulty in homiletics is that the biblical scholarship used over the centuries continues to be absorbed in an uncritical fashion. With this in mind, she offers a critique of William D. Thompson's popular book *Preaching Biblically* (1981). Thompson's method is typical of biblical scholarship, Smith claims, comprised of patriarchal authority and its narrowed, gendered interpretation. According to Smith, Thompson has the following assumptions that ought to be resisted by feminists and those who preach from that perspective:

1. *"God is predictably omnipotent, eternal, omniscient, and true. God always acts among us creatively and redemptively."* Smith resists this assumption from the point of view of language: omnipotence is not the God who has been disclosed in relation to the human community. Perhaps more radically, she questions whether God is always creative and redemptive. "For most feminists, God is not a far-removed, eternally benevolent being, but a sacred presence among and with us, more than we are but intricately interwoven with all human activity."[51]

2. *"There is continuity in human nature and experience."* Smith rejects this assumption as well, saying that, "it fails to acknowledge that the scriptures primarily document and describe male experience."[52]

3. *"There is unity and ultimate authority in biblical revelation."* For Smith, this is precisely a question for feminists because "these texts frequently perpetuate a kind of theology that serves the powerful and reinforces the present power structures."[53]

4. *"Christian experience is necessary."* This is a problem because women did not produce the Bible. So, "when we require that all preachers participate in the community of faith, to what community do we refer and whose experience does it represent?"[54]

Following liberationist preaching and the feminist biblical interpretation of Fiorenza, Smith recommends that Christian feminists approach the Bible and preaching with a "hermeneutics of suspicion" rather than submission. She finds this posture especially appropriate when preaching from the Lectionary. "Who selected the texts that are present in the lectionary? Who determines which texts will be included and which will be absent?"[55] Smith is interested in "a historical-critical reconstruction of biblical history from a feminist perspective," especially from the point of view of women "remembering."[56]

Again, like McClure's advocacy of the roundtable pulpit, Smith's feminist position on preaching will not find a friendly reception in all denominations. Yet it is not necessary to adopt Smith's stance entirely to recognize that the marginalized are often rendered invisible when it comes to interpretation and proclamation. Also, she makes a valuable critique of the way in which biblical studies have only recently broken into a more flexible hermeneutic, capable of reaching those whose voices have been silent for so long. It might be well for those churches that use lectionaries in their worship services to explore under what circumstances and in what texts women have been marginalized.[57] It is always useful to see the larger context of the scriptural text, but "filling in" what has been omitted might enflesh the role of women in the history of salvation for the congregation. Smith's argument proposes that the canonical process has been patriarchal and excised *l'écriture féminine*, and the responsible preacher shifts the textual terrain to a wider plane of vision.

We can understand Smith's points clearly enough. But it seems to me that we also need to account for the historical development that may have contributed to the silence of female writing. For instance, although the canon has been constructed by men, the canonical process does not always collude with the Lectionary as an instrument to suppress the voice of women; they are sometimes at odds. The preacher might take stock of the way in which the canon has, in fact, endorsed women's power in salvation history. Judith's exploits in the Hebrew scriptures, for example, are detailed and interesting enough to make her a heroine of considerable proportion to Israel. And the canonical process in some Christian churches reflects this reality, since the book of Judith was appropriated into the canon of the Greek, Latin, and Slavonic Bibles. Does this kind of portrait, one that represents the fullness of the scriptures, fully emerge in the Lectionary cycle? If not, then we know that the issue is not with the canon itself but the more recent choices and editorial factors in the composition of the Lectionary. There is only one passage in the *Lectionary for Mass* taken from the book of Judith (no. 737), and this reading occurs among eighteen options of readings for the Common of Holy Men and Women. And the selection of the reading itself is somewhat puzzling; it is from chapter 8 and deals with Judith as one who fasted in the days of her widowhood. There is nothing in the Lectionary about

Judith's encounter with Holofernes, in which she tricks him and then beheads him, causing the dispersal of the Assyrian army. Clearly, there is more to Judith than sackcloth and ashes, and those who collected the book of Judith into the canon of sacred texts must have thought so as well.

There may be more at stake in a feminist reading of scripture and culture than some are willing to admit, and the case of Judith, the powerful woman of Israel, virtually erased from the Lectionary (though present in the canon), is a case in point. The culture itself has recognized the importance of female power as symbolized in Judith; her victory has been celebrated through the centuries in Western art. In fact, our culture itself is already (re)writing *l'écriture féminine* in many diverse and popular ways. Consider how often popular culture has celebrated the myth of the female warrior, from Saint Joan of Arc to comic-book heroines to Hollywood *femme fatales*. Preaching must begin to account for the places that holy scripture itself is leading us—and its many reverberations in literary, visual, and popular culture.

Some of Smith's additional concerns about the Lectionary reflect the way that women often play a subservient role in patriarchal culture and that this inequality is seemingly endorsed by, of all things, God's Word and the liturgy. Although Abraham is rightly showcased in the Lectionary, Sarah has a significant part as a fully embodied character in the book of Genesis. Can the preacher re-create the text's full disclosure of Sarah? The Lectionary ought never to be treated as if it were the entirety of the revealed Word, or during the liturgy, as if this recent collection of scriptural texts (since 1969) were the equivalent of the Gospels. The Lectionary is not an object of veneration. Beyond the function of the Lectionary and its interpretation for the preacher, the still larger question remains: what features could be brought out for the assembly in order to gain a deeper appreciation for God's Word? The creativity of the living Word of God allows for diversity in preaching so that all might hear the good news of redemption.

Although she has some different perspectives on the place of women in scripture—or their overshadowing there—I take it that Smith's real benefit to even conservative interpreters is her interest

in revealing the text in its fullness and allowing a plurality of interpreters to discover its meaning. At the same time, preachers ought
to avoid strong ideological interpretations. While the tremendous
benefit of literary feminist criticism, such as that written by the
early Anglo-American feminists Susan Gubar and Sandra Gilbert,[58]
has been an imaginative exploration that cracks open the text,
preachers must exercise caution that ideology does not dominate an
interpretation of the scriptures. Such a practice would not lead to a
mutual discovery of the Word but to a closed, insulated speculation
that would be better served outside the preaching event. At the
same time, if preachers are present to interpret the Word, to mediate God's truth made present on earth, then there is no room for
fear in mining the "richer fare," the varieties of interpretations
available. The preacher is to disclose the Word to the hearts and
minds of the congregation, and such Christian witness leaves no
room for either conservative or liberal agenda or ideological slants.
A judicious approach for the preacher is to absorb the big picture—
in scripture, church, and culture—which is ever widening to
include those that have been silent.

Preaching and the Media

At roughly the same time that the New Homiletic was
beginning to stir in this country, William Kuhns was calling attention to the power of the media and its place in religious belief in
the more or less deconstructive climate of postmodernity:

> The entertainment milieu has transformed the ways in
> which we believe and are capable of believing. An
> absolute kind of belief, as well as a belief in absolutes,
> becomes increasingly difficult as the entertainment
> milieu trains people to believe tentatively and with elas-
> ticity....The very concept of faith—to believe in that
> which you cannot see and cannot understand—comes
> with difficulty to a generation that has depended, as
> perhaps no generation before, on its senses.[59]

In discussing the use of media in American religious culture, it is necessary to make confessional distinctions. For example, there has been a great deal of difference between the way in which Roman Catholics have dealt with the media compared to the evangelicals. According to Quentin J. Schultze: "While Roman Catholics generally displayed a 'profound ambivalence' toward the new media, evangelicals embraced communication technologies enthusiastically, filled with hope that mass communication was the solution to the need for worldwide evangelization."[60] According to Schultze, aside from the stunning popularity of Bishop Fulton J. Sheen's television show "Life Is Worth Living" on prime-time network TV in the 1950s, Catholic television—including Mother Angelica's EWTN network—has been largely derivative of the evangelical "rhetoric of conversion."[61] That tendency to merge television with conversion continues there and elsewhere. Indeed, EWTN regularly features those who have converted or "come home" to Catholicism and interviews people about their experience in "coming over to Rome." It may well be that conversion narratives are a fine idea, bringing the real-life story of human beings into focus to share their faith in God. But, according to Schultze, "religious television is largely the product of conversionary-minded American Protestantism."[62] Schultze himself may be as mistrustful of media as he claims the church to be. His earlier work *Televangelism and American Culture* (1991), suggested that the gospel was being "commodified" into the capitalist marketplace.[63] Unfortunately, Schultze does not fully parse the difference between the various strategies of preaching between Catholics and Protestants from the point of view of reception theory, which would make for a fascinating discussion on preaching. For example, shut-ins make up a good deal of the audience for these religious shows. How does the rhetoric of conversion work for this population, both Protestant and Catholic?

Some of the Catholic mistrust for media can be historically linked to an interest in religious liberty. The popular Jesuit magazine *America* only once over a fifty-year period expressed an optimism for the potential for radio to be an evangelical tool.[64] And the career of the so-called Radio Priest, social-activist Father Charles Coughlin, who was removed from the airways in 1939 for spreading anti-Jewish, anti-Roosevelt sentiments, confirmed that journal's suspicion "about the self-interested nature of broadcast codes."[65] Far from being an instrument of religious freedom, the airways, like the film industry before them, were subject to regulation. And it was not just liberty that was at stake. Besides *America*, other journals like *The Catholic World* complained of a strange array of offerings on the radio, from psychics to gypsies, with this powerful electronic media in the hands of the "vulgar horde, who lack good taste and intelligence."[66] The church has taken a cautious stand with regard to the media, even though a Catholic, Joseph Breen, was head of Hollywood's Production Code (the self-censoring regulatory office for the motion picture industry before the modern rating system) for years, beginning in 1934. Its position has moderated somewhat since the days when the Legion of Decency threatened to boycott the film industry if certain films were released. Some of this relaxation has occurred because our culture itself has become more permissive. But with a television in every home and computers in many, and an influx of Hollywood features now under a ratings system, the church seems to have made some peace with the media. Pope John Paul II, who was himself trained as an actor and known to have a list of favorite films, has said that "knowledge of the media, whether the more traditional forms or those which technology has produced in recent times, is indispensable. Contemporary reality demands a capacity to learn the language, nature and characteristics of mass media."[67]

Despite an occasionally adversarial relationship, religion and the media have had a much more porous exchange than the political debates about religious freedom might indicate. One of the earliest films exhibited in this country was a filming of the Oberammergau Play around 1898. These "living stations of the cross" attracted thousands of immigrants, as their descendants, the biblical epics, would do a few decades later. Hollywood often turned to religious narratives to guarantee the industry's respectability. Cecil B. DeMille and Paramount Studios became rich bringing the Bible to the screen. Moreover, Hollywood studios built enormous movie palaces in the 1920s to resemble exotic places of worship. This relationship between religion and media did not stop with the film industry. Madonna videos regularly use religious symbols, causing Mark Hulsether to claim a connection between the singer and liberation theologies.[68] Jim Trammell of the University of Georgia observes: "Although spirituality is more closely regarded as a personal experience rather than a social function, the fact that television programs have been shown to influence audiences' perception of the social norms has particular ramifications for one's perception of spirituality."[69] *Touched by an Angel* and *Joan of Arcadia*, television shows with plots that involve divine encounters, have soared in popularity. The media and religion are far from antithetical, despite the occasional pundit who finds this or that show distasteful. The fact is that the media have controlled religious discourse for years, while, at the same time, religious people have limited media, and often very successfully.

The subject of preaching and the media, then, has a history—a complicated one—entangled with politics, social regulation, and sectarian preferences that make it difficult to assess. Clearly, the evangelical churches were highly successful in their forays into radio and television over the years, and some estimates suggest that the audience was as high as forty million viewers at the height of televangelism in the mid-1980s.[70] There seems to be a natural link between evangelism and electronic media, and some people anticipated this connection long before the 700 Club and its numerous variations spread through the airways. Edward Bellamy's highly influential, utopic novel of 1888, *Looking Backward: 2000–1887*, contains the following scene between Dr. Leete and Julian West, which only approximated the success of electronic preaching:

> "Now, as to hearing a sermon today, if you wish to do so, you can either go to church to hear it or stay at home."
>
> "How am I to hear it if I stay at home?"
>
> "Simply by accompanying us to the music room at the proper hour and selecting an easy chair. There are some who still prefer to hear sermons in church, but most of our preaching, like our musical performances, is not in public, but delivered in acoustically prepared chambers, connected by wire with subscribers'

houses....I see by the paper that Mr. Barton is to preach this morning, and he preaches only by telephone, and to audiences often reaching 150,000."[71]

While the evangelical preachers were discovering their ability to spread the Word by television, they also stumbled onto the mega-church. "The 1970s witnessed the rise of super churches in America that developed alongside of, in conjunction with, and sometimes in competition with radio and television. By involving themselves in secular matters and institutions, these churches are perhaps the best example in America of the secularization of the traditional Christian institution."[72]

Like televangelism, mega-church evangelization does not fit very closely to the traditional view of Christian preaching. Indeed, the introduction of electronic media challenges the conventional notions of preaching and models of the preacher. Beyond this, electronic media can be a considerable test for liturgical preaching. Consider, for instance, how the *ethos* of a person is transformed by enlarging the preacher's image on several huge television screens for an audience of thousands. The principle is the same for movie stars. Once they were "just like us"; now they are gigantic, literally bigger-than-life images on the screen. How does the electronic transformation of the human subject change the way we perceive the message of the gospel? The use of technology is bound to cast a different light on the preacher, the text, and the congregation, as well as the way we receive these three elements of the speech-act. This is a very interesting philosophical question confronted in a somewhat different context by German Jewish thinker Walter Benjamin in the 1930s in a famous essay entitled "The Work of Art in the Age of Mechanical Reproduction."[73] Briefly, Benjamin was interested in how photography and film alter our perception. This was of special concern to him with the rise of the film industry as mass culture and, indeed, the fascist movement in Germany, where sophisticated propaganda films were changing the way people thought. What exactly are we doing when we reproduce a person or an event on a screen for a large group of people? What is the nature of the cinematic "aura," which appears to be close to what we think of as sacred? What is the difference between such imagistic activity and the use of language? Are visual prompts more "totalizing," and verbal language more pluralistic? These are questions for all of us to ponder as the media culture continues to evolve and as these forms mix with sacred space and liturgical language. A later cultural critic, Neil Postman, has the following to say about the way that photography introduces something different into our cognitive framework:

> By itself, a photograph cannot deal with the unseen, the remote, the internal, the abstract....The photograph documents and celebrates the particularities of this infinite variety. Language makes them comprehensible.... The way in which the photograph records experience is also different from the way of language. Language makes sense only when it is presented as a sequence of propositions. Meaning is distorted when a word or sentence is, as we say, taken out of context....But there is no such thing as a photograph taken out of context, for a photograph does not require one. In fact, the point of photography is to isolate images from context, so as to make them visible in a different way.[74]

When we speak of working in a multimedia environment, a lot depends on what kind of media we are talking about and how and where they are deployed. It would seem difficult to negotiate visual images into liturgical space, for instance, although some have had some success with this practice. Postman's observations suggest that with the deployment of too much visual media in church services during the homily we might experience, at the very least, a disjointed liturgy. People are distracted even during an important conversation (in a hospital visiting room, for instance) when something comes on the television, even something not very meaningful. Does the preacher want to compete with visual language? And if not, precisely how does verbal explication become integrated into visual discourse?

The age of media brings with it a shift in how we see the world. Director James L. Brooks's *Broadcast News* (1987) confronted the issue of how truth in television can be manipulated. A charming young anchorman interviews his subjects and keys his own reaction shots to them. The audience's emotions move to a higher pitch because the anchorman shows himself in a close-up reaction shot crying over the woman he is interviewing. But the anchorman's actions were really not a reaction to the woman; they were a staged event, inserted later. The editing process itself, then, forces people to perceive the woman differently. How do these dynamics play out in a worship space? Certainly the *ethos* of the preacher must be altered if he is enlarged on the screen. But here, we might remember Craddock's inductive homiletic model, which was constructed so that individual members of the congregation might be able to draw their own conclusions about the gospel. What do the various "cut aways" do to the homiletic text and, more important, how does this effect the freedom of those in the congregation to draw their own conclusions? What is the effect on a congregation that sees itself on screen? Will we resemble a football stadium with a similar media format? What is the status of the *logos* that has been enhanced by music and special effects?

For Conrad Ostwalt, the mega-church is an evacuation of sacred orientation and an absorption of internal secularization. "Internal secularization occurs when churches purposefully use 'elements of the broader culture' to eliminate a perceived cultural gap between the Christian message and the unchurched."[75] Ostwalt has been strongly influenced by the work of G. A. Pritchard and Scott Thumma, and he demonstrates at least six areas in which secularization of Christianity has occurred in the mega-church: (1) packaging through secular marketing methods; (2) organization through a business model; (3) programming through entertainment; (4) careful blending of psychological, biblical, and systematic teachings; (5) appropriation of the function of childcare, self-help groups, and other secular agencies; and (6) "a secularization of sacred space," which often duplicates or mirrors the environment of secular places.[76] I can think of one illustration in this regard that may help to underline Ostwalt's final point, such as the tendency of some preachers to duplicate a talk-show space. These preachers proclaim the gospel from the pulpit or ambo and then wander up and down the aisle with a portable microphone, asking the congregation (read: studio audience) for answers to prompts about their homily. Liturgical space no longer looks sacred because the actions there have secularized the space. Ostwalt concludes that when the wholesale adoption of popular culture becomes standard or gimmicky, the Christian message is distorted in order to make the message more attractive. "Certainly, when the tradition acculturates, it risks its prophetic voice because it can no longer speak out against the culture it has adopted."[77]

Preaching still goes on in mega-churches, but what kind of preaching is it, if it is incapable of raising its prophetic voice against the culture that surrounds it? In light of the appropriation of the tools of popular culture, it seems clear that the media are erasing the line that used to be filled by traditional Christian preaching: the unchurched were formerly brought back, say, by a dynamic retelling of the Parable of the Prodigal Son, by a change of heart brought about by an overdose of secular living. Christian preaching never tried to eliminate the distinction between the sacred and the secular, but it aimed rather to sanctify the sinner and justify the righteous. The love of God is preached when the homily addresses itself to unfathomable mercy. By contrast, an excessive use of media creates a therapeutic, safe environment with no feeling of contingency and consequently no sense of the need for God's forgiveness.

The pyrotechnics deployed in super churches are perhaps extreme examples of how preaching can become distant from its mission; over-accommodation to secular forms by naturalizing the experience of religion into something cozy, or New Age, robs the hearers of the newness required to listen to the gospel as Good news. While it is important that preachers understand the culture through and through—and, therefore, attend to video and film culture very astutely—whose gospel are we proclaiming? The "gospel" of Madison Avenue rejects the imperfect and the ugly. But the gospel of Christ embraces all and must sometimes preach against the culture, offering a Word, a life-giving alternative. As Robert Waznak writes:

> Culture is a revelation system. Culture effectively transforms, provides heroics, organizes our world, suggests human fulfillments. Culture is a gospel; it reveals an

195

alternative way of looking at ourselves and our world. Culture creates in us habits of the heart. People find in our video culture a worldview which reflects ultimate values and a way of life.[78]

And so the function of the preacher is to reveal what has been concealed. Rather than erasing the distinctions between the sacred and the secular, Christian preaching can point out the glaring conflicts in culture that go unnoticed so that the gospel becomes "fulfilled in our hearing."

The Media and Liturgical Preaching

In addition to a cooptation of media into Christian preaching, there is the additional problem of deploying electronic media in more traditional liturgical space in the context of sacramental rites. So far, we have been discussing mostly evangelical megachurches, but the use of electronics in religious traditions where the Lord's Supper is celebrated is negotiated very delicately. How do we experience *anamnesis* when photographs or film clips, taken out of context, are swimming around liturgical space? There have been some successful attempts at using media in the liturgical homily, and Lee Wilson and Jason Moore argue for a place for digital technology when preaching the Word.[79] Bernard R. Bonnot, Thomas Boomershine, and Brian Sweeney make a claim for using electronic media as a way to "energize people's experience, participation and interactivity." They say that the church has always absorbed popular media into its worship space:

> This history makes a case for integrating today's digital media into our worship. Though still young, the indomitable advance of electronic culture over the past century has already solidified certain characteristics. These include a preference for direct experience rather than abstraction as a way of knowing, multimediated sounds and images on screens as a central mode of presentation. And a participative interaction within

a community rather than private reading and reflection as the preferred way of knowing.[80]

Some scholars, such as Quentin Schultze, might argue with the authors' historical research, especially in regard to their claim that "our Catholic history is one of the appropriation and full integration of each era's new communication culture into worship."[81] Schultze's investigation finds quite the opposite.[82] Also, the media is supposed to increase church attendance, but these digital strategies have yet to be tested over the long haul. The expanding and "orthodox" young adults whom Colleen Carroll calls the "New Faithful" say they are looking for transcendence, not media in the church experience.[83] Ultimately, church attendance may not be the best reason for the deployment of media.

Without dismissing contemporary media offhand, there are some lingering questions that need to be addressed. What is the difference between entertainment and liturgy? How are the two distinguished in a media-rich environment? Finally, what about smaller, poorer churches and communities? Are these parishes the equivalent of "mom and pop" stores, destined to be driven out by superdigital liturgical franchises?

It may be naive to think that digital culture can be taken blithely into liturgical worship. In fact, Pope John Paul II says in *The Church in America* that teaching the faithful to be "critical" in the use of media requires special attention.[84] Ray John Marek, OMI, has four suggestions for preaching in a "television-saturated culture." Marek acknowledges that the first order of business is to notice the intersection between the sacred and the secular, that is, to adopt the principle of "challenging preachers to attend to God's grace revealed in much of human experience." He goes on to say: "While affirming television's potential to be revelatory of God's grace, the principle serves as a corrective to those frequent instances whereby television manipulates and distorts an authentic interpretation of human experience."[85] Marek is reiterating what we have seen as a principal function of the liturgical homily: naming grace. It is worth recommending that this naming be most vividly done is specific ways, engaging people in sparkling language that readily conjures up visual images. Second, Marek applies the theory of noted media scholar Pierre Babin to a principle of "awakening of interiority." For Babin, television is capable of fragmenting the community, of engaging deep, emotive images for its viewers, and, finally, can cause spectators to lose their attention to an inner life.[86] On the other hand, "preachers who awaken a person's interiority call attention to the very profound, deeply seated movement of a person's being as it responds to the divine and the eternal that speaks to it."[87] Preaching is an opportunity for heart to speak to heart, and that is an interchange that perhaps few people have experienced in the course of their week. The visual rhetoric of television should be used with caution.

Third, Marek says that preaching might better use stories the way television does. "To refigure effectively television narratives in our contemporary culture necessitates that preachers avail themselves of various dynamics of the communication process which television incorporates well into its own story telling capacity."[88] Marek is suggesting here that we pay attention to the way that television shapes its viewers. Consider, for example, the kind of camera work that occurs in police dramas: the quick-paced editing and handheld steadycams lend a feeling of reality to such productions. Are the stories that we use in our homilies equally real?

Fourth, preachers should be aware of modulating image and sound in their preaching. Much of Babin's research indicates that electronic media engage aural sensitivities, which might be used by the preacher. "Through their use of stories, descriptions, biblical narratives, and experiences, preachers typically convey images to their listeners....What might be missing from many preaching events is the recognition of how those images and sounds are disseminated to the listening audience."[89] Certainly, the personality of the preacher as well as the gathered assembly will modulate these aural responses in ways that will build up the experience of the homily and the liturgy. Ultimately, Marek's suggestions require a knowledge and understanding of media culture, while appropriating certain salient features of contemporary communication that work in harmony with preaching the gospel.

The homily can negotiate some of the contemporary, fundamental dynamics of media. It is possible to deploy some of the formal properties of the cinema or television in a homiletic structure in order to approximate the kind of visual language many church-goers experience daily in media consumption. Indeed, homiletic writing can be edited much the same way film is—by montage. Montage is simply cuts or slices pasted together to form some kind of idea or image or story. I am not suggesting a loose series of examples or cut-and-paste technique, but rather homiletic "clips," if you will, that are conjured by images and cohere around a single focus. The fact is that people are being educated through montage technology in advertising, sports editing, and film/television culture. The stories that are told on television and film are moving faster, and people now absorb images much faster than they did even a few decades ago. The MTV generation puts these shots together at a stunning rate. Why not use in the oral form of a homily some of the formal properties that are practiced routinely in secular culture throughout the week? Even an introduction can contain some fast-moving images, sentence fragments that suggest the world of visual montage. Other translations of the visual into a linguistic apparatus are available for discovery and experimentation.

I use as an example here of homiletic montage a weekday homily I wrote on the feast of Saint Bruno. We were in the midst of reading the story of Jonah, and I was looking for a way to incorporate the saint of the day with the scriptural text for a contemporary, young assembly.

> Clearly, it was going to be a difficult crossing, Jonah thought. There was Joppa to contend with, with its ridiculous, smelly sea merchants and scruffy unlikeables. And then, the getaway weekend to Tarshish. He could never have foreseen that storm, the nightmare, turning himself into God's peace offering, after all. Incredible!
>
> And that whale's mouth as a life raft, no less. But at least it was not for nothing; he would be coughed up in Nineveh for a reason. He would model himself after all his prophet-heroes and do the Lord's bidding. Well, anyway, at the very least now he could teach those wicked Assyrians the lessons he had learned in the

uneasy solitude of the leviathan's belly: pay up, you dirty devils, or die!

But while sitting under a fabulous gourd plant, Jonah, son of Amittai, reluctant angel, pale warrior, God's fool, heard the familiar beep of his laptop computer. (Jonah may have been a lot of things, but he always stayed in touch, even on the run).

You've got mail!

Dear Jonah, my son,

Please don't get mad but I don't think you need to be hounding after the Ninevites in quite so vengeful a fashion. They are sorry, in case you failed to notice the sackcloth and ashes, which, I think, are genuine. I have observed that your zeal sometimes turns sour. We have to do something about that, don't you think? Let's remember that you are not the only fish in the sea.

Faithfully yours,

God

Jonah became angry.

He thought he had been called to preach repentance, to tell everyone why they were headed straight for Doomsday. And he remembered, like so many Israelites, those nasty Assyrian Ninevites and what they had done to his nation. All that blood spilled. His friends and neighbors shackled.

He had thought that he had God on his side, but this God evidently preferred to include the undesirables in his camp. Even enemies of the state.

The tables had turned. And that just did not make sense.

He thought about quoting one of the cursing psalms to pass the time while he was brooding.

But right about then:

You've got mail!

Dear Jonah, my brother,

Seventy-times seven. It's a lot, but there you have it. And I have another challenge for you: forgive us our sins, for we too forgive all who do us wrong. Assyrians included.

And about people who wrong you; don't get even.

I've got good news for you. The kingdom of God is coming and it is not yours to give or take away.

Stay tuned.

In our Father's Love,

Jesus of Nazareth

How could this be happening, thought Jonah? He felt himself burn hot. This was not the fate of prophets. All the great messengers got up, they proclaimed, they got the job done. What was he supposed to do now? The shade from the gourd tree was already beginning to fade. Surely this was a world turned upside down. Forgiveness instead of fighting?

Even animals repentant in ashes. He wanted a sign.

And he felt anxiety creeping over him like the tongue of a great fish.

Fortunately, he was distracted:
You've got mail!

Dear Jonah, my confrere,

We know that we ought to see everyone as better than ourselves. That is what Benedict advises those who follow his Rule. There is no reason that humility and prophecy cannot go hand in glove.

I dived into the Grande Chartreuse like you did into the belly of the whale. But my solitude taught me joy. "Rejoice that you have escaped the manifold perils and shipwrecks of this storm-tossed world. Rejoice that you have reached a safe and tranquil anchorage in that inner harbor that many desire to reach and many make efforts to reach yet never attain. Many too, after reaching the goal, have been excluded since it was not given them from above." I hope things go better for you very soon. Pax!

In Christ Jesus,

Saint Bruno (founder of the Carthusians)

By now Jonah was more confused than ever. His little plant had shriveled up and died on him. Had it come to this? Was this the sign? Poor thing.

He looked around him and all he could see in the blazing sun was a kingdom without borders, people without class and division, well—endless endlessness. What next? he thought. Justified sinners at the same table, a thief in heaven, maybe even water to a Samaritan woman? Saints preserve us.

Jonah thought he had reached the razor's edge of his despair when, all in a flash, he realized that the screen on his laptop had suddenly gone black. For although he had become a very conscientious prophet, Jonah still had a few things to learn about communication.

The use of clearly defined segments or dramatic blocks makes this technique interesting. It is important to have a central focus, or a character to link the various segments together, so that the homily is not a patchwork of different impressions. Also, there should be a "plot," a drive toward closure, so that the whole can cohere even as the montage "snapshots" express action.

The use of images and stories go a long way toward bridging the gap between an electronic culture and a print culture. Dan Andraicco says that "preachers have the opportunity to create their own parables to compete with, for example, the Parable of the Beer that Fills Without Bloating. Like Jesus, they can use stories to challenge their listeners instead of giving instant solutions like the thirty-second parables on the TV screen."[90] Andraicco reminds his readers that much of the practical advice that comes from homiletic texts these days suggests word choices that are highly visual, such as the strategies recommended by Kenneth Untener in *Preaching Better.* Thomas H. Troeger says that writing a homily could resemble a movie script. He encourages preachers to create parables and use literary techniques used in films, such as flashbacks.[91] And Peter Malone and Rose Pacatte have written a "movie lectionary" with movie references and descriptions to fit the Sunday readings of the liturgical year.[92]

Using the media for preaching requires creative thinking more than a big budget. If the ambo is without borders, then media deployment begins before the people ever set foot in church. We might recall the explosion of publicity over the release of Mel Gibson's *The Passion of the Christ* in 2004. The cultural background of first-century Palestine, the allegedly anti-Semitic characterizations in the film, and the gospel itself were all big topics, rating a cover story in *Newsweek* magazine (February 16, 2004). There was media buzz, office conversation, school panels, and table talk before the film opened in a staggering two thousand locations on Ash Wednesday. Could we imagine such discussion around the gospel taking place after the Palm Sunday and the reading of the passion narrative? Could any parish hope to involve the parishioners in a biblical workshop with the kind of energy surrounding Gibson's *The Passion of the Christ*? We cannot fail to see that there are preaching tools available that can be used long before the congregation gathers for worship. The computer's websites, emails, interactive Bible study, and local theology chat rooms are useful tools in ministry that prepare the congregation for the Sunday homily and help listeners process it with church leaders and their peers later.[93]

Finally, it is well to remember that if the congregation seems bored, it may not be the result of a liturgy that lacks the proper media deployment or even the result of a conflicted postmodern culture but simply part of human nature. As one person observed:

> The people listen not for profit but for pleasure, like those who take their seats as critics of actors and musicians. When those who preach are obliged to contend one against another, the ability to preach eloquently, which I have just now repudiated, becomes even more an

object of ambition than it is to the sophists. The preacher, then, must be a man of soulful character far exceeding my own mediocrity if he is to be able to check the disorderly and useless whim of the crowd, and if he is to direct their attention to something more beneficial. In this way they will follow him and yield to him, without his being led by their fancies. But this cannot be attained except by two means: indifference to praise, and ability in eloquence.[94]

That was Saint John Chrysostom, writing in A.D. 387!

The Future of Preaching

If we have learned anything from the history and method of preaching, it is that the present circumstances in our own cultural milieu in North America require that the homiletics of the future be oriented toward a listener, be biblical, and "attend to the signs of the times." Liturgical preachers must be aware of the listeners, of the baptized Christian assembly gathered to hear the Word and make it a reality in their lives. Attending to the hearer is not even a question of technique; preaching is much more than an issue of style or rhetoric. A pastoral imperative grounds every homily. The church and every preaching event from the mouth of any preacher exist for the sake of *mission*, an extension of Christ's own divine mission as Son of God to spread the gospel to every nation. The opening lines of the Second Vatican Council's *Pastoral Constitution on the Church in the Modern World (Gaudium et Spes)* underlines the point that the pastoral needs of the people of God are of primary importance for the church:

> The joys and the hopes, the griefs and the anxieties of the men of this age, especially those who are poor or in any way afflicted, those too are the joys and the hopes, the griefs and anxieties of the followers of Christ. Indeed, nothing genuinely human fails to raise an echo in their hearts....United in Christ, they are led to the Holy Spirit in their journey to the kingdom of their Father and they have welcomed the news of salvation

which is meant for every man. That is why this community realizes that it is truly and intimately linked with mankind and its history. (no. 1)

The preacher's text, then, does not exist as an entity in and of itself; it comes into being in Christian preaching when it is addressed in faith to people of good will. Liturgical preaching exists for the sake of the baptized, to bring them into fuller and conscious participation in their faith and the community in which they live. To ignore the congregation—its joys and hopes, griefs and sorrows—is not only bad, ineffective preaching but contrary to the mission of the church in the modern world.

Preaching must also be biblical. The Word of God must make a difference in the day-to-day lives of those who hear it. Preaching biblically means that the sacred scriptures of our tradition—both the Hebrew scriptures and the New Testament—become the lens for a new world view, not only for the sake of personal conversion, but to enable the Church to confront issues of injustice and violence. Here again, it is not a question of style or even content as much as it is a shift in our fundamental outlook as we attend to God's activity in the world. God's own speech brought creation into existence, and so we are inevitably bound to the Word. As Judith sings her song of praise to the Lord, she says:

> for you spoke, and they were made.
> You sent forth your spirit, and it formed them;
> there is none that can resist your word. (Jdt 16:14)

As the noted biblical scholar, Donald Senior, CP, remarked recently in the Carl J. Peter Lecture at the North American College:

To take up the task of preaching is to step into a role as ancient as God's revelation and as powerful as the hurricane of faith that swept through the history of Israel and created the early Church. If the Bible teaches us nothing else about the ministry of preaching, it should teach us reverence and awe for a ministry so filled with potential power.[95]

Finally, we know that preaching must be in dialogue with contemporary culture. That dialectic may take many different forms. Indeed, a conversation with the world in which we live may give rise for a need for different kinds of preaching. We know that liturgical preaching has already been shaped around the way in which the congregation makes sense of meaning—visually, electronically, intuitively—but what of the other kinds of preaching that might effectively evangelize the world? It is axiomatic now to claim that many in the church are "under-catechized." The need for catechetical preaching by qualified men and women has never been more urgent than it is today. It is also possible to see old forms of preaching in a different light. Professor Richard R. Gaillardetz has recently argued for a new(er) apologetics. Surely, this new apologetics can take many forms: writing, teaching…and preaching. Preaching in this model gives the church an arm for evangelization in multiple places that may not be appropriate for liturgical preaching, since the task of apologetics is different from preaching in the eucharistic assembly. With a preaching that is comfortable in a multiple of environments, apologetics can get immediately to the nitty-gritty of church teaching, answering questions, raising issues, responding to problems in contemporary culture. This new(er) apologetics is not antagonistic or antithetical to the world in which we live but rather ecumenical and open to dialogue. Preachers in this mode allow the teaching of Catholic faith and its underlying concepts to invigorate and transform the difficult situation that humanity faces. The newer kind of apologetics recognizes that we are living in a graced world, mediated by God in a pluralistic environment.

> What would such a culturally engaged apologetics look like in North America today? It would have to begin with a discerning reflection on the diverse expressions of the human spirit found in modern culture. It would have to engage human culture as the setting in which humanity's glory and banality, sin and grace, despair and hope are all given expression. The effective apologist would look to political events, the visual arts, music, fiction, theater and film with an expectation that they will encounter there

the drama of human salvation and, for those with eyes to
see, intimations of the divine.[96]

The preaching of the future is a turn toward the hearer, the
Word and, finally, the cultural milieu in which these are discov-
ered. Ultimately, the preaching of the twenty-first century returns
to one of the most ancient "languages" of all: narrative. It was narrative that shaped the first listeners as they walked on this lonely
planet; it was narrative that gave shape to God's almighty Word,
made it visible, and recalls the sacred story and God's wonders
woven throughout that great story. And it is narrative that continues to animate the culture we live in—a world of stories, of
human triumphs and tragedies, of God's faithful activity among
God's people. Preaching that recognizes the power of narrative
and its origins as an instrument for sowing the Word will never
fail to tell the tale of God's wonderful works in Christ as they continue to be fulfilled in our hearing.

Notes

1. Mark I. Pinsky, *The Gospel According to the Simpsons: The Spiritual Life of the World's Most Animated Family* (Louisville, KY: Westminster John Knox, 2001), 74–75.

2. See, for example, John Fisk, *Introduction to Communication Studies* (New York: Routledge, 1990), 7–38.

3. Ibid., 31–32.

4. Graham Johnston, *Preaching to a Postmodern World* (Grand Rapids, MI: Baker Books, 2001), 27.

5. One of the most impressive studies on postmodernism remains Fredric Jameson, *Postmodernism, or, The Cultural Logic of Late Capitalism* (Durham, NC: Duke Univ. Press, 1991). Jameson covers postmodern theory from a neo-Marxist perspective.

6. Robert Venturi, Stephen Izenour, and Denise Scott Brown, *Learning from Las Vegas*, rev. ed. (Cambridge: MIT Press, 1977).

7. David Harvey, *The Condition of Postmodernity* (Cambridge, UK: Blackwell, 1989), 9.

8. Kenneth Untener, *Preaching Better* (Mahwah, NJ: Paulist Press, 1999), 42.

9. Jameson, *Postmodernism*, 9. Jameson has a particular contrast in mind: a pair of shoes painted by Van Gogh ("A Pair of Boots") and another done by Andy Warhol ("Diamond Dust Shoes").

10. Ibid., 48.

11. Jean-François Lyotard, *The Postmodern Condition: A Report on Knowledge*, trans. Geoff Bennington and Brian Massumi (Minneapolis: Univ. of Minnesota Press, 1989). Lyotard's work has become a classic in the study of postmodernism.

12. Harvey, *The Condition of Postmodernity*, 43.

13. See, for example, the essays in *The Cambridge Companion to Postmodern Theology*, ed. Kevin J. Vanhoozer (Cambridge: Cambridge Univ. Press, 2003), and in *Postmodern Interpretations of the Bible: A Reader*, ed. A. K. M. Adam, (St. Louis: Chalice Press, 2001).

14. John McClure, *Other-wise Preaching: A Postmodern Ethics for Homiletics* (St. Louis: Chalice Press, 2001), 13.

15. Ibid., 15.

16. Ibid., 16.

17. Ibid., 16–17. McClure is quoting Terry Eagleton, *Literary Theory: An Introduction* (Oxford: Oxford Univ. Press, 1982), 146.

18. See, for instance, Jacques Derrida, "Structure, Sign, and Play in the Discourse of the Human Sciences," in *Contemporary Literary Criticism:*

Literary and Cultural Studies, 2nd ed., ed. Robert Con Davis and Robert Schleifer (New York: Longman, 1989), 230–48. Derrida writes, for instance, "The center is not the center....If this is so, the whole history of the concept of structure...must be thought of as a series of substitutions of center for center, as a linked chain of determinations of the center" (231).

19. See Jacques Derrida, *Of Grammatology* (Baltimore: The Johns Hopkins Univ. Press, 1967).

20. McClure, *Other-wise Preaching*, 21.

21. Ibid., 23.

22. Ibid., 25.

23. Ibid., 32.

24. Ibid., 43–44.

25. Ibid., 51.

26. Ibid., 55. See Sandra Harding, "Subjectivity, Experience, and Knowledge: An Epistemology from/for Rainbow Coalition Politics," in *Who Can Speak: Authority and Critical Identity*, ed. Judith Roof and Robyn Weigman (Urbana: Univ. of Illinois Press, 1995) 128.

27. McClure, *Other-wise Preaching*, 63.

28. John S. McClure, *The Round-Table Pulpit: Where Leadership and Preaching Meet* (Nashville, TN: Abingdon Press, 1995).

29. Ibid., 4.

30. McClure, *Other-wise Preaching*, 62.

31. McClure, *Round-Table Pulpit*, 57.

32. McClure, *Other-wise Preaching*, 133–34.

33. Craig A. Loscalzo, *Apologetic Preaching: Proclaiming Christ to a Postmodern World* (Downers Grove, IL: InterVarsity Press, 2000). The author claims that he is interested in proclaiming confidence in a time of doubt, yet he clearly seems to be backing into a kind of modernist mode of thinking. At the same time, though, McClure has no suggestions for churches—Roman Catholic, Orthodox, and some Reformed traditions— whose teaching authority remains in contradistinction to the plurality that postmodernism offers. McClure's solution may seem like an alternative for a pluralistic age, but it may wind up something like the Tower of Babel. On the other hand, Graham Johnston, in *Preaching to a Postmodern World*, writes that dogmatism is the "postmodern kiss of death" and that one way of overcoming the obstacles of postmodernism is creating a relational network for the listener. Here, of course, Johnston is closer to Rose and McClure and the contextual theology advocated by Tisdale.

34. Lucy Atkinson Rose, *Sharing the Word: Preaching in the Roundtable Church* (Louisville, KY: Westminster John Knox, 1997), 90.

35. Ibid.

36. John McClure, *The Four Codes of Preaching* (Minneapolis: Fortress Press, 1991), 8. McClure credits Roland Barthes with directly influencing this work.

37. Ronald J. Allen, ed., *Patterns of Preaching* (St. Louis: Chalice Press, 1998), 245.

38. Ibid., 246.

39. Ibid., 247.

40. Ibid., 246.

41. *FIYH*, 7.

42. Rose, *Sharing the Word*, 90.

43. Elisabeth Schüssler Fiorenza, *In Memory of Her: A Feminist Theological Reconstruction of Christian Origins* (New York: Crossroad, 1983), 19.

44. Hélène Cixous, "The Laugh of the Medusa," in *Feminist Literary Theory: A Reader*, ed. Mary Eagleton (Oxford: Blackwell, 1986), 225. For an intelligent overview of feminist theory, see Toril Moi, *Sexual/Textual Politics: Feminist Literary Theory* (London: Methuen, 1985; repr. Routledge, 2002).

45. See, for instance, Elisabeth Schüssler Fiorenza, *Bread Not Stone: The Challenge of Feminist Biblical Interpretation* (New York: Beacon Press, 1986); and her edited volume *Searching the Scripture: A Feminist Introduction* (New York: Crossroad, 1997). See also Phyllis Trible, *God and the Rhetoric of Sexuality* (Philadelphia: Fortress Press, 1978); idem, *Texts of Terror: Feminist-Literary Reading of Biblical Narratives* (Minneapolis: Fortress Press, 2003); and Carol Newsom and Sharon Ringe, eds., *Woman's Bible Commentary* (Louisville, KY: Westminster John Knox, 1998).

46. Christine M. Smith, *Weaving the Sermon: Preaching in a Feminist Perspective* (Louisville, KY: Westminster John Knox, 1989), 92.

47. Fred B. Craddock, *Preaching* (Nashville, TN: Abingdon Press, 1985), 24.

48. Smith, *Weaving the Sermon*, 44.

49. Ibid., 92.

50. L. Susan Bond, *Trouble with Jesus: Women, Christology, and Preaching* (St. Louis: Chalice Press, 2001).

51. Smith, *Weaving the Sermon*, 93.

52. Ibid.

53. Ibid., 94.

54. Ibid.

55. Ibid., 97. A useful tool along these lines is Normand Bonneau's history of the Lectionary *The Sunday Lectionary: Ritual, Word, Paschal Shape* (Collegeville, MN: Liturgical Press, 1998).

56. Smith, *Weaving the Sermon*, 98.

57. For an overview of how the Lectionary has been used historically, see Bonneau, *The Sunday Lectionary.*

58. See, for instance, Sandra Gilbert and Susan Gubar, *The Madwoman in the Attic: the Woman Writer and the Nineteenth Century Literary Imagination*, 2nd ed. (New Haven, CT: Yale Univ. Press, 2000).

59. William Kuhns, *The Electronic Gospel* (New York: Herder and Herder, 1969), 165.

60. Quentin J. Schultze, *Christianity and the Mass Media in America: Toward a Democratic Accommodation* (East Lansing: Michigan State Univ. Press, 2003), 60.

61. Ibid., 11.

62. Ibid. Catholic programming may not be as simplistic as Schultze suggests, especially given the variety of programming available. EWTN more than likely functions on a much more subtle level of different *discourses*, attracting mostly conservative viewers, who readily recognize the ideology and signs embedded in traditional religious language. See Alf Linderman, "Making Sense of Religion in Television," in *Rethinking Media, Religion and Culture*, ed. Stewart M. Hoover and Knut Lundby (Thousand Oaks, CA: Sage, 1997), 263–82.

63. Quentin J. Schultze, *Televangelism and American Culture: The Business of Popular Religion* (Grand Rapids, MI: Baker Books, 1991).

64. Ibid., 112.

65. Ibid., 113. *America* took a particular interest in the discussion around the defense of freedom of the airways from 1920 to 1970. "The journal's support of freedom of the airways was grounded philosophically in the idea that only a free market could protect all voices and ultimately lead to reason on the airways" (Schultze, *Christianity and the Mass Media in America*, 115).

66. Ibid., 130.

67. John Paul II, *The Church in America: Post-Synodal Apostolic Exhortation* (Boston: Pauline Books, 1999), 115.

68. See Mark D. Hulsether, "Like a Sermon: Popular Religion in Madonna Videos," in *Religion and Popular Culture in America*, ed. Bruce David Forbes and Jeffrey H. Mahn (Berkeley and Los Angeles: Univ. of California Press, 2000), 77–100.

69. Jim Trammell, quoted in Pinsky, *The Gospel According to the Simpsons*, 60.

70. Conrad Ostwalt, *Secular Steeples: Popular Culture and the Religious Imagination* (Harrisburg, PA: Trinity Press International, 2003), 52.

71. Edward Bellamy, *Looking Backward: 2000–1887* (New York: Signet, 2000; orig. pub. in 1888), quoted in R. Laurence Moore, *Selling God: American Religion in the Marketplace of Culture* (New York: Oxford Univ. Press, 1994), 204. A survey in the 1930s indicated that Bellamy's book was one of the most influential of the nineteenth century.

72. Ostwalt, *Secular Steeples*, 53.

73. See Walter Benjamin, "The Work of Art in the Age of Mechanical Reproduction," in *Illuminations*, trans. Harry Zohn, ed. Hannah Arendt (New York: Schocken, 1985), 217–52.

74. Neil Postman, *Amusing Ourselves to Death* (New York: Penguin, 1985), 72–73.

75. Ostwalt, *Secular Steeples*, 62.

76. Ibid., 62–63.

77. Ibid., 63.

78. Robert Waznak, SS, "Preaching the Gospel in a Video Culture,," in Media, *Culture and Catholicism*, ed. Paul A. Soukup, SJ (Kansas City, Mo.: Sheed and Ward, 1996), 142.

79. Lee Wilson and Jason Moore, *Digital Storytellers: The Art of Communicating the Gospel in Worship* (Nashville, TN: Abingdon Press, 2002).

80. Bernard R. Bonnot, Thomas Boomershine, and Brian Sweeney, "A Liturgical via Media," *America* 185/14 (November 5, 2001), 13–14.

81. Ibid., 15.

82. Schultze, *Christianity and the Mass Media in America*, 130–31. His findings are that the Catholic Church is clearly ambivalent about new media. As *The Catholic World* said in the 1930s: "Radio is a miracle but also a menace.…The air seems to be given over to astrologists and psychologists, hillbillies and gypsies; to cheap comedy, stupid, pointless, dramatic sketches." In addition to historical misreadings, Bonnot and company too easily collapse the passive experience of church (Baroque) painting and the high entertainment qualities inherent in digital imaging and sound reproduction. Finally, the case for "appropriation" does not deal with the implications of secularization of the sacred and the questions raised by Ostwalt and others about liturgy and preaching losing its prophetic character while absorbing contemporary forms of communication.

83. See Colleen Carroll, *The New Faithful: Why Young Adults Are Embracing Christian Orthodoxy* (Chicago: Loyola Univ. Press, 2002).

84. John Paul II, *The Church in America*, 115.

85. Ray John Marek, OMI, "Turning on the Homily: Preaching in a Television-Saturated Culture," *Offerings* 1/1 (2002), 14–15.

86. Ibid., 16–17. See Pierre Babin, OMI, and Mercedes Iannone, *The New Era in Religious Communication* (Minneapolis: Fortress Press, 1991).

87. Marek, "Turning on the Homily," 16.

88. Ibid., 19.

89. Ibid., 20.

90. Dan Andriacco, *Screen Saved: Peril and Promise of Media in Ministry* (Cincinnati: St. Anthony Messenger, 2000).

91. Thomas Troeger, *Ten Strategies for Preaching in a Multimedia Culture* (Nashville, TN: Abingdon Press, 1996).

92. Peter Malone, MSC, with Rose Pacatte, FSPA, *Lights, Camera...Faith!: A Movie Lover's Guide to Scripture*, 3 vols. (A, B, C cycles) (New York: Pauline Books, 2001–3).

93. See, for instance, Angela Ann Zukowski, MHSH, and Pierre Babin, OMI, *The Gospel in Cyberspace: Nurturing Faith in the Internet Age* (Chicago: Loyola Univ. Press, 2002).

94. John Chrysostom, *The Priesthood*, trans. W. A Jurgens (New York: Macmillan, 1955), 81–82.

95. Donald Senior, CP, "What the Bible Can Teach the Preacher: The Art of a Catholic Interpretation of Scripture," Carl J. Peter Lecture, The North American College, January 7, 2004.

96. Richard R. Gaillardetz, "Do We Need a New(er) Apologetics?" *America* 190/3 (February 2, 2004), 33.

BIBLIOGRAPHY

Abbott, William, SJ, ed. *The Documents of Vatican II*. New Brunswick: New Century Press, 1966.

Adam, A. K. M., ed. *Postmodern Interpretations of the Bible: A Reader*. St. Louis: Chalice Press, 2001.

Alan of Lille. *The Art of Preaching*. Trans. and intro. Gillian R. Evans, Cistercian Studies Series 23. Kalamazoo: Cistercian Publications, 1981.

Allen, Ronald J., ed. *Patterns of Preaching*. St. Louis: Chalice Press, 1998.

Amos, Thomas L., Eugene A. Green, and Beverly Mayne Kienzle, eds. *De Ore Domini: Preacher and Word in the Middle Ages*. Kalamazoo: Western Michigan Univ. Press, 1989.

Andriacco, Dan. *Screen Saved: Peril and Promise of Media in Ministry*. Cincinnati: St. Anthony Messenger Press, 2000.

Aristotle. *Poetics*. Translated by Leon Golden. Tallahassee, FL: Univ. Presses of Florida, 1981.

———. *Rhetoric I: A Commentary*. Annotated by William M. A. Grimaldi. New York: Fordham Univ. Press, 1979.

Ascheman, Thomas J., SVD. "The Conversion of the Missionary: An Interpretation of the Guadalupan Narrative." PhD diss., Catholic University of America, 1991.

Augustine. *Teaching Christianity: De Doctrina Christiana*. Edited by Edmund Hill and John E. Rotelle. New York: New City Press, 1996.

———. *On Christian Doctrine*. Translated by D. W. Robertson Jr. Upper Saddle River, NJ: Prentice Hall, 1953.

Babin, Pierre, OMI, and Mercedes Iannone. *The New Era in Religious Communication*. Minneapolis: Fortress Press, 1991.

Barth, Karl. *Homiletics*. Translated by Geoffrey W. Bromiley and Donald E. Daniels. Louisville, KY: Westminster John Knox, 1991. Originally published in 1966.

Bausch, William J. *Story Telling the Word: Homilies and How to Write Them*. Mystic, CT: XXIII, 1996.

Bellamy, Edward. *Looking Backward: 2000-1887*. New York: Signet, 2000. Originally published in 1888.

Benjamin, Walter, "The Work of Art in the Age of Mechanical Reproduction." In *Illuminations*, translated by Harry Zohn, edited by Hannah Arendt. New York: Schocken, 1985.

Bevans, Stephen. *Models of Contextual Theology*. Maryknoll, NY: Orbis Books, 1992.

Bhabha, Homi K. "Cultural Diversity and Cultural Differences." In *The Post-Colonial Studies Reader*. Edited by Bill Ashcroft, Gareth Griffiths, and Helen Tiffin. New York: Routledge, 1994, pp. 206–9.

Bond, Susan L. *Trouble with Jesus: Women, Christology, and Preaching*. St. Louis: Chalice Press, 2001.

Bonneau, Normand. *The Sunday Lectionary: Ritual, Word, Paschal Shape*. Collegeville, MN: Liturgical Press, 1998.

Bonnot, Bernard R., Thomas Boomershine, and Brian Sweeney. "A Liturgical via Media." *America* 185/14 (November 5, 2001): 12-15.

Booth, Wayne C. *The Rhetoric of Fiction*. Rev. ed. Chicago: Univ. of Chicago Press, 1983. Originally published in 1961.

Brilioth, Yngve. *A Brief History of Preaching*. Translated by K. E. Mattson. Philadelphia: Fortress Press, 1965.

Broadus, John A. *A Treatise on the Preparation and Delivery of Sermons*. 4th ed. Revised and edited by Vernon L. Stanfield. San Francisco: HarperCollins, 1979. Originally published in 1870.

Brueggemann, Walter. *Cadences of Home: Preaching Among Exiles*. Louisville, KY: Westminster John Knox, 1997.

Bugnini, Annibale. *The Reform of the Liturgy, 1948-1975*. Collegeville, MN: Liturgical Press, 1990.

Burghardt, SJ, Walter. *Let Justice Roll Down like Waters: Biblical Justice Homilies Throughout the Year*. New York: Paulist Press, 1997.

Burke, John, OP, and Thomas P. Doyle, OP. *The Homilist's Guide to Scripture, Theology, and Canon Law*. New York: Pueblo, 1986.

Buttrick, David. *Speaking Parables: A Homiletic Guide*. Louisville, KY: Westminster John Knox, 2000.

———. David. *Preaching the New and the Now*. Louisville, KY: Westminster John Knox, 1998.

———. *A Captive Voice: The Liberation of Preaching*. Louisville, KY: Westminster John Knox, 1994.

———. *Homiletic: Moves and Structures*. Philadelphia: Fortress Press, 1987.

Campbell, T. A. *The Religion of the Heart*. Eugene, OR: Wipf and Stock, 2000.

Carroll, Colleen. *The New Faithful: Why Young Adults Are Embracing Christian Orthodoxy*. Chicago: Loyola Univ. Press, 2002.

Carroll, Thomas K. *Preaching the Word*. Wilmington, DE: Michael Glazier, 1984.

Casarella, Peter, and Paul Gomez, SDS. *El Cuerpo de Cristo: The Hispanic Presence in the U.S. Catholic Church*. New York: Crossroad, 1998.

Casey, Michael, OCSO. *Sacred Reading*. Ligouri, MO: Triumph Books, 1996.

Chávez, Denise. "The Closet." In *Growing Up Latino: Memoirs and Stories*, ed. Ilan Stavans and Harold Augenbraum, 85-100. Boston: Houghton Mifflin, 1993.

Childers, Jana. *Performing the Word: Preaching as Theater*. Nashville, TN: Abingdon Press, 1998.

Chevalier, Tracy. *The Girl with the Pearl Earring*. New York: Plume Books, 2001.

Chrysostom, John. *The Priesthood*. Trans. W. A. Jurgens. New York: Macmillan, 1955.

Clements, Keith W. *Friedrich Schleiermacher: Pioneer of Modern Theology*. Philadelphia: Fortress Press, 1991.

Code of Canon Law: Latin-English Edition. Washington, DC: Canon Law Society of America, 1983.

Connors, Joseph M., SVD. "Catholic Homiletic Theory in Historical Perspective." Ph.D. diss. Northwestern Univ., 1962; Ann Arbor, MI: UMI.

Cox, James W., ed. *Best Sermons*, vol. *1*. San Francisco: Harper & Row, 1988.

Craddock, Fred B. *As One Without Authority*. 4th ed. St. Louis: Chalice Press, 2001. Originally published in 1971.

———. *The Cherry Log Sermons*. Louisville, KY: Westminster John Knox, 2001.

———. *Luke*. Louisville, KY: Westminster John Knox, 1990.

———. *Preaching*. Nashville, TN: Abingdon Press, 1985.

———. *Overhearing the Gospel*. Nashville, TN: Abingdon Press, 1978.

Crawford, Evans E., and Thomas Troeger. *The Hum: Call and Response in African American Preaching*. Nashville, TN: Abingdon Press, 1995.

Davis, Cyprian, OSB. *The History of Black Catholics in the United States*. New York: Crossroad, 1990.

Davis, H. Grady. *Design for Preaching*. Philadelphia: Fortress Press, 1958.

Davis, Kenneth G., OFMConv, and Jorge L. Presmanes, eds. *Preaching and Culture in Latino Congregations*. Chicago: Liturgy Training Publications, 2000.

Davis, Kenneth, OFMConv, Eduardo C. Fernández, and Verónica Méndez. *United States Hispanic Catholics: Trends and Works, 1990–2000*. Scranton, PA: Univ. of Scranton Press, 2002.

Davis, Robert Con, and Robert Schleifer, eds. *Contemporary Literary Criticism: Literary and Cultural Studies*. 2nd ed. New York: Longman, 1989.

DeBona, Guerric, OSB. "Preaching for the Plot." *New Theology Review* 14/1 (February 2001): 14-22.

Deck, Allan Figueroa, SJ. *The Second Wave: Hispanic Ministry and the Evangelization of Cultures*. New York: Paulist Press, 1989.

DeLeers, Stephen Vincent. "The Place of Preaching in the Ministry and Life of Priests." In *The Theology of Priesthood*, edited by Donald J. Goergen and Ann Carido, 87-103. Collegeville, MN: Liturgical Press, 2000.

Della Torre, L. *"Homilía."* In *Nuevo Diccionario de Liturgia*. 3rd edicion. Ed. D. Sartore, A.M. Triacca, and J.M. Canals. Madrid: San Pablo, 1987, 1015-1038.

Derrida, Jacques. *Of Grammatology*. Baltimore: The Johns Hopkins Univ. Press, 1967.

Dewey, John, and Arthur F. Bentley. *Knowing and the Known*. Westport, CT: Greenwood Press, 1976. Originally published in 1949.

Diamant, Anita. *The Red Tent*. New York: Picador, 1998.

Dodd, C. H. *Apostolic Preaching and Its Developments: Three Lectures with an Appendix on Eschatology and History*. Grand Rapids, MI: Baker Books, 1982.

Ebeling, Gerhard. *Word and Faith*. Trans. James W. Leitch. Philadelphia: Fortress Press, 1963.

Edwards, O. C., Jr. *Elements of Homiletic: A Method for Preparing to Preach*. New York: Pueblo, 1982.

Eagleton, Mary, ed. *Feminist Literary Theory: A Reader*. Oxford: Blackwell, 1986.

Elizondo, Virgilio P. *Christianity and Culture: An Introduction to Pastoral Theology and Ministry for the Bicultural Community*. Huntington, IN: Our Sunday Visitor, 1975.

Elliot, Mark Barger. *Creative Styles of Preaching*. Louisville, KY: Westminster John Knox, 2000.

Eslinger, Richard L. *The Web of Preaching*. Nashville, TN: Abingdon Press, 2002.

———. *A New Hearing*. Nashville, TN: Abingdon Press, 1987.

Fairbanks, Sarah Ann. "Displaced Persons: Lay Liturgical Preachers at the Eucharist." *Worship* 77/5 (September 2003): 439-57.

Farris, Stephen. *Preaching That Matters: The Bible in Our Lives.* Louisville, KY: Westminster John Knox, 1998.

Fiorenza, Elizabeth Schüssler. *Bread Not Stone: The Challenge of Feminist Biblical Interpretation.* New York: Beacon Press, 1986.

———. *In Memory of Her: A Feminist Theological Reconstruction of Christian Origins.* New York: Crossroad, 1983.

Fisk, John. *Introduction to Communication Studies.* New York: Routledge, 1990.

Foley, Edward, OFMCap. "The Homily Beyond Scripture: *Fulfilled in Your Hearing Revisited.*" Worship 43/4 (July 1999): 352-58.

Foley, Nadine, OP, ed. *Preaching and the Non-Ordained.* Collegeville, MN: Liturgical Press, 1983.

Forbes, Bruce David, and Jeffrey H. Mahn, eds. *Religion and Popular Culture in America.* Berkeley and Los Angeles: Univ. of California Press, 2000.

Frei, Hans. *The Eclipse of Biblical Narrative.* New Haven, CT: Yale Univ. Press, 1980.

Funk, Virgil C. "The Liturgical Movement." In *The New Dictionary of Sacramental Worship,* ed. Peter Fink, 695-715. Collegeville, MN: Liturgical Press, 2000.

Gaillardetz, Richard R. "Do We Need a New(er) Apoplogetics?" *America* 190/3 (February 2, 2004): 26-33.

Goizueta, Roberto S. *Caminemos Con Jesús: Toward a Hispanic/Latino Theology of Accompaniment.* Maryknoll, NY: Orbis Books, 1995.

Goldberg, Natalie. *Writing Down the Bones.* Boston: Shambhala, 1986.

González, Justo L., ed. *Alabadle! Hispanic Christian Worship.* Nashville, TN: Abingdon Press, 1996.

———. *Santa Biblia: The Bible through Hispanic Eyes.* Nashville, TN: Abingdon Press, 1996.

Grasso, Dominic, SJ. *Proclaiming God's Message: A Study in the Theology of Preaching.* Notre Dame, IN: Univ. of Notre Dame Press, 1965.

Green, Garrett. *Imagining God: Theology and the Religious Imagination.* San Francisco: Harper & Row, 1989.

Greidanus, Sidney. *The Modern Preacher and the Ancient Text: Interpreting and Preaching Biblical Literature.* Grand Rapids, MI: Eerdmans, 1988.

Grossberg, Lawrence, Cary Nelson, and Paula Treichler, eds. *Cultural Studies.* New York: Routledge, 1992.

Harding, Sandra. "Subjectivity, Experience, and Knowledge: An Epistemology from/for Rainbow Coalition Politics." In *Who Can*

Speak: Authority and Critical Identity, edited by Judith Roof and Robyn Weigman. Urbana: Univ. of Illinois Press, 1995.

Harvey, David. *The Condition of Postmodernity.* Cambridge, UK: Blackwell, 1989.

Hilkert, Mary Catherine. *Naming Grace: Preaching and the Sacramental Imagination.* New York: Continuum, 1997.

Hitz, Paul, CSsR. *To Preach the Gospel.* Translated by Rosemary Sheed. New York: Sheed and Ward, 1963.

Hoover, Stewart M., and Knut Lundby. *Rethinking Media, Religion and Culture.* Thousand Oaks: Sage, 1997.

Huels, John M. "Canonical Observations on *Redemptionis Sacramentum.*" *Worship* 78/5 (September 2004): 404-420.

Iser, Wolfgang. *The Act of Reading: A Theory of Aesthetic Response.* Baltimore: Johns Hopkins Univ. Press, 1980.

Jameson, Fredrick. *Postmodernism, or, The Cultural Logic of Late Capitalism.* Durham, NC: Duke Univ. Press, 1991.

Janowiak, Paul. *The Holy Preaching: The Sacramentality of the Word in the Liturgical Assembly.* Collegeville, MN: Liturgical Press, 2000.

Jensen, Richard A. *Thinking in Story.* Lima, OH: CSS Press, 1993.

Jeter, Joseph R., Jr., and Ronald J. Allen. *One Gospel, Many Ears: Preaching for Different Listeners in the Congregation.* St.Louis: Chalice Press, 2002.

John Paul II. *The Church in America: Post-Synodal Apostolic Exhortation.* Boston: Pauline Books, 1999.

———. *Pastores Dabo Vobis.* Washington, DC: USCCB, 1992.

Johnson, Graham. *Preaching to a Postmodern World.* Grand Rapids, MI: Baker Books, 2001.

Kennedy, George A. *Classical Rhetoric and Its Christian and Secular Tradition from Ancient to Modern Times.* Chapel Hill: Univ. of North Carolina Press, 1980.

Kuhns, William. *The Electronic Gospel.* New York: Herder and Herder, 1969.

LaRue, Cleophus James. *The Heart of Black Preaching.* Louisville, KY: Westminster John Knox, 1999.

Lischer, Richard, ed. *The Company of Preachers: Wisdom on Preaching, Augustine to the Present.* Grand Rapids, MI: Eerdmans, 2002.

Long, Thomas. "Edmund Steimle and the Shape of Contemporary Homiletics." *The Princeton Seminary Bulletin* 11(1990): 253–69.

Long, Thomas G. *The Witness of Preaching.* Louisville, KY: Westminster John Knox, 1990.

————. *Preaching and the Literary Forms of the Bible*. Philadelphia: Fortress Press, 1989.

Loscalzo, Craig A. *Apologetic Preaching: Proclaiming Christ to a Postmodern World*. Downers Grove, IL: InterVarsity Press, 2000.

Lowry, Eugene L. *Doing Time in the Pulpit: The Relationship Between Narrative and Preaching*. Nashville, TN: Abingdon Press, 1985.

————. *How to Preach a Parable*. Nashville, TN: Abingdon Press, 1989.

————. *The Homiletic Plot*. Rev. ed. Louisville, KY: Westminster John Knox, 2001. Originally published in 1980.

Lyotard, Jean-François. *The Postmodern Condition: A Report on Knowledge*. Translated by Geoff Bennington and Brian Massumi. Minneapolis: University of Minnesota Press, 1989.

Malone, Peter, MSC, and Rose Pacatte, FSPA. *Lights, Camera...Faith! A Movie Lover's Guide to Scripture*. 3 vols. (A, B, and C cycles). New York: Pauline Books, 2001-3.

Marek, Ray John, OMI. "Turning on the Homily: Preaching in a Television-Saturated Culture." *Offerings* 1/1 (2002): 13-22.

Maynard-Reid, Pedrito U. *Diverse Worship: African-American, Caribbean and Hispanic Perspectives*. Downers Grove, IL: InterVarsity Press, 2000.

McCullough, Peter E. *Sermons at Court: Politics and Religion in Elizabethan and Jacobean Preaching*. Cambridge, UK: Cambridge Univ. Press, 1998.

McClure, John. *Other-wise Preaching: A Postmodern Ethics for Homiletics*. St Louis: Chalice Press, 2001.

————. *The Round-Table Pulpit*. Nashville, TN: Abingdon Press, 1995.

————. *The Four Codes of Preaching*. Minneapolis: Fortress Press, 1991.

Melloh, John Allyn, SM. "On the Vocation of the Preacher." In *Ars Liturgiae: Worship, Aesthetics and Praxis*, edited by Claire V. Johnson, 161-90. Chicago: Liturgy Training Publications, 2003.

Meyers, Robin R. *With Ears to Hear: Preaching as Self-Persuasion*. Cleveland: Pilgrim Press, 1993.

Mitchell, Henry. *Celebration and Experience in Preaching*. Nashville, TN: Abingdon Press, 1990.

————. *Black Preaching: The Recovery of a Powerful Art*. San Francisco: Harper & Row, 1979; Nashville, TN: Abingdon Press, 1990. (Originally published in 1970 by Lippincott.)

Moi, Toril. *Sexual/Textual Politics: Feminist Literary Theory*. London: Methuen, 1985.

Moore, R. Laurence. *Selling God: American Religion in the Marketplace of Culture*. New York: Oxford Univ. Press, 1994.

Moyd, Olin P. *The Sacred Art: Preaching and Theology in the African-American Tradition.* Valley Forge, PA: Judson Press, 1995.

Naremore, James, and Patrick Brantlinger, eds., *Modernity and Mass Culture.* Bloomington: Indiana Univ. Press, 1991.

National Council of Catholic Bishops (NCCB). *Sunday Celebration in the Absence of a Priest.* Washington, DC: USCCB, 1996.

————. *Fulfilled in Your Hearing.* Washington, DC: USCC, 1982.

Nieman, James R., and Thomas G. Rogers. *Preaching to Every Pew: Cross-Cultural Strategies.* Minneapolis: Fortress Press, 2001.

O'Day, Gail R., and Thomas G. Long, eds. *Listening to the Word: Studies in Honor of Fred B. Craddock.* Nashville, TN: Abingdon Press, 1993.

Old, Hughes Oliphant. *The Reading and Preaching of the Scriptures in the Worship of the Christian Church.* 5 vols. Grand Rapids, MI: Eerdmans, 1998-2004.

Organ, Deborah. "Immigrants and Inculturation." *America* 189/15 (November 10, 2003): 12-14.

Ostwalt, Conrad. *Secular Steeples: Popular Culture and the Religious Imagination.* Harrisburg, PA: Trinity Press International, 2003.

Parachini, Patricia A. *Lay Preaching: State of the Question.* Collegeville, MN: Liturgical Press, 1999.

Parker, Dorothy. "A Telephone Call." In *Points of View: An Anthology of Short Stories.* Edited by James Moffett and Kenneth R. McElheny. New York: Penguin, 1985, pp. 15–20.

Pinsky, Mark I. *The Gospel According to the Simpsons: The Spiritual Life of the World's Most Animated Family.* Louisville, KY: Westminster John Knox, 2001.

Pontifical Council for Culture. *Toward a Pastoral Approach to Culture.* Boston: Pauline Books, 1999.

Postman, Neil. *Amusing Ourselves to Death.* New York: Penguin, 1985.

Power, David, OMI. *"The Word of the Lord": Liturgy's Use of Scripture.* Maryknoll, NY: Orbis Books, 2001.

Rahner, Karl, SJ, ed. *The Renewal of Preaching: Theory and Practice.* New York: Paulist Press, 1968.

Resner, Andre, Jr. *Preacher and Cross: Person and Message in Theology and Rhetoric.* Grand Rapids, MI: Eerdmans, 1999.

Ricoeur, Paul. *Figuring the Sacred: Religion, Narrative, and Imagination.* Translated by David Pellauer. Edited by Mark I. Wallace. Minneapolis: Fortress Press, 1995.

Rimmon-Kenan, Shlomith. *Narrative Fiction: Contemporary Poetics.* New York: Methuen, 1983.

Rogers, Thomas G., and Mauro B. deSouza. "Preaching Cross-Culturally to Spanish Speaking U.S. Hispanic Americans." *Homiletic* 28/1 (Summer 2003): 1-10.

Rose, Lucy Atkinson. *Sharing the Word: Preaching in the Roundtable Church.* Louisville, KY: Westminster John Knox, 1997.

Said, Edward. *Cultural Imperialism.* New York: Vintage, 1994.

Sartore, Domenico. "The Homily." In *Handbook for Liturgical Studies.* Vol. 3, *The Eucharist,* edited by Ansgar J. Chupungco, 189-208. Collegeville, MN: Liturgical Press, 2000.

Satterlee, Craig Alan. *Ambrose of Milan's Method of Mystagogical Preaching.* Collegeville, MN: Liturgical Press, 2002.

Schleiermacher, Friedrich. *Hermeneutics and Criticism.* Edited by Andrew Bowie. Cambridge, UK: Cambridge Univ. Press, 1998.

Schultze, Quentin J. *Televangelism and American Culture: The Business of Popular Religion.* Grand Rapids, MI: Baker Books, 1991.

———. *Christianity and the Mass Media in America: Toward a Democratic Accommodation.* East Lansing: Michigan State Univ. Press, 2003.

Schreiter, Robert. *Constructing Local Theologies.* Maryknoll, NY: Orbis Books, 1985.

Scott, Bernard Brandon. *Hear Then the Parable: A Commentary on the Parables of Jesus.* Minneapolis: Augsburg Fortress Press, 1989.

———. *Jesus: Symbol-Maker for the Kingdom.* Philadelphia: Fortress Press, 1981.

Shannon, Claude Elwood, and Warren Weaver, *The Mathematical Theory of Communication.* Urbana: Univ. of Illinois Press, 1963.

Siegfried, Regina, and Edward Ruane, eds. *In the Company of Preachers.* Collegeville, MN: Liturgical Press, 1993.

Skudlarek, William. *The Word in Worship: Preaching in a Liturgical Context.* Nashville, TN: Abingdon Press, 1981.

Sloyan, Gerard. "What Kind of Canon Do the Lectionaries Constitute?" *Biblical Theological Bulletin* 30 (Spring 2000): 27–35.

———. "Some Thoughts on Liturgical Preaching." *Worship* 71/5 (September 1997): 386-99.

———. *Worshipful Preaching.* Philadelphia: Fortress Press, 1984.

Smith, Christine M. *Weaving the Sermon: Preaching in a Feminist Perspective.* Louisville, KY: Westminster John Knox, 1989.

Soukup, Paul A., ed. *Media, Culture, and Catholicism.* Kansas City, MO: Sheed and Ward, 1996.

Spencer, Jon Michael. *Sacred Symphony: The Chanted Sermon of the Black Preacher.* Westport, CT: Greenwood Press, 1987.

Stackhouse, Max L., Tim Dearborn, and Scott Paeth, eds. *The Local Church in a Global Era: Reflections for a New Century.* Grand Rapids, MI: Eerdmans, 2000.

Staiger, Janet. *Interpreting Films: Studies in the Historical Reception of American Cinema.* Princeton, NJ: Princeton Univ. Press, 1992.

Steimle, Edmund A., Morris J. Niedenthal, and Charles Rice. *Preaching the Story.* Rev. ed. Eugene, OR: Wipf and Stock, 2003. Originally published in 1980.

Stern, Richard C. "Preaching as Listening: Good Preachers Listen First." *Church* (Winter, 1999): 21-26.

———. *Preaching for Today and Tomorrow.* Handbook and video. St. Meinrad, IN: Abbey Press, 1996.

———. "Communication Perspectives in Teaching Preaching." Ed.D. diss., Northern Illinois Univ., 1990. Ann Arbor: UMI.

Stewart-Sykes, Alistair. *From Prophecy to Preaching: A Search for the Origins of the Christian Homily.* Boston: Brill, 2001.

Swears, Thomas R. *Preaching to Head and Heart.* Nashville, TN: Abingdon Press, 2000.

Taylor, Barbara Brown. *The Preaching Life.* Cambridge: Cowley, 1993.

Thomas, Frank, and Henry Mitchell. *They Like to Never Quit Praisin' God: The Role of Celebration in Preaching.* Cleveland: United Church Press, 1997.

Tisdale, Leonora Tubs. *Preaching as Local Theology and Folk Art.* Minneapolis: Fortress Press, 1997.

Tracy, David. *Plurality and Ambiguity.* Chicago: Univ. of Chicago Press, 1987.

———. *The Analogical Imagination: Christian Theology in the Culture of Pluralism.* New York: Crossroad/Herder and Herder, 1998.

Trible, Phyllis. *Texts of Terror: Feminist-Literary Reading of Biblical Narratives.* Minneapolis: Fortress Press, 2003.

———. *God and the Rhetoric of Sexuality.* Philadelphia: Fortress Press, 1978.

Troeger, Thomas. *Ten Strategies for Preaching in a Multimedia Culture.* Nashville, TN: Abingdon Press, 1996.

Untener, Kenneth. *Preaching Better.* Mahwah, NJ: Paulist Press, 1999.

United States Conference of Catholic Bishops (USCCB). *New General Instruction on the Roman Missal.* Washington, DC: USCCB, 2003.

———. (Bishop Wilton Gregory). "Three Decrees of Promulgation on Lay Preaching and Radio, TV Teaching on Faith." *Origins* 31/33 (January 31, 2002): 550-52.

———. *Encuentro and Mission: A Renewed Pastoral Framework for Hispanic Ministry.* Bilingual Edition. Washington, DC: USCCB, 2002.

———. *Welcoming the Stranger among US: Unity in Diversity.* Washington, DC: USCCB, 2000.

———. *Strangers No Longer on the Journey of Hope.* Washington, DC: USCCB, 2003.

———. *Hispanic Ministry: Three Major Documents.* Washington, DC: USCCB, 1995.

———. "U.S. Bishops' Guidelines for Lay Preaching in Churches and Oratories." *Origins* 18/25 (December 1, 1988): 402-4.

Vanhoozer, Kevin J. *The Cambridge Companion to Postmodern Theology.* Cambridge: Cambridge Univ. Press, 2003.

Venturi, Robert, Stephen Izenour, and Denise Scott Brown. *Learning from Las Vegas.* Rev. ed. Cambridge: MIT Press, 1977. Originally published in 1972.

Wallace, James A., CSsR. *Preaching to the Hungers of the Heart: The Homily on the Feasts and Within the Rites.* Collegeville, MN: Liturgical Press, 2002.

———. "Guidelines for Preaching by the Laity: Another Step Backward?" *America* 161/6 (September 9, 1989): 9-16.

———. *Imaginal Preaching: An Archetypal Perspective.* Mahwah, NJ: Paulist Press, 1995.

Waznak, Robert P., SS. "Homily." In *The New Dictionary of Sacramental Worship,* edited by Peter E. Fink, SJ, 552-58. Collegeville, MN: Liturgical Press, 1990.

———. *Introduction to the Homily.* Collegeville, MN: Liturgical Press, 1998.

Whateley, Richard. "Elements of Rhetoric." In *The Rhetorical Tradition,* edited by Patricia Bizzell and Bruce Herzberg, 828-53. Boston: Bedford, 1990.

Williams, Raymond. *Keywords: A Vocabulary of Culture and Society.* Rev. ed. New York: Oxford Univ. Press, 1983. Originally published in 1976.

Willimon, William H., and Richard Lischer, eds. *Concise Encyclopedia of Preaching.* Louisville, KY: Westminster John Knox, 1995.

Wilson, Lee, and Jason Moore. *Digital Storytellers: The Art of Communicating the Gospel in Worship.* Nashville, TN: Abingdon Press, 2002.

Wilson, Paul Scott. *The Four Pages of the Sermon.* Nashville, TN: Abingdon Press, 1999.

———. *A Concise History of Preaching.* Nashville, TN: Abingdon Press, 1992.

Wisdom, Andrew Carl, O.P. *Preaching to a Multigenerational Assembly.* Collegeville, MN: Liturgical Press, 2004.

Wood, Susan K, ed. *Ordering the Baptismal Priesthood: Theologies of Lay and Ordained Ministry.* Collegeville, MN: Liturgical Press, 2003.

Zukowski, Angela Ann, MHSH, and Pierre Babin, OMI. *The Gospel in Cyberspace: Nurturing Faith in the Internet Age.* Chicago: Loyola Univ. Press, 2002.

INDEX OF NAMES